CANADIAN CAMPING & CARAVANING

CANADIAN CAMPING & CARAVANING

Claudette and Robert Cope
Authors of EUROPEAN CAMPING AND CARAVANING

DRAKE PUBLISHERS INC.
NEW YORK · LONDON

Published in 1975 by
Drake Publishers Inc.
381 Park Avenue South
New York, N.Y. 10016

Library of Congress Cataloging in Publication Data

Cope, Claudette and Robert.
  Canadian camping and caravaning.

  1. Camp sites, facilities, etc. —Canada. I. Cope,
  Bob, joint author. II. Title.
GV191.44.C67   917.1'04'644   74-22619
ISBN: 0-877490765-6
ISBN: 0-87749-846-6 (Paper)

Printed in The United States of America.

CONTENTS

Preface

Chapter One: Introduction   1

Chapter Two: Strategies   4

Chapter Three: Planning   10

Chapter Four: Different Modes/ Different Equipment   13

Chapter Five: Potpourri   32

Chapter Six: Different Tours/ Different People   66

Chapter Seven: Selected Campgrounds   102

Chapter Eight: Coping With Camp Cooking   132

Appendix   154

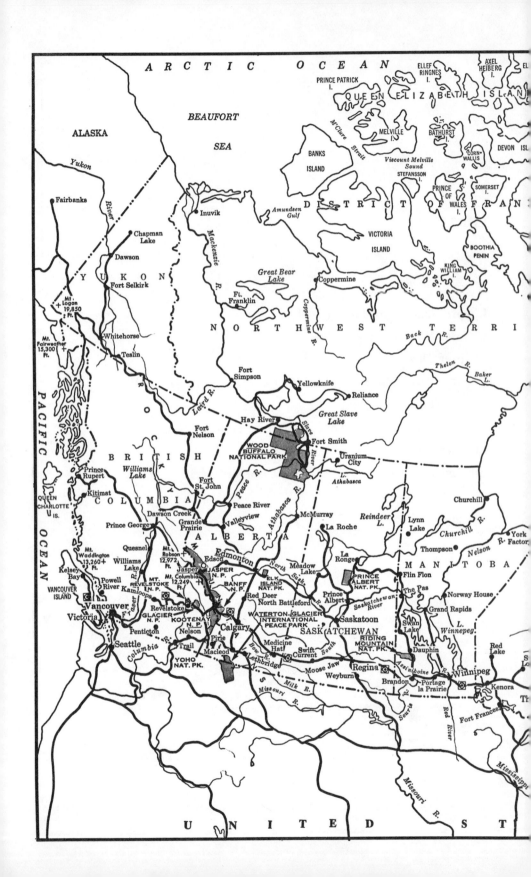

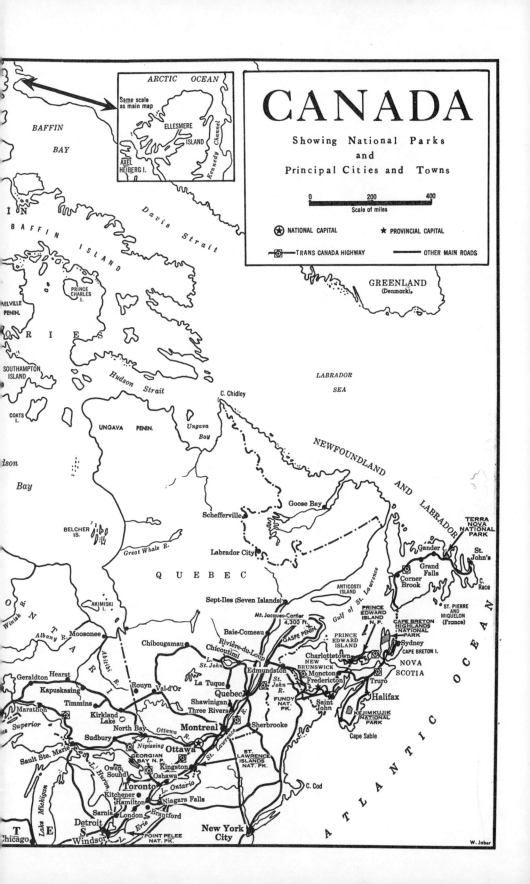

ARCTIC OCEAN

Same scale
as main map

ELLESMERE
ISLAND

AXEL
HEIBERG I.

Kennedy Channel

N

BAFFIN

BAY

CANADA

Showing National Parks
and
Principal Cities and Towns

0   200   400
Scale of miles

★ NATIONAL CAPITAL   ★ PROVINCIAL CAPITAL

TRANS CANADA HIGHWAY   OTHER MAIN ROADS

Davis Strait

BAFFIN ISLAND

PRINCE
CHARLES
I.

GREENLAND
(Denmark)

MELVILLE
PENIN.

R I E S

SOUTHAMPTON
ISLAND

COATS
I.

Hudson Strait

LABRADOR
SEA

C. Chidley

UNGAVA   PENIN.

Ungava
Bay

son

Bay

NEWFOUNDLAND AND LABRADOR

BELCHER
IS.

Goose Bay

TERRA
NOVA
NATIONAL
PARK

Great Whale R.

Schefferville

Gander

St.
John's

Labrador City

Grand
Falls

C.
Race

Q U E B E C

Corner
Brook

ANTICOSTI
ISLAND

ST. PIERRE
AND
MIQUELON
(France)

O

Winisk R.

AKIMISKI
I.

Sept-Iles (Seven Islands)

Gulf of St. Lawrence

PRINCE
EDWARD
ISLAND
N.P.

CAPE BRETON
HIGHLANDS
NATIONAL
PARK

Albany R.   Moosonee

Mt. Jacques-Cartier
4,300 Ft.

GASPE PENIN.

PRINCE
EDWARD
ISLAND

Sydney

CAPE BRETON I.

Abitibi R.

Chibougamau

Baie-Comeau

Rivière-du-Loup

Chicoutimi

Charlottetown

NOVA
SCOTIA

Geraldton   Hearst

Rouyn   Val-d'Or

L.
St. John

NEW
BRUNSWICK

Moncton

St.
Lawrence

Kapuskasing

La Tuque

Edmundston

St.
John
R.

Fredericton

Truro

Halifax

Marathon

Timmins

Quebec

FUNDY
NAT.
PK.

Saint
John

Superior

Kirkland
Lake

Shawinigan

Three Rivers

St. Lawrence R.

KEJIMKUJIK
NATIONAL
PARK

ce

North Bay

Ottawa R.

Sudbury

Sherbrooke

Cape Sable

Sault Ste. Marie

L.
Nipissing

Montreal

St. Lawrence R.

C. Cod

GEORGIAN
BAY N.P.

Ottawa

ST.
LAWRENCE
ISLANDS
NAT. PK.

Owen
Sound

Kingston

L. Huron

Oshawa

T

S

Toronto

L. Ontario

Kitchener

Hamilton

Niagara Falls

Sarnia   London   Brantford

Detroit

Erie

Chicago

Lake Michigan

Windsor

L.

E

New York
City

POINT PELEE
NAT. PK.

ATLANTIC OCEAN

W. Jaber

It's the fresh air that does it...
Wonderfully fine air it is, out here.
—LEWIS CARROLL

PREFACE

Camping and caravaning in Canada is obviously not new; however, it is only since the early 1970s that in-the-know Canadians and Americans have turned on by the million to this least ostentatious and yet in many aspects most fulfilling way to experience adventure, discovery, and economy. This guidebook represents our small effort to encourage you not to miss out, using camping as a means for doing things by and for yourself, as a free person, as a family of free persons, as vagabonds.

The campgrounds, equipment stores, and other agencies mentioned, and sometimes highly recommended, were chosen for inclusion in this guide on merit alone. No payment of any kind has been received. The only criteria are known service and evidence they come up to standards. Most agencies and campgrounds recommended will, in fact, be surprised to learn that our visits were for more than browsing and camping.

Assistance from every provincial office of tourism and the national tourist office in Ottawa has made this guide possible. We know of no country in the world where there is such complete official willingness to help the traveler with printed material and personal advice.

Despite our best effort we are certain a few mistakes have crept into our work. We are certain, too, that others will have points of view differing from ours on matters discussed. We, therefore, encourage you to correspond with us so the next edition will be even more useful.

Claudette and Bob Cope
S.E. 72nd Pl.
Mercer Island, Wash. 98040

A PERSONAL NOTE ON CAMPING WOMAN TO WOMAN CLAUDETTE

O heart, be at peace, because
Nor knave nor dolt can break
What's not for their applause,
Being for a woman's sake.
—WILLIAM YATES

Most women have an aversion to camping, even before trying it. And with good reason. We're concerned about cleanliness of facilities, cramped quarters, lack of privacy, how we'll prepare food, wash clothes, and the like.

What noncampers may not realize is even the smallest recreational vehicle (the British, French, and other Europeans call them *caravans)* is ingeniously converted into what amounts to a small home, with ample cupboards, storage, and work space, and comfortable beds. In deference to aesthetics most caravans are designed with attention to detail, creating a pleasing, cozy appearance, besides having the luxury of sink, refrigerator, stove, table, curtains, and so on.

Even tents have changed a lot from the days of rough-and-tumble, ax-and-survival camping. Many tents are equipped like small cottages with folding tables, cots, and chairs—not to mention cupboards and other fold-down storage chests that can be assembled to form the furniture of the traveling home. A vase of fresh flowers, a clean tablecloth, and a light or candle centered on the table are a modern-day indication that nature can be enjoyed with some of the comforts of home. Yes, these homes away from home can be made pleasant indeed.

One of the best features about camping is keeping our "home" in the kind of order we wish to keep. Rather than hoping the hotel employees have removed other people's germs and aired the smoke-laden furnishings, we can clean our own "home," wash our own dishes, care for our own linen—live by our own standards. And with the addition of hot showers, laundry facilities, and efficient little stoves, camping becomes a comfortable way of traveling.

A NOTE ON COSTS

There is some ill
A-brewing towards my rest,
For I did dream
Of money-bags tonight.
—SHAKESPEARE

It is important to everyone using this guide to know how much reliance he can place on quoted prices. Since there is considerable time between collecting price information and publishing the book, we have avoided stating any price as exact. Instead we give approximate prices that are increased from what we know in 1975, taking inflation into consideration. For example, when we know the charge for camping at Esker Lakes Provincial Park in Swastika, Ontario, is now $3.50 per night, we round out the amount, giving more than due credit to inflation and record the cost at $4.00. All 1975 costs are increased 15-25%, so this guide will still be reasonably accurate in 1976 and 1977. We felt it would be better to estimate on the high side so the reader may be surprised by a saving.

One touch of nature
Makes the whole world kin.
—SHAKESPEARE

CANADIAN CAMPING & CARAVANING

-1
INTRODUCTION

What prevents most persons from vacationing more frequently has been the high cost of hotels, motels, transportation, and food. Now, however, millions of people in North America, like those of Europe and Australia, are discovering the joy of low-cost, long vacations—as well as many weekends and holidays away from home—because they are all camping. Millions of sturdy and not so sturdy souls are learning that camping is no longer the smoky, wilderness experience we used to associate with getting away from it all. Camping is now available in or very near the major cities of Toronto, Montreal, Vancouver, Quebec, Victoria, and the like. Camping is available everywhere; for example, there are more than 60 campgrounds on little Prince Edward Island. Even British Columbia, with over 500 campgrounds, has far fewer than either Ontario or Quebec; the east-west road through Banff and Yoho National Parks has, on the average, a campground every seven miles; make-your-own-campsite camping is possible away from major roads on millions of square miles of crown (public) lands; Canada already has more than 3,000 organized campgrounds and new camp-grounds are opening currently at the rate of about 200 per year.

Camping in Comfort

In addition to their convenient location and their great number, the *quality* of most campgrounds comes as a surprise even to the experienced. It is no longer unusual to find campgrounds with beaches and swimming pools, asphalt roads, flush toilets, hot and cold showers, a laundry, a small supermarket, and a games room. Of course, not all areas have high-caliber campgrounds like this (if convenience is what you want), but most of the new camps are surprisingly comfortable. Some of the new private developments are like Europe's low-cost resort campgrounds and the new camping-resort facilities of Florida—they have everything from riding horses to convenience stores. Camping *has* changed! Of course it is still possible to pitch a tent in some uncrowded spot in the shade of the forest, to roam and explore, to fish and hunt, to breathe the fragrance of flowers in bloom on cool mountainsides, and to chop wood and keep warm by a fire at night, but the options are much wider today.

Camping Costs Less

The following chart gives a general idea of costs, comparing touring by recreational vehicle (owned or rented) and shopping for food in a supermarket; touring by car (with tent in trunk) and shopping in roadside markets and supermarkets; with touring by car, staying in modest motels and eating in restaurants.

Comparing Approximate Costs of Travel
per Day by 4 Persons with
Car and Motels, with Rented and Own Recreational Vehicle (RV), and Own
Car and Tent

	Car & Motels	Rented RV	Owner's RV	Owner's Car & Tent
Meals (4 persons)				
Breakfast: Juice, eggs toast, and coffee	$5.00	$1.25	$1.25	$1.25
Lunch: Hamburger deluxe, potato chips, milk, fruit	6.00	3.75	3.75	3.75
Dinner: Steak, potato, salad, milk, wine	25.00	7.50	7.50	7.50
Motel or Hotel	25.00			
Campsite		3.00	3.00	3.00
Camper Rental		35.00		
Gasoline: 100 miles at 80¢/gal., assuming 20 mpg for car, 15 mpg for RV	4.00	5.35	5.35	4.00
Misc. Expenses: Ferries, museum fees, boat rental, horseback riding	5.00	5.00	5.00	5.00
TOTAL PER DAY	$70.00	$60.85	$25.85	$24.50

Look at the figures. Camping is about $10 a day less expensive than moteling, even when using a rented motorhome costing $35 per day—and you have greater fun and flexibility besides. Motel costs are at an estimated minimum and could easily run up to $40 per day in the better motels and hotels during the summer; eating in the better restaurants would add 30% more.

With a recreational vehicle, or a car and tent, there is greater flexibility, travel anywhere, anytime. There are no motel worries, no reservations. With a recreational vehicle you can stay almost anywhere. You need not even go to a campsite at night, and during the day you can drive into the city center, do your sightseeing, and return to the motorhome for lunch and rest. No packing and unpacking. No fixed itinerary. No schedules to keep. Carefree!

The intent of this guide is to share what we learned, often through trial and error, while camping in Canada from coast to coast. We have traveled and camped in almost every province with both tent and campmobile, with and without children, in almost all seasons, and for a variety of purposes from simply seeing an eclipse (Bob has taught astronomy), to vacationing (we prefer the Maritime Provinces), to studying cultures (for this we prefer the western provinces), to gathering material for this book.

This guide book is *not* for those who believe travel consists of knowing that someone else will see to it they have a place to stay each night with three well-planned meals catered in the best places, or for those who want their time filled by sightseeing, arrivals and departures, television and the daily paper, or for those who believe that modernity consists of steady progress, more leisure, comfort, and security. This is

for people who know that in a lifetime they could never become acquainted with so much, yet are starting the venture. These are people who generally place emphasis on life-seeing. They want more than sightseeing. They tend to prefer the small, distinctive places, the ghost towns, the glimpses of nature, the pleasure of canoeing, the luxury of a down-filled sleeping bag, the wilderness birds, the richness of ethnic differences, the ocean waters, the farmers' markets, and quiet log-sitting. They savor independence over security, not mistaking comfort for civilization, while sharpening their senses and their learning.

W hen we ask further, what is conduct?
Let us answer:...Conduct is three-fourths
Of our life and its largest concern.
—MATTHEW ARNOLD

-2
STRATEGIES

Canadian coast-to-coast travel is a one-time experience, with some travelers feeling compelled to tour all the major cities, all the natural wonders: an afternoon is spent in Victoria, an evening in Vancouver, a day in Winnipeg, two days in Ottawa, two days in Montreal, and one day in Quebec City. The well-publicized museums, government buildings, formal gardens, souvenir shops are visited; Lake Louise, Banff, Jasper, Niagara Falls, the Laurentians, and Cape Breton are sandwiched in between.

More frequently, because of Canada's immense size and because it is realized there will be opportunities to return, travelers choose to limit travel to one or two provinces: a summer tour of the Maritimes, a fall visit to the Gatineaus, a skiing encounter in the Rockies, a springtime holiday in Victoria. Most sportsmen frequently see little but the immediate environs of their destinations in the woods.

With increased leisure, more people are traveling and traveling more frequently. Europeans are visiting relatives who have emigrated to Canada, Canadians are revisiting family "back on the farm," Americans are getting better acquainted with their northern neighbor, and the Japanese are visiting everything, everywhere.

For my part,
I travel not to go anywhere,
but to go.
I travel for travel's sake.
The great affair is to move.
—ROBERT LOUIS STEVENSON

Modern travelers have progressed from Stevenson's 19th-century philosophy, determining reasons for travel, then determining location—putting the *why* before the *where*.

If your main goal is to find a spot where sunning, beachcombing, and bikini watching will fill your days, you are ready to determine a destination. If antique collecting is your *why* you are ready for the *where*. We, like others, have made the mistake of putting the trailer before the car—deciding to visit Vancouver, then getting there and wondering what to do.

Special interests, unusual modes of travel, off-beat places, and various forms of purposeful travel are where it's at.

Special Interests

While it is impossible to imagine all the alternatives or illustrate the following more or less off-beat travel ideas—because we have not tried most of them—we would like to suggest some purposes for travel for those who desire a 20th century approach.

If you are interested in the ethnic groups of Canada and their cultures, you can experience a grand tour (used only in the pleasurable sense) by planning travels around large concentrations of Scandinavians, Ukrainians, Eskimos, Scots, Germans, French, Italians, Indians. You have over 60 ethnic groups to choose from. Foods, handicrafts, foreign language newspapers, festivals, museums experienced while traveling add new understanding of the culture, new intrigue to travel.

If you are interested in history, you might choose to follow historic trails by land or water—canoeing along MacKenzie's fur trading routes, driving the Cabot Trail of Nova Scotia, following the Cariboo Trail of British Columbia. Theater and performing-arts buffs might emphasize the cultural cities—Winnipeg, Montreal, Ottawa, Vancouver, Stratford, London, Niagara-on-the-Lake; the more earthy festival fancier might plan his tour to include the Folk Arts Festival at St. Catharines, Ontario, in late May; the Eskimo and Indian festival in Inuvik in the Northwest Territories in mid-July; the Icelandic Festival at Gimli, Manitoba, the Nova Scotia Gaelic Mod at St. Anns, or the Ukraninian Festival in Dauphin, Manitoba, in early August before heading for an Octoberfest at Kitchener-Waterloo, Ontario, or Winnipeg, Manitoba, in mid-October. The appendix includes a lengthy list for the pleasure of the festival follower.

Old West enthusiasts can concentrate their travels on the rodeo towns of Saskatchewan, Alberta, and British Columbia, making certain to arrive early for the mid-July granddaddy of all rodeos, the Calgary Stampede. And the fisherman may want to try his luck in Vancouver in mid August ($25,000) goes to the winner of the Salmon Derby) after tempting the tuna (sometimes 1,000 lbs. each), the lobster, the trout in more easternly waters.

The possibilities are surprisingly varied for planning a trip around a specific interest. Perhaps this list will trigger a travel theme for you:

ghost towns	gold panning
winetasting	cheese tasting
archeological sites	battlegrounds
churches	hospitals
animals	flowers
botanical gardens	historic routes
festivals	handicrafts
muskets, guns of yesteryear	schools, universities
hot springs	rockhounding
pottery	painting
weaving	forts
curling	golf
hunting	fishing
skiing	sailing
canoeing	racing
antiques	architecture
theater	logging events
bottle collecting	pioneering artifacts
agricultural fairs	rodeos
covered bridges	curiosities*

For further inspiration and suggestions write for an annual list of events throughout Canada (Canadian Government Travel Bureau, Ottawa, KlA Oh6), or name your special interest, ask for their brochures and suggestions on where these interests are best persued.

---

*For a start, visit an operahouse never playing an opera (Moosomin); fossils of dinosaurs, crocodiles, and palm trees (Cypress Hills, Saskatchewan); the river Manitoba that flows backwards (St. John).

Purposeful Travel

The point is to give travel some purpose or purposes; then, while rock-hounding or ghost towning in British Columbia you will undoubtedly visit the Provincial Museum or the Butchart Gardens and sample afternoon tea and crumpets in the English tradition at the Empress Hotel in Victoria as a natural adjunct to your purpose. If collecting Eskimo handicrafts is your hobby and you are in the city of Quebec, after visiting L'atelier Galerie de Peintures et d'art Canadien and examining far north artifacts, perhaps you'll take a walking tour of Upper and Lower towns allowing your mind to reflect on the exhibits and discussions about soapstone carvings, your first love.

Decide on some purpose, or combination of purposes, that fits your interests. Then visit those places where your interests can best be enjoyed. That kind of advice leaves one with little advice to give. You know yourself best. The choice of what to do and where to go is therefore quite personal. It is simply too easy to say, "Do not miss camping at Upper Queensland," to find out later the recipient of your advice found Upper Queensland is better missed. If told that Lower Queensland is a waste of time, the person will probably go there anyway and find it a highpoint of the trip. Let us put it this way: If you are going to experience life with the local people, to seek out the folk art of the provinces, to wander on foot through little ghost towns, to frequent the local bakery shops, to take in an occasional undulating belly button, to picnic at a wayside lobster stand, to spend an Ontario evening with Shaw or Shakespeare, to savor alder-smoked salmon prepared in Indian-style, to camp where there is serenity, beauty, *and* hot showers, we will be happy to go along. We will stay home to reseed the front lawn and paint the trim on our house, however, if you are determined to see hundreds of ecclesiastical edifices, botanical gardens, houses of the famous, municipal buildings, fortifications, monuments, and the 5,000 miles of Trans One.

> *I have no time*
> *to be in a hurry.*
> *—JOHN WESLEY*

Miscellaneous Recommendations

At the risk of sounding overly prescriptive, let us offer some suggestions:

1. *Simplify.* One of the most admirable attributes of Europeans is their ability to take pleasure in simple foods and simple activities enjoyed in leisure. For example,

when Americans visit a historical place, they customarily hop into a car and drive. When they arrive at their destination, they seek a parking space nearest the entrance, and then after visiting the historical site, they eat a quick meal at the nearest restaurant and drive home.

Another way of experiencing the historic site might include walking at least part of the way, enjoying the weather, the landscape, possibly picnicking enroute or cooling tired feet in a stream, then approaching the object of travel as it was approached by the people who built, worked, and lived in it. This is one way to sense the texture of a past way of life; this is the way to reflect on what you are experiencing. You will remember a place to the extent you sensed it when planning it and shared in its environment while there.

2. *A day in transit is only that.* Do not plan any lengthy visits or experiences on a day devoted to travel.

3. *When traveling on main highways you can estimate 350-450 miles a day;* on other roads 250-350 miles a day is reasonable—assuming no mud, ice, or snow, of course. *Note:* After summer rains some back roads in Manitoba and Saskatchewan become impassably muddy.

4. *Even when a trip must follow a fairly tight schedule, allow for the occasional freedom to explore the inconceivable discovery.* Sprinkle in a liberal number of absolutely free days, at least two a week on a lengthy trip.

5. *If crossing several time zones within a short time span, allow a day or so on arrival in Canada to adjust.* When you have a fly-drive arrangement, the day you get off the plane should be free. Rest! Some of us require several days to adjust to time changes.

6. *On a lengthy trip have two or three prearranged points at which you check the money supply.* Half the trip over and three-quarters of the money gone is usually our problem.

7. *If pressed for time—and who isn't—you may find it better not to make a series of short stops, but rather concentrate on one objective.* For example, if you wish to do some canoeing and can only spare five days for it, two days in one area, one day driving, and two days somewhere else would leave you totally exhausted. Better to decide on a home base in one area having many possibilities and then getting to know that area well.

8. *For a lengthy trip, as an aid in considering alternate trip routes, take an 8-1/2 X 11 map of Canada, and cover it with a celeloid sheet.* Sketch with china marker possible routes, one by one, filling in driving times and optimum days at each destination. This technique quickly eliminates those side trips that clearly become too time-consuming.

9. *If planning to rent a vehicle or equipment on arrival, check both provincial and national holiday lists to avoid arriving on a holiday, or on a Saturday prior to a Monday holiday.* To arrive thinking you can take immediate delivery of a camper or car only to find offices closed for several days is very upsetting. A list of Canadian holidays is included in the appendix.

10. *To gain a sense of living in an area, whenever possible ride the local metro or walk.* Who knows whom you will meet or what unique experience you may have.

11. *For all the glory, costliness, and world attention given to monuments, we find they are usually beautiful, historic, mighty, massive, monumental—and only that.* Better to spend an afternoon at the water's edge examining the sand dollars, the cockles, the anemones of the sea or chatting with an old-timer about the days he panned for gold, pioneered the West.

12. *Seek out the flea markets, the auctions, the craft sales, and avoid the gift shops, the tourist traps—unless it is the ordinary souvenir you desire.*

13. *And when you feel a desire to move indoors, rather than heading for the nearest motel, consider calling at a farm family, guest ranch, or rooming house with bed-and-breakfast.option, where you can experience other individuals, perhaps another style of life.* See the appendix for more information.

14. *Allow time at the conclusion of a lengthy journey to unwind.* Pick a quiet, attractive place where you can relax at least two days before returning to the hassle of school, housekeeping, or office.

Conclusion

The art of viewing and experiencing Canada *au naturel* is to key your living to the out-of-doors, to the local peoples, to the local way of life. With eyes observing and pace relaxing, an educational and enjoyable journey can be had.

-3
PLANNING

*Pleasant memories must be
arranged for in advance.*
—ANONYMOUS

Advance Planning

We travel three times: as a mind plagued with uncertainties and romanticized with expectations (before), as a physical object moved from place to place at considerable expense (during), and again as a mind, retracing steps in a distant place (afterward).

Get involved early. The planning is as pleasurable as the traveling: the more painstaking the preparation, the most lasting the learning.

Before suggesting books to read and suggesting a plan for organizing travel notes, a time schedule for decision making is offered. Before continuing, however, we feel it important for you to understand the mode of presentation. Since you make the decisions according to your interests, time, and money, we wish only to suggest alternatives you might consider. And since it is impossible in a book of this size to discuss details associated with all the decisions you make, our emphasis is on providing recommendations, names, and addresses. We will not, however, shrink from an obligation: making our personal feelings known to you. We definitely have preferences in life styles, equipment, places to visit, and the like. Insofar as you, too, share these points of view—that is, what we euphemistically call *biases*—you will have greater confidence in our recommendations.

A Countdown

6 months-1 year prior to departure. Write provincial tourist offices, ferry, airline, railroad, or rental companies for maps, tourist literature, rates, and reservation information. Mention your vocational or avocational interests, inquire about camping, farm vacations, guest ranches. Ask for listings of festivals, special events, crafts shows.

Read everything you can about Canada, its history, its ethnic groups, its sports, its scenic, and cultural attractions.

Study French?

Set up a filing system for brochures, maps, clipped articles.

5-6 months. Plan a tentative route after your goals are determined.

Decide whether to take the children along, whether they should attend camp, stay at home, or travel with a teenage tour group.

Write to specific outfitters, guest ranches, farms for their current rates and reservation procedures.

Start preparing your own travel notebook (discussed later in this chapter).

3-4 months. Make plane, ferry, or rail reservations.

Arrange for purchase or rental of vehicle, if required for all or a portion of tour.

Make hotel reservations for first day or two if getting to your destination involves crossing several time zones by plane.

Arrange for passport or visa if required by some special reason.

Arrange for rental of your home or apartment if traveling three months or longer.

Check your medical coverage to see if it includes Canada.

Decide whether to take major camping/sporting items from home or whether to purchase or rent en route.

1-2 months. Purchase needed clothing, luggage, camera, film, hobby equipment.

Check expiration date of your driver's license.

Write Canadian friends you plan to visit, establish contacts with "People Meet People" programs.

Write provincial office again for latest listing of events, if your listing is no longer current.

Obtain your Canadian nonresident interprovincial motor vehicle liability card (Americans can obtain it from their own insurance companies); this yellow card is not essential but indicates your financial responsibility.

If your dog travels with you, be certain his rabies certificate indicates he was vaccinated less than 12 months prior to entry into Canada.

3-4 weeks. Prepay all insurance policies, mortgage payments, utilities that will come due while you're away.

Prepare a first aid kit with your regular prescriptions, addresses, and phone numbers in case of emergency, extra pair of eyeglasses, and usual first aid items.

Plan gifts to take to friends along the way.

Make money arrangements. Buy travelers checks, and record numbers in your traveling notebook. Get at least $50 in Canadian currency before leaving home.

Continue to record vital information in your traveling notebook.

Prepare mailing addresses and itinerary with approximate dates where friends and relatives at home can contact you if your trip is a lengthy one.

1-2 weeks. Type addresses of friends and relatives on gummed stickers for easy removal onto postcards when on the road.

Arrange for discontinuation of services: milk, mail, newspapers, garbage removal, phone (?).

Arrange for house check, care of lawn, pets, plants.

If flying into Canada, pre-order duty-free items for airport pickup at departure time.

Have own vehicle checked for optimum performance.

1-2 days. Notify police.

Give house and car keys to neighbor.

Confirm plane (boat) departure time if not driving own vehicle.

If flying, tape closed all covers to liquid containers and fountain pens before packing.

Defrost refrigerator.

Store valuables, outdoor equipment.

Day of departure. Ask yourself if carrying: tickets, passport or visa, if required, Canadian money, travelers checks, savings account numbers, credit cards usable in Canada, travel notebook, maps, books, keys to house, luggage, car, driver's license, motor vehicle liability card, car registration certificate, rabies certificate for dog, addresses, reservation confirmations for rental agency, outfitter, hotel, ferry, ranch, theater, farm or private campground.

Check to see that doors and windows are locked, electrical appliances are disconnected,the automatic timer for lights is connected, the furnace thermostat is adjusted, and the hot water tank thermostat is turned down.

At airport or pier, check in, keeping only what you'll need en route plus photographic equipment and film. Mail traveler's and luggage insurance. Pick up duty-free items. Relax, get acquainted with others. Forget what you forgot.

Each venture is a new beginning,
A raid on the inarticulate
With shabby equipment
Always deteriorating.
—THOMAS ELIOT

-4

DIFFERENT MODES/
DIFFERENT EQUIPMENT

The means of camping have expanded greatly in the last ten years. Options now vary from simple backpacks to trailers, along a continuum that includes backpacking and hitchhiking, bike camping, car with tent, car with tent trailer, truck campers (pickup campers), motorized recreational vehicles, car pulling a trailer, and the new mania for the well-heeled, the fifth wheel trailers. The continuum goes from least cost to most, most freedom to least, younger to older age, individual to larger family, least luggage to most. The purpose of this chapter is to provide some guidelines to what may be most appropriate for your situation and objectives.

BASIC MODES OF CAMPING

Mode One Backpacking and hitchhiking	Two Car and tent(s)	Three Car and tent trailer	Four Recreational vehicle	Five Car and trailer
Younger-		AGE		-Older
Least-		LUGGAGE		-Most
Smaller-		FAMILY		-Larger
Least-		COST		-Most

Backpacking and hitchhiking (Mode One), and its variant, bicycle camping, are the fastest growing means of travel among college-age youth of North America and Europe. Car-and-tent combinations (Mode Two) are most common among the newly married. A car pulling a tent trailer (Mode Three) is especially popular in the eastern and middle western states and provinces and is growing in popularity with fuel-conscious families.

Most American couples and families, however, seem to prefer the attributes of pickup campers (especially in the west) and recreational vehicles, such as the Volkswagen campmobile (Mode Four). Car (or truck) pulling a trailer (Mode Five) is common among older, wealthier Canadians and their American counterparts. In the sections that follow we outline some of the basic considerations associated with each of these major ways of camping.

MODE ONE: BACKPACKING AND HITCHHIKING

Unquestionably the least expensive and most vagabonding in character is the backpacker—walking, biking, or hitchhiking. Clearly this is *the mode* among a large proportion of the approximately half million American and Canadian college and near college-age youths who descend on the western provinces each summer. While it is possible to get along with as little as a pair of jeans, a shirt, a sweater, a swim suit, half a towel, a comb (optional), a toothbrush, a bed roll, and a skimpy rucksack, this is perhaps a little too spartan.

BASIC EQUIPMENT FOR BACKPACKING

Backpack

The two most important items are something to carry your gear in and a sleeping bag. Do not waste time considering a suitcase or even a duffle bag for carrying your gear; they are too cumbersome, too easy to steal, too fragile, and you will feel like a burdened tourist. A backpack is the only way to go; however, the choice of backpack is not so simple. The primary decision is whether the nylon, rigid-metal frame, or the soft canvas varieties will give you the best service. Equal numbers of each are seen on the backs of girls and guys. The critical variable is how much is to be carried. With the metal-frame variety you will carry more gear comfortably. With the softer varieties you will have more freedom because they are usually smaller; thus, you will have less difficulty getting in and out of automobiles and crowded buses; because they are soft you will be able to sit on them easily without worrying about bending the aluminum frame; and because they fold, they are easier to store when empty. On balance, the softer variety is recommended, unless you plan to carry a lot of gear—which usually means you have too much—or plan on some distant, backcountry, off-the-road camping. Plan to pay $40-$80 for a good pack. The cheaper ones will have straps that break, zippers that stick, and insecurely sewn seams.

Sleeping Bag

A good sleeping bag is *the* vital item. It is your security blanket, cozy home, essential tie with the sandman. You want something that is warm, lightweight, compressible, and durable. Nothing fills these requirements better than goose-down bags. Ounce for ounce, goose down is still the warmest insulation known to science, and since it breathes, goose down also provides a substantial comfort range of temperature, without a buildup of moisture. They do, however, take much longer than a synthetic fiber to dry if you are caught unprotected in a rainstorm. (Drying a down item in front of an open fire can cause irreparable damage. (See p. 20 for suggestions for cleaning down-filled items.) Other materials tend to wear out and lose thickness after each cycle of compression and release; not so with down. Nothing, when unpacked and given a brisk shaking, springs back to its original buoyancy like down. Plan to pay $75-$125 for the right bag. If goose down is too expensive, you can get a bag filled with dacron for about one-third the cost.

Shelter

A lightweight, nylon, two-person pup tent (sometimes called *ridge tents*) with enough room inside for your gear will cost between $50 and $150 for adequate to good quality. It will take up about as much space as the sleeping bag. There are some plastic cheapies which will cost as little as $20, while some specially designed mountaineering tents require a $250 layout. Plan to get something for about $75; this should include a sewn-in ground sheet (floor), mosquito netting, aluminum poles, pegs, guy lines, and storage bag. For approximately $50 you can expect to find a similar but minimum-quality, lightweight, cotton tent with wooden poles; it will require a separate ground sheet if you want a floor.

Stove

A miniature portable stove is recommended if you plan to cook. There are stoves weighing only a few ounces to those tipping the scales at a full pound and a half. International Camping Gaz, Optimus, Svea, and Primus are the brand names we prefer. Our favorite, lightweight stove is the Optimus; it is made in Sweden and burns white gas or regular automobile gas, if you cannot find white gas. For dependable burning, get the model #8R, weighing 1-1/2 lb., and coming in a lightweight metal box. (Certain fuels burn better in cold temperatures than others; if this concerns you, read the section on stoves,

Other Items

A knife is almost indispensable. Our recommendation is the Swiss Army knife, made with Swedish steel. Each knife is a collection of assorted tools with sizes which fairly boggle the mind. Look for the red handles and the Swiss Army Medallion (as seen on the Swiss flag); these are available through most of the better equipment dealers. The fanciest model contains two blades, a can opener, small screwdriver, scissors, scaler and disgorger, course saw, fine saw, cap opener, Phillips screwdriver, file, punch, tweezers, and toothpick—too much, too heavy. Get one with the blades, screwdriver, and can opener, about $10.

A foam pad will increase sleeping comfort substantially and is warmer than an air mattress. The thin, dense foam pads are light, compact, and comfortable. Expect to pay $10 to $12 for best quality.

A miniature flashlight is handy, even in dimly lighted campgrounds. Reverse the batteries when not in use or you are certain to discharge them unknowingly.

The Spanish leather wine bag *(bota)*, because of its flexibility, is excellent for liquid refreshments. Avoid syrupy mixes, however. If two are traveling together, try water in one, wine in another. You will grow accustomed to the slight off taste.

Aside from these standard items, a dry marker pen is useful for making hitchhiking signs; an alarm clock is useful for making you less than popular with late-sleeping vagabonds; a poncho is more versatile than rain jackets and trousers because it gives you all-purpose rain protection and a ground cloth; and finally, an over-the-shoulder or around-the-waist bag with variable-length straps is handy for those items you will use during the day: guidebook, stamps, pen, lunch, map, camera, and so on.

This may seem like a lot of stuff and, with even the minimum of clothing, ought to require at least a VW Super Beatle for transport. Not so. A standard metal-frame backpack will carry it all; if you can live—as many campers do—without a tent, you can get by with one of the soft backpacks.

Bicycle Camping

Bicycle camping is growing in popularity, but may be one of the difficult variations to use in Canada because of the mountains and great distances. Although that did not deter a group of middle-aged Vancouver women we met one summer in the Rockies near the top of a steady five-mile climb; they were going to Banff with their dogs.

Despite the mountains and distances British Columbia and Alberta are good for cyclists because the roads have unusually wide, paved shoulders. The cyclist, however, finds a much narrower gravel shoulder in Manitoba and Saskatchewan and just plain narrow roads in the eastern provinces.

There are now many good books on the market that deal with bicycle touring; we suggest some elsewhere in this guide. Your local bicycle dealer will also give you advice. Your car dealer sells racks, so that bikes may be mounted on your camper or car; thus, the bike may be a means to camp away from a base camp reached by automobile. For the most part, however, you must simply get a bicycle with low enough gearing to make pulling the extra weight easier (some cyclists are now hauling small trailers). Aside from this it is only necessary to select the same lightweight camping equipment developed for backpackers.

MODE TWO: CAR WITH TENT

While backpacking, hiking, biking, and hitching are the most common mode of transit among the young, car-and-tent camping is practiced by all ages and incomes. One virture of camping is economic, but for many who have the means, the main advantage of the car is freedom of movement: it is not necessary to rely on leg power, the weather, or the passing motorist; and after the tent is pitched, the car is free to wander. Furthermore, the millions who annually take their tent on vacation are insisting it should also be a comfortable experience.

Much of the comfort is provided by the facilities, cleanliness, and security of the organized campground, which are often equal to that provided in most motels and hotels; much of the personal comfort is, however, provided through wisely chosen equipment.

BASIC EQUIPMENT FOR TENTING

Tent
Since the tent is your home, it is the most important item. Incidentally, you may consider purchasing or renting. Check the yellow pages for a rental agency or inquire at the large sports shops. Either way, the choice of the right tent depends on the interaction of a number of variables, most of which are common sense considerations. We will mention them, anyway, since many who choose this means will be camping for the first time, and because even experienced campers should rethink their camping strategy occasionally.

A major variable is the type of vacation anticipated. Since a big, roomy, frame tent can require one to two hours to set up, and not much less to take down, it may not be worth your time and energy, unless you are planning to stay at each site at least five days. If planning to move a lot, think of something less adequate in size which can be put up or taken down in a short time. Some tenters use two tents: a large frame tent to use at their destination, and a smaller, quick-to-erect model for use en route.

How large is the group or family? Children? By North American standards the largest European tents, sometimes seen in Canada and the United States, are incredible, incorporating a separate kitchen, up to three bedrooms, a toilet and shower compartment, several doorways, picture windows, and more than one veranda. If you have young children, it is especially important to have a tent with at least one separate bedroom so they can go to bed early. Or if the family is large, and big tents seem too expensive or simply too cumbersome, consider using several small tents. Two small tents go up faster than one big one because everyone works at the same time. Some families are even moving to separate tents for mom and dad, the girls and boys. Separate tents make it easier to bring friends too.

The size of the car will be an important consideration as the tent may well be the largest item to be carried; not all tents will fit in the trunk of small cars, although all except the tents with unusually long, nontelescoping or unjointed poles can be carried on a roof rack.

The other major variable, of course, is cost. The largest frame tent, with several bedrooms, described above, costs between $400 and $500; a modest family tent that sleeps four in one bedroom costs about $225; a family tent with two bedrooms, sleeping six costs about $300. On the other hand, touring tents providing overnight sleeping accommodations for three or four people, with room for standing but little or no extra space inside, range from $100 to $200. It is becoming more common for groups of youths traveling together, to pitch several touring-style tents on one site, or one or more pup tents with one large tent. As a rough guide, try to acquire at least 25 to 30 feet of floor space for each person in the party.

General Tent Specifications and Cost

Type	Specifications	Approximate cost
Pup or ridge (small size)	Sleeps 2, sewn-in floor Dimensions: 8′ long, 4′ wide, 3½′ high Packed size: 20″ X 7″ Weight: 15 lb.	$50-$60
Pup or ridge (large size)	Sleeps 2-3, sewn-in floor Dimensions: 8′ long, 6′ wide, 6′ high Pack size: 30″ X 9″ Weight: 25 lb.	$70-$100

Touring or umbrella (medium size)	Sleeps 3-4, sewn-in floor, canopy Dimensions: 10' X 12' base, 7' high Packed size: 36" X 12" X 12" Weight: 35 lb.	$130-$200
Frame or cabin tent (no separate inner bedroom)	Sleeps 3, plus space for camp furniture, sewn-in floor Dimensions: 14' long, 7' wide, 7' height at center, 5' height at eaves Packed size: 30" X 10" X 10" Weight: 25 lb.	$130-$200
Medium-size frame or cabin tent with 1 inner bedroom	Sleeps 3-4 in inner tent, kitchen area, sewn-in floor Dimensions: Outer tent is 14' long, 10' wide, 7' high in center; inner tent, 7' X 7' Packed size: 36" X 10" X 10" Weight: 60 lb.	$200-$260
Large frame or cabin tent sometimes with 2 inner bedrooms	Sleeps 6, sewn-in floor, picture windows, kitchen and lounge area Dimensions: 14' long, 14' wide, 7' high at center; two inner tents each 6½' X 6½' Packed size: 36" X 16" X 16" Weight: 80 lb.	$250-$330

What about fabrics? Nylon is for backpackers. Cotton fabric, whether it is called drill, twist, poplin, duck, or just plain canvas, is still best for families. The different names are for different cotton weaves. Most good tents are of drill and are treated with mildew and water repellents. Cheap tents have repellents that rub off and tend to have a musty smell, even before you use them. The best tents smell like the out-of-doors, clean and fresh.

Avoid an all-nylon tent for family camping. It doesn't breathe, so the air inside nylon tents, unless well ventilated, gets very uncomfortable. Moisture may even condense on the ceiling and walls and drip! Nylon's light weight and strength, however, are ideal for backpacking and trail use.

One of the best means for deciding which type of tent is best for your situation is to examine mail order catalogs or brochures. Write to several of the following for information:

Tent Catalogs

Sears, Chicago, Ill. 60607.
Ask for the catalog of recreational vehicles and camping.

Thermos Division of King-Seeley Thermos Co.
Norwich, Conn. 06360.

The Coleman Company
Wichita, Kan. 67201.

The Wenzel Company
St. Louis, Mo. 63132.

Recreational Equipment, Inc.
1525 Eleventh Ave., Seattle, Wash. 98122.

Eastern Mountain Sports, Inc.
1041 Commonwealth Ave., Boston, Mass. 02215.

Eureka Tent, Inc., subsidiary of
Johnson Diversified, Inc.
P.O. Box 966, Binghamton, N.Y. 13902.

Camel Manufacturing Co.
329 South Central St., Knoxville, Tenn. 37902.

White Stag, Hirsch-Weis Div.
5203 S.E. Johnson Creek Blvd.
Portland, Ore. 97206.

Eddie Bauer
P.O. Box 3700, Seattle, Wash. 98124.

Gerry Products, division of Outdoor
Sports Industries, Inc.
5450 North Valley Highway, Denver, Col. 80216.

Pacific Tent
P.O. Box 2028, Fresno, Cal. 93718.

Sleeping Bag

Next to the tent, the most important accessory is the sleeping bag, which has been discussed as part of the gear required by the backpacker. In that section we advocated the down-filled bag because of its weight and compressibility; the car-and-tent camper has greater latitude, however, so weight and size are not as important. Therefore, you might consider any of the many varieties of bags filled with dacron or similar fiber. The best feature about dacron bags is their quick wash-and-dryability. Another good feature about modern sleeping bags is their colorful design. Since they are attractive (this is especially true of those manufactured in Europe), you can use them year-round as bed quilts. Almost all bags can now be zipped together to form a large sleeping bag for two.

You can expect a good sleeping bag to cost between $30 and $50, unless you select down, in which case the price will triple. Bags in children's sizes are available for about $20. The addresses given for tents will also provide catalogs with sleeping bag options.

Stove

Earlier, when we were discussing camping via the road (hitchhiking, biking) we recommend our favorite stove, the Optimus (#8R), from Sweden. Well that's fine for lightweight stoves may be adequate for a couple or small family that doesn't do much cooking (like us), but we are "old school" when it comes to a really rugged and reliable stove: the Coleman two-burner (#413 G 499) is not glamorous, but it certainly is dependable. We have one of each.

We are not even a little impressed with the fancy propane models coming out in great profusion in recent years: they usually leak and are cumbersome to carry; they sometimes are difficult to find replacements for and do not work well in high altitudes. Three-burner stoves have one burner too many.

For advice on fuels, see the table on the advantages and disadvantages of the common fuels. For trouble-shooting problems with stoves, see the table on stove problems, causes, and solutions.

WHITE GAS

Advantages	Disadvantages
Light weight stove	Priming required
Spilled fuel evaporates readily	Spilled fuel very flammable
Stove fuel used for priming	Self-pressurizing stoves must be insulated from snow or cold
Fuel readily available in U.S.	Difficult to start in wind

KEROSENE

Spilled fuel will not ignite readily	Priming required
Stove can be set directly on snow	Spilled fuel does not evaporate readily
Low cost fuel	
Fuel available throughout the world	Difficult to start in wind

BUTANE

No priming required	Higher cost fuel
No fuel to spill	Empty cartridge disposal a problem
Immediate maximum heat output	Fuel must be kept above freezing for effective operation
	Bleuet cartridges cannot be changed until empty
	Lower heat output

Accessories

There is now a full range of options for internal sanitation (toilets), if you wish to supplement the facilities available in campgrounds, if you have young children, or if you plan considerable primitive camping. The most noteworthy improvement has come in the form of chemicals that no longer merely mask unpleasant odors, but actually destroy them, and are free of odor themselves. The chemical action is so efficient that the toilet is self-cleaning and the liquid waste is harmless to any water-flush drainage system. A simple, folding-seat model with disposable bags costs between $10 and $15. Most flushing models are available for about $100. (We have found a barrel-shaped variety—about $40—that fits neatly beneath the jump seat in our VW camperbus.)

Coolers (ice chests) come in all sizes. We recommend the plastic-exterior types you can use as a seat, that are as durable as the metal-exterior types and cost less. Get a large one if space is not a problem because you can store more ice and extra perishables, allowing you to spend more time camping and less time looking for ice and supermarkets. (We have found an Igloo brand cooler that serves as an added seat and fits conveniently between front seats of the camperbus. Most coolers are too wide.)

On long trips we find a covered bucket useful. A bucket? Yes. To badly soiled clothes, add water, soap and agitation from rough roads, and the bucket almost becomes a washing machine.

Of course, you will have stakes for the tent, but remember to include a variety of lengths and at least twice as many as you need for tent, dining fly, and canopy. Tent stakes are not really indestructible: We have left lower halfs in half of North America and most of Europe. Stakes that seem long enough in the store are short when you are trying to anchor one in soft wet or sandy ground, so have a few extra long stakes. (More suggestions for tent camping are included in Chapter 5.)

There are water cans, tent hangers, first aid kits, clotheslines, portable showers, clothes driers which hook to windows, portable ovens, and a host of other less essential items, but according to your circumstances may be desirable. All of these items and more are illustrated in the catalogs obtained from the stores already recommended. The more complete list of outlets is given later in this chapter. Many of these items also appear in the checklist at the end of the chapter.

MODE THREE: CAR WITH TENT TRAILER

If backpacking is not for you and living in a tent puts your wife off, then you may wish to consider the compromise between a motor caravan and a car-hauled trailer. The car pulling a tent trailer, sometimes called a *folding camper*, is probably the most common camping rig found throughout Canada.

These lightweight campers are roomy, set up fast, have a solid floor, provide storage space, and are less costly than a recreational vehicle that often does not get much use after the vacation and, thus, does not justify the greater expense.

There are a few basic things one should be aware of, however, since it is not as simple as just putting a trailer hitch on the back bumper and driving away. Except for the lightest folding trailers, such as the Minuteman by Coleman and the Danish import, the Combi-Camp, towing cars usually require at least heavy-duty radiators and batteries, and often benefit from power brakes as well. Not all folding tent trailers are safely towed by compacts and subcompacts, as these cars are usually capable of towing trailers only up to about 2,000 lb. (fully loaded) with no more than 200 lb. tongue weight.

The energy crisis has forced companies to offer some new mini-sized travel trailers. These offer a bit more convenience than the folding camper, but, of course, are heavier, requiring a larger car, and need more space for out-of-season storage. We feel you are getting away from *real* camping when you go "solid state." The best way to get information on folding campers and minitrailers is to attend the annual sport-and-outdoor shows in the late winter and spring. One folding trailer we like is the Combi-Camp, mentioned above. Danish-built, it stands on its end when not in use. The Combi-Camp only weighs 420 lb., has a low profile, and requires little storage space; the manufacturer is Frenderup Maskinfabrik, Grevinge, Denmark. One nice feature about this piece of equipment is that recently it has gone on sale in the larger cities of the United States, so you may be able to take a look at it near home. To find out which dealers are now displaying the Combi-Camp write: in the east, Thomas Nemet, Nemet Auto International, 153-03 Hillside Ave., Jamaica, N.Y. 11432; in the midwest, Combi-Camp Midwest, Inc., 13840 W. Warren, Dearborn, Mich. 48126; in the west, Hansen Brothers, 1500 Highway 99 North, Eugene, Ore. 97402. The delivered cost in the United States is about $1,300.

Other firms manufacturing folding caravans include:

Trailer	Manufacturer
Apache	Veseley Company
Coleman	Coleman Company
Nimrod	Nimrod Company
Polomino	Vanguard Industries
Skamper	AMP Skamper Corp.
Trail King	Trail King, Inc.
TrailStar	American Sterling Corp.

MODE FOUR: MOTORIZED CARAVAN

The term *motorized caravan* is a European term, referring to a camping vehicle with its own engine. Most North Americans call them *recreational vehicles*, or simply *RV's*. The most familiar motorized caravan across the country is the Volkswagen Campmobile, although the big three automobile manufacturers each offer a number of RV options. They perform and handle almost like cars, are comfortable to ride in and visibility is good because the driver is able to see over cars and roadside hedges. Like small mobilehomes they also fulfill the role of a large family car. RVs are particularly suitable for two persons or a young family of four, since they require minimum time for readiness and can go anywhere a medium-sized car can go.

For lengthy stays in one place, however, they are not convenient, for it is necessary each time you want to drive out of camp to take your bedroom and kitchen with you. Occasionally, you lose a site this way.

TYPES OF MOTOR CARAVANS

There are four main types of medium-sized motor caravans: fixed roof, elevating roof, coachbuilt, and pickup camper.

1 FIXED ROOF

2 ELEVATING ROOF

ACHBUILT MODELS

4 PICKUP CAMPER

The pickup camper, a camping unit mounted on back of a pickup truck, is particularly popular in the west where the truck becomes a second car, and for any handyman-sportsman is the most useful vehicle imaginable. The pickup campers have all the attributes of RVs except they frequently lack aesthetic appeal.

Beyond the medium-sized motorized caravans, there are, of course, the luxury motor coaches and motorhomes. The biggest is the Winnebago Chieftain; this motorhome sleeps six in comfort, has central heating and air conditioning, hot and cold running water, seven-cubic-foot refrigerator-freezer, four-burner stove with eye-level oven, shower, bath tub, flush toilet, stereo unit with AM/FM radio, and so on. Too much.

Extra tent or motorchalet?

If the family is larger than can be accommodated in the recreational vehicles illustrated here, it is possible to take an extra tent along; put the extra gear on a roof rack, or tow a small storage trailer. If small children are to be accommodated, it is possible to sleep two children in a bunk intended to accommodate one adult.

A free-standing annex tent is also useful to extend the bounds of either motor caravan or stationwagon. Motor chalets usually come without a floor, but do provide standing room and plenty of extra storage or sleeping space: size is approximately 9' X 7', and cost about $120.

Finally, while we can provide some general advice, only you are aware of the requirements appropriate to your circumstances, so write to manufactuers for descriptive brochures. Their literature customarily includes color pictures, diagrams, size and weight specifications as well as the latest prices. In the last few years libraries and bookstores are responding to consumer demand, so a little search will net many detailed guides to new equipment that go beyond our advice here, beyond the information salesmen provide, and even beyond that contained in the books we recommend to you.

MODE FIVE: CAR OR TRUCK HAULING A TRAILER

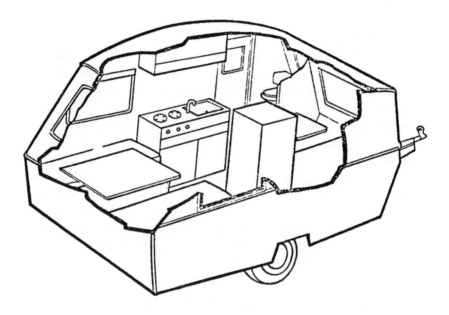

We must express a bias. We are generally opposed to the rolling penthouse. As more disposable income became available, almost insatiable appetites called for larger, more luxurious, more expensive equipment. Industry responded. Today trailers over 40 feet in length are available; they can and do include such items as fireplaces, wet bars, built-in vacuum cleaners, and fold-out dining rooms; they have central heating and air conditioning, elaborate baths, and power plants with enough electrical equipment to outfit a small factory. Small amenities—as described in an advertising brochure—included in a bath are items such as a stylish towel bars, cosmetic box with sliding mirror doors, three large wall mirrors and a pair of fashionable multi-bulb complexion lights. Other factories include a deluxe rotary TV antenna, an intercom system (really! an intercom system), a battery-operated clock, and much more. It sounds like a home in an exclusive neighborhood.

EQUIPMENT

Compared with our European cousins, North Americans are in the bush league when it comes to tent camping. You probably would feel inadequately equipped after camping with the English, the Germans and the French, because they spend a great deal of time camping, and it is not uncommon for them to spend as much as $600 for a tent. Some go to excesses. For example, we saw a German family with a canvas garage to complement their three-room, multi-colored tent, which had windows all around and two arched doorways; next to the German family was an Austrian with a comparable tent, inflatable motorized boat, and electric rotisserie. When it rained, they both went into their tents to enjoy television. If you think this is unusual, let us tell you it is possible to see a family of Germans set up their *kamping platz* with a tent for the parents, separate units for the children, and a puqntent for schnauzer. After the tents are assembled, out will come the folding chairs, several tables (indoor and outdoor), matching floral printed air mattresses and sleeping bags, and sundry items such as stove, refrigerator, radio, and TV. Then for outdoor living they put in place their three-position lawn and beach chairs, lanterns, lawn games and bright orange, inflatable kayaks. It is not unusual for the wealthier European camper to have a maid along to care for the children and handle food preparation and dishes.

So much for the European—more of whom are seen in North American campgrounds every year. Our concern is locating equipment found between the Pacific and Atlantic, so the remainder of this chapter provides addresses, checklists, and a few hints.

ESPECIALLY RECOMMENDED
SOURCES OF EQUIPMENT

On our west coast, where camping has for many become a way of life, there are a number of suppliers we can recommend with confidence. The very best in selection and price is Recreation Equipment of Seattle. They have a fine selection of European camping stoves at prices no higher than in Europe; an excellent selection of backpacks; and a good selection of tents, cookware, sleeping bags, camp lights, and picnicware. Catalog and mail orders are available. Write to: Recreation Equipment, 1525 11th Ave., Seattle, Wash. 98122. For higher-quality goods and higher prices Eddie Bauer, Inc., also of

Seattle, is highly recommended—especially for the best in down-filled sleeping bags. Get the Eddie Bauer mail order catalog by writing to 1737 Airport Way South, P.O. Box 3700, Seattle, Wash. 98124. The Seattle showroom is at 1926 Third Ave. In San Francisco see the equipment at Eddie Bauer's new store and also check Sierra Designs, at 4th and Addison St. in Berkeley.

Midwest

In Denver it is Holubar and Gerry, especially for backpacks, and Alpine Design at 6185 E. Arapahoe, Boulder, Col. 80303. In the midwest, Eddie Bauer, Inc., has a new store in Minneapolis at the Foshay Tower. In or near Cleveland, check Wilderness Ways, 12417 Cedar Rd., Cleveland Heights, Ohio 44106.

East

L.L. Bean of Freeport, Me. 04032, has a wide selection of camping equipment and will also send the mail order catalog on request. In New York, check at Abercrombie and Fitch, and Camp and Trail Outfitters; the latter provides mail order service from 112 Chambers St., New York, N.Y. 10007. In Ogdensburg, N.Y., it is Thomas Black & Sons for English equipment. Ask for their catalog: 930 Ford St., 13669. In Massachusetts, Eastern Mountain Sports have outlets in Wellesley, Amherst, Boston, and Conway; their catalog is excellent. Write: EMS, Inc., 1041 Commonwealth Ave., Boston, Mass. 02215.

Southeast

In the southeast, write to Hi-Camp, P.O. Box 17602, Charlotte, N.C. 28211, or to Trailblazer, Taylorsville Rd., Statesville, N.C. 28677.

EQUIPMENT CHECKLIST

While planning and packing, jog your mind with this checklist—add or delete where appropriate.

Example. On each line: cross out what you don't wish to take, circle what you need to purchase, check when packed.

Take	Purchase	Packed	
	Will	Did	
			Flashlight, lantern, candles, extras—mantels, generator, batteries

Take Purchase Packed

Tent, stakes, ropes, repair kit

Extra canopies, stakes, ropes

Ground cloths (interior, exterior)

Sleeping bags, blankets, quilts, pillows

Sleeping bag linings, sheets, pillow cases

Foam pads, cots, air mattresses (pump, repair kit)

Folding table, table covering

Folding chairs, stools

Chaise lounges, hammock

Grid, hibachi, grill, charcoal, wood, fire starter, extinguisher

Stove, fuel, funnel

Ropes, clothespins, braided expandable clothesline

Flashlight, lantern, candles, extras—mantels, generator, batteries

Hammer, hatchet, and sheath

Folding shovel and saw, ice pick

Pocket knife, sharpening stone

Pliers, screwdriver, nails

Whisk broom, dust pan

Wash basin

Portable toilet, disposable bags, disinfectant

Assorted plastic bags

Aluminum foil, paper toweling, napkins, cheesecloth

Matches in moisture-proof container, newspapers for insulation

Cleanser, detergent, cold-water soap, laundry (and mesh) bags

Water carriers (collapsible)

Assorted plastic screw-top containers, plastic egg carrier

Pressure cooker, Dutch oven, reflector oven, foil pans

Nested saucepans (Teflon?) with covers—one large for lobsters

Skillet, griddle, skewers

coffeepot, teabob, kettle

Tongs, wooden spoon, slotted spoon, soup ladle, spatulas, pancake turner, pot holders

Cutting board, grater, strainer (collapsible), funnel

Corkscrew, bottle opener, bottle caps, can opener-punch

Paring and slicing knives, vegetable peeler

Fish scaler, nut cracker and picks (for lobsters, crabs), oyster knife

Measuring devices, timer; toaster (collapsible)

Dishpan, dishtowels, dishcloth, apron, pot scrubber, dish scraper

Covered salt and pepper shakers, assorted spice containers

Nesting cups (Sierra and disposable)

Plates, bowls (plastic and disposable)

Glasses (plastic, disposable nested—wine and liqueur, too)

Flatware (rust-free)

Water purification tablets, bleach

Bar soap and container, disinfectant

Coat hangers, inflatable

Toiletries: toobhbrush, deodorant, safety pins, mirror, etc.

First aid kit and book, vitamins, prescriptions

Sunglasses, extra pair reading glasses

Insect repellent (liquid, spray)

Suntan lotion, Calamine lotion

Toilet and facial tissues

Towels, washcloths, wash n'dry

Backpacks

Recreational equipment: balls, tackle, swim suits, etc.

Binoculars, compass, nature books

Camera equipment, film

Radio, cassette recorder, alarm clock

Heater

Portable cooler, refrigerator

Maps, guidebooks (see Countdown in chapter on planning)

Sewing and writing equipment

Toys and supplies for children

-5
POTPOURRI

It is the little bits of things,
That fret and worry us;
We can dodge an elephant,
But we can't a fly.
—JOSH BILLINGS

It seems there are always a lot of things needing mention so we will try to handle them in a question-and-answer format, grouping by topic whenever possible.

What is meant by "Old World Charm?"
No bathroom.

Any problems using U.S. electric shavers, etc., in Canadian outlets?
No.

When are long distance rates for telephoning least expensive?
All day on Sunday and 6 P.M. to 6 A.M. other days—or is it nights?

Can we use U.S. dollars?
Yes, but you will get a much better exchange if you visit a bank and receive the prevailing rate. Restaurants and stores usually charge for their inconvenience.

Can U.S. stamps by used from Canada?
No! No! Canadian postal rates differ from those in the States, and, in any case, you must use stamps of the country where the mail originates.

Can we use credit cards?
Yes, the most common are the American Express, Diners' Club, and Carte Blanche. Wherever Chargex is accepted, your Bank Americard will also be honored. Bancardchecks are also common. At service stations, credit cards from the major oil companies will buy gas, oil, tires, batteries, and even minor repairs.

Is a Canadian called an American?

"North American," yes, but he prefers "Canadian."

Where do most Canadians live?

Along a band that is about 3,000 miles long and 100 miles wide or stated another way, 80% of all Canadians live within 100 miles of the Trans-Canada Highway.

Which cities have the largest population?

Montreal has a population approaching three million, only slightly more than that of Toronto; Vancouver's is approximately a third their size, and the remaining major cities hover roughly around the half-million mark.

What is a Canadian Nonresident Interprovince Motor Vehicle Liability Insurance Card, and is it really required?

They may never ask to see it—unless there is an accident—but American motorists are advised to get this yellow card showing their financial responsibility from their insurance agent before leaving home.

Is a special driver's license required?

Driver's licenses from any state or any country are recognized, as is the International Driver's License.

Can any vehicle be driven into Canada—even if rented or loaned?

Vehicles and trailers used for touring up to 12 months can enter without custom's assessment. If a permit is required, it is issued at the border. Rented trailers of the u-haul luggage variety may be subject to a small refundable deposit. Rented vehicles should be accompanied by a motor vehicle registration form and a copy of the rental contract stating that the vehicle can be used in Canada. If a tourist is using a vehicle that is not registered in his name, he should carry a letter from its registered owner authorizing use of the vehicle.

When crossing the Canadian border is it necessary to have passport, visa, or documents showing citizenship?

Native-born U.S. citizens do not need a passport or visa but should carry some identifying paper such as a birth, baptismal, or voter's certificate. *Naturalized* U.S. citizens should carry their naturalization certificate, and *permanent residents* of the United States who are not Americans should carry their Alien Registration Receipt Card.

Customs regulations are so ho-hum, but do you know—or care—about the restrictions on transporting tobacco or alcohol into Canada?

"Up to 50 cigars, 200 cigarettes, and 2 lb. of manufactured tobacco, and up to 40 oz. of spirituous liquor or wine may be allowed entry in this manner. If beer or ale is substituted for the aforementioned beverages, 24 pints or the equivalent thereof up to 288 imperial ounces may be imported." These quantities are admitted free of duty if used by visitor, not resold. To import tobacco products a person must be 16 years or over, and ti import alcoholic beverages the visitor must have reached the legal age established by authorities of the province or territory into which the beverages are entering. U.S. customs regulations differ and we'll get to those at the end of the chapter.

Should recreational equipment be declared?

Yes, declare your fishing tackle, portable boat, outboard motor, ice boat, motorized tobaggan, snowmobile, skidoo, equipment for camping, golf, tennis, and the like, radio, portable TV, musical instrument, typewriter, and camera. To simplify your entry prepare a duplicate list of all durable items carried, with a description of each and serial numbers where possible. All will need to be reported when leaving Canada. Normally these items are all admitted free of duty although occasionally a refundable deposit is requested to ensure exportation.

Traveling with pets?

No restrictions on *cats*, but *dogs* from the United States must be accompanied by a certificate signed by a licensed veterinarian certifying that the dog has been vaccinated against rabies during the preceding 12 months. The certificate should carry an adequate and legible description of the dog and date of vaccination. *Puppies* under six months may be vaccinated with a reduced dosage recorded on the certificate. Suckling puppies accompanied by a mother dog who has been vaccinated are admitted without restrictions. *Birds* of the parrot family are admitted if found healthy and if owner certifies in writing that the birds have not been in contact with other birds for 90 days immediately preceding importation. *Other pets* such as canaries, cage birds, monkeys, skunks, hamsters, guinea pigs, rabbits, and the like enter without restrictions.

Are tourists entering Canada faced with food restrictions?

Two days' food per person is allowed, duty-free. (British Columbia prohibits the importation of fruit trees other than citrus and pine unless the trees have been fumigated. The same is true for fresh apricots, nectarines, and peaches.) Meats are generally prohibited as personal effects or as gifts; however, uncertified meats from the United States are permitted in quantities of not more than 20 lb. and provided the importer gives verbal assurance that the meat is for personal or family use, not for resale.

Concerned about importing plant material into Canada?

All plants and plant material must be *declared* at time of entry. "The Plant Protection Division prohibits or restricts the importation of plants, their unprocessed byproducts and related material including seeds, bulbs, fruits, and vegetables, without prior authority. Soil, plants with soil, and implements and articles contaminated with soil are prohibited entry from all countries except the continental United States, excepting the states of Delaware and New York. From other states, such importation must meet the requirements of federal and state quarantines applying the area of origin."

Visitors planning to bring in plants or plant material are advised to write in advance to the Director, Plant Protection Division, Department of Agriculture, Ottawa, Ontario K1A OC5.

Interested in the regulations on firearms and fishing tackle?

Canadians are quite conservative when it comes to carrying guns, so unless you feel it is absolutely necessary to have them with you, better to leave them at home—hunt with a camera, there are fewer controls!

"Revolvers, pistols, fully automatic firearms, and 'any firearm that is less than 26 in. in length or is designed or adapted to be fired when reduced to a length of less than 26 in. by folding, telescoping, or otherwise,' are prohibited." Neither rifles and shotguns (other than fully automatic) nor fishing tackle require special permit, although customs must be provided with a description of the equipment and serial numbers of the guns so that articles can be readily cleared again for exportation.

A visitor 16 years or older does not need a federal permit to possess most sporting rifles and shotguns or fishing tackle but anyone under "16 years is not permitted to import any firearm including air pistols, CO_2 pistols, rifles, shotguns, and revolvers." Two hundred rounds of ammunition per person are admitted duty-free.

Gaining admission, however, doesn't entitle one to hunt or fish without a license—nonresident licenses are required for *each* province or territory where hunting or fishing is done.

If *in transit to Alaska* over the Alaska Highway, the western provinces allow revolvers, pistols, and semi-automatic weapons to be imported under customs permit on the condition they are placed in a container capable of being sealed by Canadian customs officials at port of entry. This is not so east of the Ontario-Manitoba border.

It is illegal at all times to carry loaded firearms in vehicles. It is also illegal to carry or use firearms in any place frequented by game except under the authority of a license.

Do the regulations governing hunting and fishing in Canada vary from one province to another?

Yes, there are no uniform regulations covering Canada as a whole. For the most current information regarding regulations, licenses, fishing conditions, and game species write directly to the province you intend to hunt or fish in. (See the appendix for the addresses.)

How many time zones cross Canada?

Would you believe seven? A difference of 5-1/2 hours exists between the Yukon and Newfoundland. As we understand it, there is only a half-hour difference between the Newfoundland and Atlantic time zones so when it is 12 noon in the Yukon zone, it is 1 P.M. in the Pacific zone, 2 P.M. in the Mountain zone, 3 P.M. in the Central zone, 4 P.M. in the Eastern zone, and 5 P.M. in the Atlantic zone, it is 5:30 P.M. in the Newfoundland zone—and 9 P.M. in London.

The various zones correspond with the time zones in the United States; a more detailed description defines the zones in this way:

Newfoundland Standard Time	Newfoundland and Labrador
Atlantic Standard Time	Maritime Provinces, Gaspe Peninsula, Anticosti Island, Quebec province east of Comeau Bay
Eastern Standard Time	Remaining part of Quebec, all of Ontario except the far northwest
Central Standard Time	Northwest Ontario west of 90^0 longitude, Manitoba, southeast Saskatchewan (Keewatin area)
Mountain Standard Time	Remaining part of Saskatchewan (except SE) including Regina, Alberta, and the N.W.T. to the north of Saskatchewan and Alberta
Pacific Standard Time	British Columbia
Yukon Standard Time	Yukon Territory

Asking about daylight saving time only clouds the issue, for it appears there is no consistent way except in Quebec of knowing what cities or areas follow it. Many cities within Alberta, British Columbia, and Prince Edward Island do not use D.S.T.

Montreal and Quebec plus a host of other cities and towns in the province of Quebec do follow D.S.T., as do Halifax, Saint John, Winnipeg, and Regina.

If you forget—as we usually do—when daylight saving time takes effect, here it is: from the last Sunday in April to the last Saturday in October, all timepieces are advanced one hour.

How many national parks exist, and how can we learn more about them?

Canadian National Parks, originating in 1885 in Banff, now number 28 encompassing more than 50,000 square miles with another 30 parks in the planning stage. Over 16 million people in 1973 visited the Canadian National Parks, so there is no doubt about their popularity.

If you would like more information than what is provided here, write to one of the following five regional offices or directly to the headquarters of the park in question.

Parks Canada—Western Region
131 Customs Bld.
11th Ave. and 1st St. S.E.
Calgary, Alberta T2G OX5
(Tel. 403-265-6380)

Parks Canada—Prairie Region
114 Oarry St.
Winnipeg, Manitoba R3C 101
(Tel. 204-985-2131)

Parks Canada—Ontario Region
P.O. Box 1359
Cornwall, Ontario K6H 5V4
(Tel. 613-933-7951)

Parks Canada—Quebec Region
P.O. Box 9578
Ste. Foy, Quebec G1V 4C2
(Tel. 418-694-4042)

Parks Canada—Atlantic Region
5161 George St.
Halifax, Nova Scotia B3U1M7
(Tel. 902-426-3405)

Western Region

Of the nine national parks in the region (five in British Columbia and four in Alberta) are some of the oldest and one of the newest in the nation. Banff, Glacier, Yoho, and Waterton Lakes were all established in the late 1800s.

Pacific Rim in British Columbia: The major feature of this 150-square-mile park on the west coast of Vancouver Island is its fabulous Long Beach. Only established in 1971, this park's plans include an opportunity to view sea lions and other marine life, an interpretive program, a historic Lifesaving Trail. The park is accessible by highway, has a campground in the park and other accommodations nearby. Address: P.O. Box 280, Ucluelet, British Columbia VOR 3A0. Tel. 604-726-7721.

Mount Revelstoke in British Columbia: Situated on the west slope of the Selkirk Mountains, this 100-square-mile rolling, mountain-top park has alpine meadows and lakes as well as an interpretive program. It is accessible by Trans-Canada Highway, and although only picnic facilities are within the park, other accommodations are found in the nearby towns of Revelstoke. Address: P.O. Box 350, Revelstoke, British Columbia VOE 2SO. Tel. 604-837-5155.

Glacier in British Columbia: Also in the Selkirk Mountains, this rugged landscape encompasses towering peaks, rushing streams, over 100 glaciers, and forests of hemlock and cedar. This 521-square-mile park has an interpretive program, motor hotel, and campgrounds, and is accessible by the Trans-Canada Highway. Address: P.O. Box 350, Revelstoke, British Columbia VOE 2SO. Tel. 604-837-5155.

Yoho in British Coluvbia: Situated on the western slopes of the Rockies, Yoho Park encompasses lofty peaks, glaciers, waterfalls, lakes, and the Yoho and Kicking Horse Valleys. The facilities include lodges, chalets, campgrounds, and an interpretive program. The 507-square-mile park is accessible by the Trans-Canada Highway. Address: Field, British Columbia VOA 1GO. Tel. 604-343-6324.

Kootenay in British Columbia: Also situated on the western slopes of the Rockies, this spectacular area has two river valleys of differing characters—high glaciers and deep canyons, icy alpine lakes and hot springs. The facilities include chalets, campgrounds, an airstrip just outside the park at Radium Hot Springs, and an interpretive program. This 532-square-mile park is accessible by a highway, although not Trans One. Address: P.O. Box 220, Radium Hot Springs, British Columbia VOA 1MO. Tel. 604-347-9615.

Waterton Lakes in Alberta: This northern section of the Waterton-Glacier International Peace Park is a blending of mountains and meadows, lakes and vistas. The facilities include hotels, motels, chalets, and campgrounds as well as an interpretive program with its 203-square-mile area. Address: Waterton Park, Alberta TOK 2MO. Tel. 403-859-2262.

Banff in Alberta: This 2,564-square-mile park is noted for its ice-capped peaks, deep valleys, glaciers and lakes, its famous ski center and hot springs, and the well-known resorts of Banff and Lake Louise. Park facilities include all accommodations plus campgrounds, an interpretive program, and a park museum. It is accessible by both railroad and Trans-Canada One. Address: Banff, Alberta TOL OCO. Tel. 403-762-3324.

Jasper in Alberta: This 4,200-square-mile park is one of the largest in North America. It is noted for its alpine landscape, ice fields, hot springs, and ski area. Campgrounds and all types of accommodations are available with easy access by rail or highway. Address: Jasper, Alberta TOE lEO. Tel. 403-852-4401.

Elk Island in Alberta: Lakes and forests of aspen and spruce make up most of this 75-square-mile park which serves as home for a large bison herd. Facilities include a campground, a fine beach, and an interpretive program. Other accommodations are available in Edmonton with highway access from the park. Address: Site 4, R.R. #1, Fort Saskatchewan, Alberta TOB lPO. Tel. 403-543-3781.

Prairie Region

Of the five national parks in the prairie region, three were established in the 1920s, two in 1972 (Kluane and Nahanni).

Kluane in the Yukon: Still in the planning stages, this 8,500-square-mile park in the southwest corner of the Yukon Territory has Canada's highest mountains, as well as extensive ice fields and glaciers. A campground has not yet been established but accommodations are available nearby. There is highway access. Address: Mile 1019, Alaska Highway, Haines Junction, Yukon Territory YlA 3A4. Tel. 3371.

Nahanni in the Northwest Territories: Three deep river canyons, hot springs, and spectacular Virginia Falls are included in this wilderness park along the South Nahanni River in the southwest corner of the Northwest Territories. No campgrounds are yet developed within the park since it is still in the planning stages, but accommodations are available nearby, with highway access. Address: Fort Smith, Northwest Territories XOE OPO. Tel. 403-872-2349.

Wood Buffalo in Alberta and Northwest Territories: Largest of the national parks, this region of forests and open plains straddles the border between the two provinces between Athabasca and Great Slave Lake. It serves as the home for the continent's largest bison herd and is a nesting ground for the rare whooping crane. The 17,300-square-mile area is accessible by highway and developed camping is available. Address: Fort Smith, Northwest Territories XOE OPO. Tel. 403-872-2349.

Prince Albert in Saskatchewan: Providing an interesting transition between the northern forests and the prairie grasslands, this 1,496-square-mile area, is interlaced with streams, lakes, and forests. Facilities include an interpretive center and program, campgrounds, and other accommodations. Accessible by highway. Address: Box 100, Waskesiu Lake, Saskatchewan SOJ 2YO. Tel. 306-663-3511.

Riding Mountain in Manitoba: With a blending of western grasslands and nothern and eastern forests we find fine lakes, a good interpretive program with center, and a variety of accommodations including campgrounds within the 1,149-square-mile park. Address: Wasagaming, Manitoba ROJ 2HO. Tel. 204-848-2811.

Ontario Region

Three of the parks in the region were established between 1900 and 1929; the remaining one (Pukaskwa) was established in 1971.

Pukaskwa in Ontario: Not yet accessible by highway this 725-square-mile park contains many lakes and rivers plus a wide variety of wildlife as it is situated in the wilderness area of northern Ontario, along the northern shore of Lake Superior. Since the park is still under development, accommodations must be sought nearby. Address: Box 550, Marathon, Ontario POT 2EO. Tel. 807-229-0801.

Georgian Bay Islands in Ontario: This 5.5-square-mile park is accessible by boat from nearby mainland points. There is a small mainland park area but the uniqueness of this park is to be seen in the 40 picturesque islands which provide a varied landscape of glacier-scraped rock, weathered pine, and dense maple-beech-oak woodland. Flowerpot Island has remarkable rock pillar formations; Beausoleil Islands have campground facilities. An interpretive program is established and accommodations are available on the mainland as well. Address: Honey Harbour, Ontario POE 1EO. Tel. 705-756-2415.

Point Pelee in Ontario: This six-square-mile park is a birdwatcher's paradise, for it is located on the path of two major migration flyways. Large cattail marshes, some forested areas, and a 14-mile beach are included within the park limits. There is highway access and an interpretive program and center, but accommodations have to be sought elsewhere.

St. Lawrence Islands in Ontario: The tiniest of the national parks (1.6 square miles), it has a small mainland area, 18 heavily treed islands, and 80 rocky islets all located in the famous Thousand Island region, known for its scenery and water recreation opportunities. Park campgrounds are found at Mallorytown Landing and on Grenadier Island. Address: P.O. Box 469, R.R. #3, Mallorytown, Ontario KOE lRO. Tel. 613-923-5241.

Quebec Region

The national parks within the Quebec region have all been established in the 1970s, making this the region with the fewest and the newest parks.

La Mauricie in Quebec: This heavily wooded 210-square-mile park is situated in the largely unspoiled section of the Laurentian Mountains in the Grand-Mere and Shawinigan area, almost equidistant from Montreal and Quebec City. Although still under development, there are lakes and campgrounds to enjoy, plus an interpretive program; highway access and additional accommodations available nearby. Address: P.O. Box 758, Shawinigan, Quebec G9N 6V9. Tel. 819-536-2638.

Baffin Island in the Northwest Territories: Currently in the planning stage, this 8,290-square-mile tract is located on the Cumberland Peninsula of Baffin Island. The area abounds with fiords, deeply carved mountains, glaciers, and arctic wildlife. It is accessible from Montreal by air. Address: Pangnirtung, Northwest Territories, XOA ORO. Tel. 962.

Forillon in Quebec: Situated on the scenic tip of Forillon Peninsula on the Gulf of St. Lawrence the 92.8-square-mile park is planned to reflect both the unique coastal environment and the rich human history of the famous Gaspe region. Accessible by highway and already functioning with campground and interpretive center and program. Address: P.O. Box 1220, Gaspe, Quebec GOC lRO. Tel. 418-368-5505.

Atlantic Region

Of the seven parks in this region, two were established in the mid-1930s (Cape Breton Highlands and PEI), and one in each of the following decades, with Kouchibouguac being the newest.

Kouchibouguac in New Brunswick: The most outstanding feature of this 87-square-mile park is the 15-1/2 mile of off-shore sandbars which provide protected swimming, quiet lagoons, and bays off of Kouchibouguac Bay, along the northern section of Northumberland Strait. Accessible by highway, it is functioning with campground and interpretive program. Address: Kouchibouguac, Kent County, New Brunswick EOA 2AO. Tel. 506-876-3973.

Fundy in New Brunswick: This nearly 80-square-mile area provides a fine example of the rugged shoreline surrounding the Bay of Fundy with sandstone cliffs, coves, inlets, forests, waterfalls, streams, and lakes providing variety in landscape. All accommodations including campgrounds are available and an interpretive program is operating. The highest tides in the world are operating, too. Address: Alma, New Brunswick EOA 1BO. Tel. 506-887-2000.

Prince Edward Island: With a 25-mile coastal strip on the Gulf of St. Lawrence this park on the island of the same name is abundant with sand dunes, cliffs, salt marshes, and fine bathing beaches. Campgrounds, lodge, and bungalows are available plus an interpretive program within the limits of the 7-square-mile park. Address: P.O. Box 487, Charlottetown, Prince Edward Island C1A 7L1. Tel. 902-672-2211.

Kejimkujik in Nova Scotia: Indian rock carvings can be studied in this 147.3-square-mile park with its rolling landscape, numerous lakes, and countless islands and bays. Accessible by highway with campgrounds and an interpretive program in operation. Address: P.O. Box 36, Maitland Bridge, Nova Scotia BOT 1NO. Tel. 902-242-2770.

Cape Breton Highlands in Nova Scotia: Beautiful seascapes along the Cabot Trail, rugged coastlines, and forested hillsides untouched by fire dominate this 367-square-mile region. Campgrounds and an interpretive program are functioning. Address: Ingonish Beach, Nova Scotia BOC 1LO. Tel. Ingonish 31.

Gros Morne in Newfoundland: Situated in the most scenic section of the Long Range Mountains on Newfoundland's western coast, about 50 miles northwest of Corner Brook, are fiord-like lakes, dense forests, rugged seacoast, and beautiful beaches. The 750-square-mile park is accessible by highway, and although still under development, an interpretive program is in operation. Address: P.O. Box 130, Rocky Harbour, Bonne Bay, Newfoundland AOK 4NO. Tel. Rocky Harbour 2417.

Terra Nova in Newfoundland: Accessible by Trans One, this 153.1-square-mile park is made up of a rugged, deeply indented coastline with spectator inlets, a boreal forest of spruce and bogs, and a display of icebergs or along the sides of roads or highways is not permitted either. A two-week limit on occupancy is enforced in most campgrounds.

Is it possible to make reservations at national park camp-grounds? Are there particular restrictions we should be aware of?

No reservations are possible for camping as all campsites are allocated on a first-come, first-served basis. Camping within the park but outside the established ·campgrounds is not permitted unless special permission is granted and the necessary camping and fire permits are obtained from a park warden; camping in picnic areas or along the sides of roads or highways is not permitted either. A two-week limit on occupancy is enforced in most campgrounds. Free firewood is usualy available, but fires are permitted only in stoves, grills, and fireplaces.

More specific information regarding the various parks and their facilities is available in *Accommodation National Parks* obtainable from the Canadian Government Travel Bureau. Specify the provinces you intend to visit, as there are two volumes available for Eastern and Western Canada.

Although we have not seen it yet, we have recently learned of a booklet—available at all Information Canada offices (75¢) which discusses camping techniques. It is titled *Family Camping*.

What regulations apply to firearms within a national park?

A person entering a national park must have his firearms, or any devices for capturing or destroying game, sealed by the park officials. One exception is made for persons traveling through Elk Island, Fundy, Prince Edward Island, Cape Breton Highlands, Glacier, Mount Revelstoke or Terra Nova National Parks during the hunting season of the province where the park is located, if all firearms and devices in his possession are kept within the vehicle and dismantled.

You will probably see more animals in the wild of Canada than you have ever seen anywhere in the States. Do you know what to do when you encounter a bear, for instance, or how to avoid inviting them to your campsite?

In the national parks and even in some of the provincial parks not far from the Trans-Canada Highway, bear often roam. Because of their protected status many have lost the fear of man and appear tame, although actually in this state they are more dangerous. Often bear are seeking food when they approach a person or a car and then may attack without warning and for no apparent reason. Because of this, *NEVER* feed or approach a bear—in fact, for your protection and the bear's, it is *unlawful to feed bears.*

Bear will eat almost anything. In established campgrounds we are told to:

Keep campsite clean.

Use prepared food, avoiding bacon and ham as they are greasy and odorous.

Lock food in the trunk of your vehicle—*NEVER* in the tent.

Never leave dirty utensils around.

Never eat or cook in the tent, as the smell lingers.

Place all garbage in covered garbage containers or burn all food scraps.

Store food in airtight containers; a good deodorizer is also effective in eliminating food odors from your campsite.

In the backcountry it is suggested we:

Camp off animal or walking trails and near large, sparsely branched trees you can climb if the occasion arises.

Choose another area if signs of bear are evident (fresh tracks, diggings, droppings).

Cache food away from the tent, preferably hanging 10-12 ft. off the ground from a strong limb.

NEVER cook or store food in the tent.

BURN food scraps—burying is useless and dangerous.

Carry out all noncombustible garbage to nearest covered container.

Several more things can be done to avoid encountering a bear: Watch for bear signs; stay out of berry patches and away from carcass remains or other food sources; avoid walking alone; carry a noisemaker (bells, a can with stones inside, a whistle); remain alert and aware that a strong wind may carry your scent away, enabling you to surprise a bear unaware of your presence; and never go near a cub. Finally, don't take your dog into bear country—just the sight or smell of a dog has been known to infuriate bears. When in trouble, the dog is likely to run to you, with the bear close behind.

However, if worse comes to worse and the bear confronts you, it does not necessarily mean it will attack. If you see a bear, try to keep your cool and try to assess the situation. Many bear can run as fast as a racehorse, so running is not recommended. Quick, jerky movements may prompt an attack. Remain still and speak in low tones, and he may understand you mean no harm. *If it is a grizzly* (prominent humps over shoulders, grizzled, white-tipped fur, big), slowly back towards a sturdy tree, removing your pack or loose garment to distract him. Although grizzlies cannot climb trees they can reach eight to ten feet—so keep climbing! *If it is a black bear* (straight shoulder-rump line, brown tapered nose with long nostrils, flat-soled feet with short, curved claws, smaller), the tree won't do you much good as he probably can climb better than you can. If you have no escape, we are told to "play dead": Drop to the ground face down, lift legs to the chest, and clasp hands over back of neck (if your pack is still on, pray it will serve to protect your back). It takes courage to lie still, but bears have been known to inflict only minor injuries under these circumstances. Sometimes bear will bluff their way out of a threatening situation by charging and then veering away at the last second.

Very few attacks by bear occur considering the number of people in the woods and parks these days. The majority of these attacks are brought on by ignorance or carelessness.

For more complete information about types of bear, where they are likely to be located, footprint illustrations, write for *You Are in Bear Country,* published by Parks Canada and available from the Canadian Government Travel Bureau in Ottawa.

One day after discussing safety precautions concerning bear with our daughters, this little piece of poetry was composed:

> *He may be brown,*
> *He may be black,*
> *You bother him,*
> *He'll get you back!*
> *—KATHY COPE*

Proper care and cleaning of down-filled clothing and sleeping bags prolong their serviceability. We'll try to anticipate your questions.

Quoting information learned from tests conducted by Recreation Equipment, Inc.—a reputable manufacturer and dealer of down sleeping bags—we emphasize that proper use, care, and cleaning of a down item will prolong its years of service. After being compressed, restore its insulating efficiency before using it by shaking and fluffing it well enabling the down to achieve its maximum loft. Air down items thoroughly after each use and after dry cleaning; then store loosely folded or draped over a hanger and protected in a clean, dry place.

Sometimes dry cleaning is recommended for down items, but in latest tests at Recreation Equipment, best scores came from *careful hand laundering.* They suggest filling a bathtub half full of warm water and adding one capsule of Fluffy Down soap (manufactured in Holland). Then gently press the down item into the water, sponging the heavily soiled areas. Soak for about 12 hours, carefully turning the item a few times. Gently agitate by hand to remove loosened dirt.

Down absorbs great amounts of water so *do not lift the sleeping bag or garment out of the water.* Instead, drain water from the tub pressing gently on the article to remove the excess water. Then refill the tub with fresh water and agitate gently by hand to remove the remaining soap. Drain and repeat the rinsing process until all traces of soap are removed. Gently press out as much water as possible.

You have a choice for drying, depending upon your circumstances. The preferred method appears to be air drying the article for 1 to 1-1/2 days on a *flat surface that permits air to pass through the item.* Hanging may damage it. Then, after it has partially dried, it may be placed in a commercial clothes dryer with a few clean tennis balls or tennis shoes added the last ten minutes or so to help down achieve loft.

The other method of drying is lifting the garment or bag from the tub by placing both hands under it—you may need an octopus—and carrying it to a (hopefully) nearby washing machine. After distributing the garment evenly around the tub, use the spin cycle to remove the excess water. Final drying may be done in a large commercial dryer at low heat.

If the facilities for hand laundering are not available, a reputable drying cleaning establishment can be visited but only if you are assured they will use a clean solvent.

Both methods of cleaning will likely remove the water repellency of outer covering. You may wish to have the water repellency commercially reapplied, or you may choose to use Scotch-Guard spray, as we do, at home—out-of-doors.

Are you an inexperienced tent camper?

If so, perhaps a few hints will be useful. Open terrain is best. Nestling beneath tall trees can be hazardous because of falling limbs and lightning. Bird stains, sap drippings, roots where you'd like stakes, and insects when you'd prefer breezes all encourage one to move out into a location that is near enough to get shade from trees when sun is at an angle, yet not near enough to have acorns, or fruit dropping on the rooftop during the dead of night.

A level site is fine when ditching is possible. Most established campgrounds ask that you not ditch, however. If you can't locate a level site with soil that will drain well, look for one with a slight slope. Avoid the base of hills unless rain is impossible, the ground is sand—or you like to swim in a sleeping bag. Have wooden stakes 2 to 3 ft. in length for those nights on the beach when the winds start blowing!

If a storm starts to threaten:

Loosen ropes and canvas (they shrink when wet);

open tent windows and door, if wind gets healthy;

when the rains begin, avoid touching the walls or roof to avoid capillary action.

Before ducking out, a couple more quick reminders: insect spray removes some kinds of waterproofing and may cause nylon to deteriorate; clay soils, we are told, frequently contain acids detrimental to canvas, so ground cloths should be used but not allowed to extend beyond the edge of the tent. Clipping the ground cloth to the edge of tent floor is recommended.

Do you get the sleeping bag chills?

If so, you may wish to invest in a heavier-weight bag, and possibly filled with down, which is the best insulation for any given amount of weight. The warmth of a sleeping bag depends on the thickness of the insulation material, and is affected by such factors as insulation under the bag, protection from the wind, clothing worn inside the bag, and the metabolism or heat-generating capacity of the person. A hot meal helps to increase the heat generated by the body and helps insure a warm night's sleep.

Can you consume alcoholic beverages in campgrounds? What liquor establishments should women avoid with or without, escort?

We have had difficulty finding answers relating to liquor consumption. Until recently in many segments of Canadian society a stigma was attached to the consumption of alcoholic beverages—in fact, until the 1960s the liquor laws were quite puritanical in all provinces with the possible exception of Quebec. We found a Northwest Territory regulation of just a few years ago stating, "Liquor may not be given or sold to Indians or Eskimos." Many provinces required that individuals be permit-holders before they could purchase alcoholic beverages. So with that warning of attitude, we will share what current regulations we were able to find.

In a Manitoba Parks Department leaflet we learned that, "The Liquor Control Act says that a residence is in part a house trailer, tent or vessel that is bona-fide and actually occupied and used by the owner, lessee or tenant solely as a private dwelling. Thus: If you are going to visit our Provincial Parks or Recreation Areas you may consume alcoholic beverages only within your own tent or trailer and upon the assigned lot on which the tent or trailer is located." Although some private and public campgrounds forbid any consumption of alcohol, unless clearly posted, the assumption is that consumption of moderate amounts on your own campsite is socially acceptable. Elsewhere in the campground is considered public and an unacceptable location for liquor consumption.

Alberta: Liquor supplies can only be purchased through Alberta Liquor Stores. Many are closed on Mondays, but during the summer are open six days a week, excluding holidays and election days and many from 11 A.M. to 6 P.M. Alberta prices are reported the best of all the provinces.

British Columbia: Women are permitted to frequent any establishment of their choice; the legal drinking age is 19.

Manitoba: Mixed drinking is permitted everywhere except beer parlors where only men are permitted; the legal drinking age is 18. Open liquor must not be transported in a vehicle unless it is stored in the trunk or space designed for carriage of baggage. Hours when liquor stores and approved vendors are open are 8:30 A.M. to 4:30 P.M., Monday through Friday.

New Brunswick: Minimum drinking age appears still to be 21, and women are still not permitted to enter taverns. Liquor stores are open Monday through Saturday, usually 9 A.M. to 5 P.M.

Newfoundland: The legal drinking age is still 21, as far as we know, but women are now permitted in taverns and cocktail lounges.

Northwest Territories: The legal drinking age is 19, and "an eligible person may personally import into the Territories 40 ounces of liquor or wine, or one dozen of beer, without an Import Permit."

Nova Scotia: Women beware! The taverns are for men only; beverage rooms are open to women if escorted by a male companion; only cocktail lounges allow unescorted women.

Ontario: The legal age for purchasing alcoholic beverages is 18. Government liquor stores sell spirits, imported and domestic wines, and imported beer. Domestic wine is also available from retail wine stores in most large cities; domestic beer is sold through brewer's outlets. The sale of *any* alcoholic beverage is restricted in some communities. Liquor stores are open in most communities five days a week, 10 A.M. to 6 P.M., closed Sundays, holidays, and often Wednesdays.

Prince Edward Island: The legal drinking age is 18; liquor stores are usually open four days a week, 10 A.M. to 5 P.M.

Quebec: Liquor laws have always been liberal here, although the taverns are still for men only. Liquor stores are usually difficult to find and close at 6 P.M.

Saskatchewan: The legal drinking age is 18, and mixed drinking is permitted in any establishment with a permit to sell alcoholic beverages. A purchase permit is no longer necessary, nor is there a limitation on the quantity purchased at retail liquor outlets. In addition to the usual liquor stores, small liquor outlets exist in some drug stores and other "suitable establishments at country points." Liquor store hours are usually 11 A.M. to 6 P.M., except on Sundays and holidays. Some stores are open only 1-6 P.M. or 1-10 P.M.

Yukon: Mixed drinking is permitted in taverns and other public drinking places. Most government liquor stores, except in Whitehorse, are open 10 A.M. to 6 P.M., Tuesday through Saturday. Whitehorse store hours are 9 A.M. to 6 P.M., Monday through Saturday.

How many ounces in a fifth of liquor?

If bottle sizes have you confused, perhaps these equivalents quoted from a Quebec brochure will be of some help when computing for customs:

40 oz.	=	1-1/4 qt.
25-26 oz.	=	1/5
10 and 12 oz.	=	About 1/2 of 1/5

How can we find out about ferries, cruises, and so on?

The Canadian Government Travel Bureau in Ottawa will send you on request an excellent booklet entitled *Ferries, Bridges, Cruises,* listing times, rates, length of vehicle restrictions. Or you can write:

Ferry Services
Canadian Pacific Rail
Vancouver, British Columbia

Coastal service

Nootka Sound Service Ltd.
P.O. Box 28
Port Alberni, British Columbia

Vancouver Island coast

British Columbia Ferries
816 Wharf Street (Head Office)
Victoria, British Columbia

Coastal service

Tsawwassen Terminal (Reservations)
Delta, British Columbia

Ministry of Transportation
Information Services
1201 Wilson Avenue
Downsview, Ontario M3M 1J8

Georgian Bay

Manager-Ferry Services
Canadian National Railways
Moncton, New Brunswick

Between Borden, Prince Edward Island, and Cape Tormentine, New Brunswick

Northumberland Ferries Ltd.
P.O. Box 634
Charlottetown, Prince Edward Island

Between Wood Islands, Prince Edward Island, and Caribou, Nova Scotia

Co-operative de Transport
    Maritime et Aerien
P.O. Box 245
Cap-aux-Meules, Quebec

Between Souris, Prince Edward Island, and Magdalen Island, Quebec

Manager Passenger Sales & Public Relations East Coast Marine & Ferry Service CN Railways Moncton, New Brunswick	Between Yarmouth, Nova Scotia, and Bar Harbor, Maine
Lion Ferry AB P.O. Box 4216, Station A Portland, Maine 04101	Between Yarmouth, Nova Scotia, and Portland, Maine
Bay of Fundy Service P.O. Box 3460 Saint John, New Brunswick	Digby, Nova Scotia, and Saint John, New Brunswick
CN Railways Newfoundland Services St. Johns, Newfoundland	North Sydney, Nova Scotia, and Argentia, Newfoundland; North Sydney, Nova Scotia, and Prot-aux-Basques, New- foundland; coastal services
Puddister Trading Co. Ltd. P.O. Box 5353 St. Johns, Newfoundland	St. Barbe, Newfoundland, and Blanc Sablon, Quebec

Is it possible to transport cars and recreational vehicles via rail?

Yes, Canadian National Railways has a "car-go-rail" arrangement for those who want to avoid the long drive, but wish the use of their vehicle at their destination. A recent schedule indicates your vehicle can be left in Vancouver on Monday and you can pick it up in Toronto by Saturday for less than $250. For current scheduling and prices write to your nearest CNR agent, or to:

> Canadian National Railways
> Passenger Sales & Service Headquarters
> 935 Lagauchetiere St. West
> P.O. Box 8100
> Montreal, Quebec

Are there family, youth, or senior discount plans if riding the rails?

Yes, at time of writing, CNR offered a 10-20% reduction on certain days of the week for senior citizens, youth, families, and groups. (Air Canada also has reduced rates for senior citizens and youth on their flights.)

To whom can we write for information and rates regarding car and recreational vehicle rental?

The Canadian Government Travel Bureau in Ottawa will send a list of companies offering camper rental service; however, it is our experience in writing to a few from the CGTB list that these companies come and go frequently, causing the Ottawa listing often to be out of date. You would likely do better if you visited a large metropolitan or university library in the States and checked the yellow pages in the telephone directory for any Canadian metropolitan area. The following are a few firms we have seen advertising recently and a few firms from the CGTB list (some are part of a chain of rental agencies):

Tilden Rent-A-Car
209 Bear St.
Banff, Alberta

Maple Lead Motor Home Holidays
2720 Barlow Trail N.E.
Calgary, Alberta
(ca. $250/wk. plus 10¢/mi.)

Bay Trailer Sales Ltd.
Northbrook Mall
Nanaimo, British Columbia

H. & H. Trailer Sales Ltd.
1789 Clearbrook Rd., R.R. 5
Abbotsford, British Columbia

Holiday Rentals & Sales Ltd.
17840 56th Ave.
Cloverdale, V3S 1C7
Surrey, British Columbia

Voyager Rentals Ltd.
c/o Rentabug
11 Alberni St.
Vancouver 5, British Columbia

Abbey Rents
2124 McPhillips
Winnipeg, Manitoba

Host Rent-A-Car
228 Queen St.
Fredericton, New Brunswick
($16/day/no mileage)

Mobile Homes & Trailer Sales Ltd.
Topsail Road, P.O. Box 25
St. Johns, Newfoundland

Fader's Trailer Rentals
P.O. Box 180
Sackville, Nova Scotia

Vardon's Rentals
1026 Adelaide
London, Ontario

Toronto Drive-Away Service
Nationwide Ltd.
5385 Yonge St., Suite 34
Willowdale, Ontario

Roll-A-Long Trailers
747 Richmond Rd.
Ottawa, Ontario

P.E.I. Mobile Homes & Trailer Sales
78 Kensington Rd.
Charlottetown, Prince Edward Island

At major air terminals:
Avis
Budget Rent-A-Car
Hertz

If traveling to the Yukon you will find Avis Rent-A-Car & Truck Rental (Mile 916, Alaska Highway, Whitehorse) with a variety of options:

Cars $70-100/wk. plus 14-20¢/mi.
Trucks $110-150/wk. plus 18-25¢/mi.;
              canopy shell $1.00 a day more.

Dropoffs at locations other than Whitehorse are possible for an additional charge. Other Yukon dealers with auto rentals are:

Tilden Rent-A-Car Service
2089 2nd Ave. & Lambert
Whitehorse

Yukon Auto Rentals Ltd. (Hertz)
4th Ave. & Ogilvie St.
Whitehorse

Yukon Travel Agency
212 Main St.
Whitehorse

Where can we get canoeing information?

Almost all of the provincial tourist offices have booklets on canoeing and lists of outfitters. Besides the books listed in the appendix on the topic, request the following free ones: *Canoe Trips in Canada* from the Canadian Government Travel Bureau in Ottawa and *Hunting, Fishing and Canoe Trips in Canada* from the Canadian National Railway (935 Lagauchetiere St. West, P.O. Box 8100, Montreal, Quebec, or from a branch office). *The Field and Stream Guide to Family Camping*, in our book list, has a chapter on boat camping where regions are suggested for canoeing and many addresses are provided for requesting information.

Some of the larger outfitters include:

Hudson's Bay Co.
Northern Stores Department
79 Main St.
Winnipeg 1, Manitoba

Canadian Quetico Outfitters
P.O. Box 910
Atikokan, Ontario

Wilderness Expeditions Ltd.
11445 143rd St.
Edmonton, Alberta

For more ideas on where to canoe, read the Ontario and Quebec sections in the selected campground chapter.

Interested in hiking with a group in Alberta?

For over 40 years the Skyline Hikers of the Canadian Rockies (P.O. Box 5905, Station A, Calgary, Alberta T2H 1Y4) have taken groups on five-day hikes. For around $100 per person you receive meals, tent accommodations, and transportation to the trail head.

Interested in joining a group camping tour of Alaska and the Yukon, the Canadian Rockies, or the Maritime Provinces?

Write: Camping Guide Tours Inc.
Rt. 1 Box 877, McCourtney Rd.
Grass Valley, Cal. 95945

Interested in rock-hunting but lacking in information?

British Columbia is endowed with a generous variety of gem stones and provides its tourists and *amateur rockhounders* with these suggestions: "When going into untravelled country always let someone know where you are going and for how long. If you are not an experienced wilderness traveller take someone with you who is. Your preparations should include maps, a compass and adequate provisions. Safety glasses are vital when chipping or hammering hard materials. Proper books, clothing and tools can mean the difference between a successful hunt and a wasted journey."

Etiquette: "If you are hunting on private property, the permission of the owner must always be obtained. Never spoil the natural beauty of the country by littering. When digging in grazing country always fills your excavation so that cattle will not be harmed. Close all gates. Never take more material than you need for your own purpose."

Since British Columbia is one of the earth's most prolific rockhounding areas, lapidary opportunities are endless: jade, agate, garnet, hematite, jasper, lazulite, obsidian, opal, quartz, rhodonite, tourmaline, and zircon are just a few of the many hundreds of different minerals found so far.

For more information on rockhounding in British Columbia, write: The Lapidary Rock & Mineral Society of British Columbia, Box 194, Postal Station A, Vancouver. While in British Columbia you might enjoy visiting the Hope Tourist Bureau, where you can examine over 600 different varieties of rock specimens found near or along the Fraser River.

Newfoundland, too, has a fair variety of gem stones: labradorite, jasper, alabaster, marble, copper, xonotlite, barite, garnet, amazonite, orthoclase, fluorite, quartz, chert, felsites, pyrophyllite, pyrite, agate, virginite, serpentine, and beryl. You might enjoy reading the tourist bureau's booklet, *Gemstones of Newfoundland and Labrador.*

Confused over the size of the Canadian gallon?

The Canadian and Imperial gallons are a fifth again as large as the U.S. gallon. You will get the equivalent of six U.S. gallons when you order five Imperial gallons.

What distinction does the Trans-Canada Highway have?

It is the longest national road in the world.

Are there any toll roads in Canada?

None—but there are toll bridges!

International road signs are becoming more commonplace in Canada as well as in the United States. Are you familiar with all of them?

Watch for rock
on Road
Attention au roc
sur la route

No Stopping

Arrêt interdit

No Parking
Stationnement
interdit

Do Not Enter

Entrée interdite

Watch for
Wild Animals
Attention aux
animaux sauvages

School Bus Stop

Autobus scolaire,
arrêt

No Motor Vehicles
Allowed
Accès interdit,
aux automobiles

No Passing

Dépassement
interdit

Trucks Entering

Passage de
camions

Do you know the metric system is beginning to be used in Canada?

Kilometer signs are appearing gradually, so with that in mind we are offering the following:

Table of Equivalents

1 in.	=	2.5 cm.
1 ft.	=	3.0 dm.
1 yd.	=	0.9 m.
0.6 mi.	=	1.0 km.
1 mi.	=	1.6 m.
25 mi.	=	40 km., approx.
1 oz.	=	28.35 g.
1 lb.	=	0.45 kg.
1 pt.	=	0.57 l.
1 qt.	=	1.14 l.
1 gal.	=	4.54 l.
1 Canadian gal.	=	1.2 U.S. gal.
1 gal. water	=	10 lb. or 4.5 kg.
Fahrenheit degrees	=	9/5 degrees C plus 32
Celsius degrees	=	(Degrees Fahrenheit minus 32)5/9

How are kilometers converted to miles, or vice versa? (You will need to know for Quebec, at least.)

Five miles are equal to eight kilometers; therefore, the kilometer is shorter than the mile. There are a number of complicated ways of converting kilometers to miles, but the simplest method is to multiply the number of kilometers by six and drop the last figure. For example, 20 kilometers is 12 miles (6 times 20 equals 120); 180 kilometers is 108 miles (6 times 180 equals 1080); and 45 kilometers is 27 miles (6 times 45 equals 270).

For a more accurate conversion, the number of kilometers should be multiplied by 0.62137. Unless you are mathematically inclined, however, the simple rule of multiplying by six should serve you well; the error is only about two miles in every 100 kilometers.

DISTANCE CONVERSION

From Kilometers	1	5	10	15	20	30	50	100	200	300	400	500
To Miles	.62	3.1	6.2	9.3	12.4	18.6	31	62.1	124.2	186.4	248.6	310.7

Will we need to convert U.S. gallons to liters anywhere?

Chances are you will only encounter this problem in Quebec.

GASOLINE CONVERSION

From U.S. Gallons	1	2	3	4	5	6	7	8	9	10	15	20
To Liters	3.8	7.6	11.4	15.1	18.9	22.7	26.5	30.3	34.1	37.9	56.8	75.7

How are mile and kilometer speeds converted?

The principle is the same as for conversions of distance, but this table may save calculating, especially if you are behind the wheel:

MPH to KPH Conversion

KILOMETERS PER HOUR	M.P.H.	M.P.H.	KILOMETERS PER HOUR
10	6	10	16
20	12	20	32
30	19	30	48
40	25	40	64
50	31	50	80
60	37	60	96
70	43	70	113
80	50	80	129
90	56	90	145
100	62	100	161
110	68	110	177
120	75	120	193
130	81	130	209
140	87	140	225
150	93	150	241
160	99	160	257

Is there a good method for estimating driving time?

One quick method of obtaining an estimate of driving time is to figure one kilometer per minute. It is too easy to overestimate the number of miles you can cover in any one day.

Plan to spend much time on gravel roads? Maybe a couple of hints will be helpful.

Dust and flying gravel will probably be more of a problem than rough roads. Your car's gas tank can be protected from gravel damage by fastening a rubber mat to the underside of the tank. A wire mesh or fabric screen will prevent insect or gravel damage to the radiator. Travel trailers are best equipped with rockguards and tough protectors for areas where wiring is exposed.

Will AAA membership be of any value in Canada?

Yes, the automobile clubs are affiliated and the Canadian Automobile Association (CAA) services for AAA members as the AAA clubs do in the United States. Both CAA and AAA have met the same inspection requirements. Triptiks are available for most parts of Canada as well as an emergency service directory, maps, camping and trailering directories, tour book, and the like. Their many services are worth investigating if a lengthy Canadian trip is anticipated.

Are your days incomplete without a good cup of coffee and a hot cinnamon roll or freshly glazed doughnut?

That's us! We usually are too lazy to brew a good cup of coffee in the campground so our habit is to seek out the local bakeries with coffee bars. Not only is this practice satisfying to the palate, but satisfying to those of us who enjoy meeting European immigrants, who are frequently owners and operators of small-town bakeries. We also have had good coffee breaks at the Voyageur restaurants scattered across Canada along the tourist routes.

Interested in making good coffee over the campfire?

We are too lazy to prepare "real" coffee; however, this is the way grandmother did it: For each cup of water, add one heaping tablespoon of regular grind coffee (if over ten cups of water, add an extra teaspoon coffee—for the pot). Put the pot on the fire (or stove) after stirring gently to mix. Allow the coffee to almost boil, then remove from the fire, and keep in a warm spot for three to five minutes while the grounds settle. (A little cold water added to hot coffee helps grounds to settle. Another method of keeping the grounds oux of your cup is to put the coffee grounds in a cotton muslin bag, and an even better method is just to use a strainer when pouring coffee into your cup.)

As a space-saver while traveling you might consider storing your coffee can inside the coffee pot, your tea inside your teapot. We never dreamed anyone camped with a teapot until one afternoon about 4 o'clock we were invited to a neighboring site for tea, and there it was—a real teapot brewing bulk tea while snuggled in a cozy! You guessed it—the family was from England.

Are there organizations that operate "people-meet-people" programs?

The Travel Industry Association of Canada (Suite 1016, 130 Albert St., Ottawa, Ontario K1P 5G4) used to operate a "Meet the Canadians at Home" program in about 20 cities. Although the program is no longer administered nationally, there is a strong chance that cities that once took part may still have such programs within their areas. Addresses of former hosts were:

Kamloops Chamber of Commerce
775 West Columbia St.
Kamloops, British Columbia

Calgary Tourist & Convention Association
Hospitality Centre, Mewata Park
Calgary, Alberta

Edmonton Chamber of Commerce
South Side Visitor Information Bureau
5068 103rd St.
Edmonton, Alberta

Saskatoon Board of Trade
Room 100, Bessborough Hotel
Saskatoon, Saskatchewan

Regina Chamber of Commerce
2145 Alberta St.
Regina, Saskatchewan

Tourist & Convention Association of Manitoba
Room 707, 177 Lombard Ave.
Winnipeg, Manitoba

Thunder Bay Convention Bureau
857 N. May St.
Thunder Bay, Ontario

Kitchener Chamber of Commerce
Visitor & Convention Bureau
68 King St. East
Kitchener, Ontario

Hamilton Visitors & Convention Bureau
Suite 820, 155 James St. South
Hamilton, Ontario

The Ottawa office suggested writing to the above addresses and also indicated the following had relevant programs: St. Johns, Newfoundland has a hospitality program where members of service clubs can meet with local members of their club (write St. John's Tourist Commission & Convention Burku.yCity Hall, P.O. Box 5416, St. John's, Newfoundland A1C 5W2; and in Calgary, Alberta, write Calgary Tourist & Convention Association, Hospitality Centre, 1300 6th Ave. S.W., Calgary, Alberta T3C OH8.

If you are visiting areas not serviced by one of these programs we remind you of the farm vacations, guest ranches, and bed-and-breakfast arrangements. (See the appendix.)

Are there student travel organizations sponsoring intra-Canada air charter flights?

Check with:
Tourbec
112 ouest, rue St. Paul, Suite 500
Montreal 125, Quebec

Tourbec
35, rue Richilieu
Quebec 4, Quebec

Association of Student Councils
44 St. George St.
Toronto 5, Ontario

Club Jeunesse, Inc.
5450 Cote-des-Neiges, Suite 304
Montreal, Quebec H3T 1Y6

Club Jeunesse, Inc.
30 Deerfield Rd.
Wyckoff, N.J.

What about hitchhiking?

Although there is no federal legislation concerning hitchhiking, provincial legislation does vary. Generally, it is considered illegal to hitchhike along the transcontinental routes, but you commonly see many young people hitchhiking both along the highways and along the access ramps leading to highways. Students from Canada, the United States, and Europe find hitchhiking an easy way to travel, combining it with camping at roadside sites or using the many hostels for shelter.

How can we learn more about Canadian hostels?

Write:
Hostels
Department of the Secretary of State
110 O'Connor St., 3rd Fl.
Ottawa, Ontario K1A OM5

Canadian Youth Hostels Assn.
333 River Rd.
Vanier City, Ottawa, Ontario K1L 8B9

The hundred or so hostels scattered about the country are generally located in summer camps, farm houses, or buildings donated or specially built for the purpose. They provide simple sleeping accommodations—a bed, mattress, pillow, and blankets in separate dormitories for men and women. Some provide showers, and some have kitchens equipped with a stove and cookware. Although each hostel is supervised by house parents, standards vary considerably. The charge per night is usually around 50¢.

For regional information, write to CYHA at:

6405 Quinpool Rd. Halifax, Nova Scotia	For Nova Scotia, New Brunswick, Prince Edward Island, and Newfoundland
1324 Sherbrooke St. W Montreal 109, Quebec	For province of Quebec
270 MacLaren St. Ottawa, Ontario	For Ottawa area
86 Scollard St. Toronto 185, Ontario	For province of Ontario except Ottawa area
P.O. Box 135 Postal Station C Winnipeg R3M 357, Manitoba	For Manitoba and Saskatchewan
10922 88th Ave. Edmonton 61, Alberta	For province of Alberta north of Red Deer
455 12th St. N.W. Calgary 41, Alberta	For province of Alberta south of Red Deer
1406 West Broadway Vancouver 9, British Columbia	For province of British Columbia except Vancouver Island
Room 106 1951 Cook St. Victoria, British Columbia	For Vancouver Island in British Columbia

The Canadian Government Travel Bureau is reported to have a free publication, *Canada—Youth Accommodation*, listing hotels, guest ranches, and farms (we have not yet seen a copy). However, a comprehensive listing is found in *The Canadian Youth Hostels Association Handbook*, which can be secured for 50¢ from either the United States or Canadian Youth Hostel organization. A free leaflet distributed by the secretary of state's office entitled *Youth Hostels*, also gives addresses, dates open, and facilities of hostels along Trans-Canada routes. *Handbook Canada* (particulars are included in the book list in appendix) provides addresses for the 20 or so Salvation Army hostels across the country, and for universities and YM/YWCAs where inexpensive shelter can be sought—when the weather turns cool or wet.

Did you buy a first-aid kit, put it in an out-of-the-way place in the car, and forget about it?

Guess that's probably what most of us do—unintentionally—without considering that a hiking and mountain climbing kit should vary from a beach and desert kit. Perhaps a wise procedure is to ask your doctor for his recommendations on inclusions for your family's first-aid needs, depending upon where you are going, and then prepare your own kit, becoming familiar with each item, how and when it should be used, perhaps even reacquainting the family with the first-aid book.

We are told basic necessities for the home first-aid kit should include: assorted sizes of adhesive bandages and pads, gauze bandaging and pads, plus tape that won't hurt when coming off, an oral thermometer in protective case, mineral oil, antiseptic soap, rubbing alcohol, boric acid eye wash, aspirin or equivalent, a triangular bandage, and a icebag-hot water bottle. In a traveling situation, the last two may be improvised.

A leading manufacturer of travel kits includes these items: several sizes of adhesive bandages and pads, gauze pads and roller bandage, antibacterial cleaning wipes, tape, pain killer (acetaminophen), a small pair of scissors, and a concise first-aid guide. Adapting to your family's needs and preferences, you may choose to include a general antiseptic such as hydrogen peroxide, a first-aid spray or ointment, sun tan lotion, baking soda, burn ointment, safety pins, tweezers, soda mint tabs, laxative, medicine dropper, absorbent cotton, petroleum jelly, calamine lotion, and a snake bite or a wasp sting kit. Perhaps iodine, ammonia inhalant, lip or skin salve, insect repellent, water-purification tablets, salt tablets, and wilderness storm kit would be included.

We consider outselves anything but authorities on the subject of first aid and list the above possible kit inclusions more as a reminder to the informed than anything specifically informative. Robert Elman's *The Hiker's Bible* is full of practical first-aid tips for the person spending considerable time in the out-of-doors. And of course, there is always the American Red Cross first-aid book.

Are there special things children visiting Canada should see?

We're sure there must be a long list of children's attractions, but we haven't recorded them even though we have found some occasional goodies. Our suggestion is to find a paperback copy of Percy Rowe's *Travel Guide to Canada*, for it is the best source we know for children's attractions. Sallie Ann Robbin's *See Canada Free* might also be useful in suggesting plant tours, museums, and the like. Ask the provincial tourist offices for suggestions for children.

During travels with our daughters, we have frequently developed games around sights along the route, nature and animal bingos, and so on. We like tongue twisters, too, and would like to share a few we had fun with:

The ragged rascal ran around the rugged rock.

The mad milkman, Mr. Marvin Merman, missed Ms. Marion Moon's mansion Monday.

The big, black bug bit the big, black bear and made the big, black bear bleed blood.

Sixty-six sick chicks sat on six slender sapplings.

Moses supposes his toes were roses but Moses supposes erroneously for Moses knows his toes aren't roses as Moses supposes he toes to be.

Big, black Ben bounced the blue ball in the bleak, blowing blizzard.

Rubber baby buggy bumpers.

A white-eared little wool weirdo. (Our little wool-loving black dog after getting his ear doused with flea powder.)

Are you familiar with U.S. customs regulations for residents returning to United States?

We wish a quick referral to the *Know Before You Go* booklet distributed by the many customs offices would suffice. However, if you are like us, acquiring the booklet may be low on your list of things to do before departing—and an easily forgotten request at the border. Thus, we will try to summarize some of the U.S. regulations to help in your decision making regarding acquisitions made in Canada. Reminder: This is not likely the everlasting word, even though it has come directly from customs just prior to time of printing. To obtaim the most current and complete information write: Office of Information & Publications, Department of the Treasury, Washington, D.C. 20226.

Declarations and Exemptions

All articles acquired while out of the country and in your possession at the time of return must be declared. This includes gifts presented to you, repairs or alterations made to any article taken with you and returned (whether or not a charge was made for the repair), items you are carrying that were requested by another person, and any article you intend to sell or use in your business. The price actually paid for each article must be stated in U.S. currency, and if not purchased, its fair retail value where acquired must be named. (The wearing or use of any article does not exempt it from duty, and it must be declared at original price. The customs officers will adjust value for wear and tear.)

A written declaration is necessary when the total retail value of articles acquired abroad *exceeds $100 per person;* when more than *1 qt. of alcoholic beverages* or more than *100 cigars* are included; when some of the items are intended *for sale* or for use in your *business* rather than for personal or household use, and when a customs duty or internal revenue *tax* is *collectible on any article* in your possession.

The head of a family may make a joint declaration for all members residing in the *same household and returning* with him or her to the United States. A family of four may bring in articles free of duty valued up to $400 retaul value on one declaration, even if the articles acquired by one member of the family exceeds his $100 and regardless of the ages of the family members. An oral declaration can be made to the customs officer if the articles acquired abroad have not exceeded the duty-free exemption; however, he may choose to ask you to prepare a written list if he thinks it is necessary.

WARNING: If you underestimate the value or otherwise misrepresent an article, it may be subject to seizure and forfeiture. If you fail to report an item, not only might it be seized, but you will be liable for a penalty equal to the value of the article in the United States and liable to criminal prosecution. If in doubt, declare it, then ask questions regarding value.

Articles purchased abroad but left for alterations, cannot be applied to your $100 exemption. You must also have been *out of the country for 48 hours and have not received the $100 exemption within the last 30 days.* Your exemption is not cumulative, so even though you may have used only a small portion of that exemption sometime during the last 30 days, you only have a $10 exemption available to you until the 30-day period has expired.

In the 30-day, $100-exemption requirement is the stipulation that not more than 100 cigars or 1 qt. (31 oz.) of alcoholic beverages can be admitted free. There is *no limitation on cigarettes* imported for personal use (the only exception is the prohibition of Cuban tobacco). The 1 qt. exemption applies to anyone *21 years* or over, and any excess of that quantity is subject to duty and internal revenue tax. Also, the liquor must be for personal use or a gift and must not violate the law of the state in which you arrive. (Alcoholic beverages are prohibited shipment through the U.S. mail.)

If you cannot claim the $100 exemption because of the 30-day or 48-hour minimum limitations, you may bring in duty-free articles akquired abroad if the total value does *not exceed $10.* This is an individual exemption and may not be grouped with other members of a family. You may include: *50 cigarettes, 10 cigars, 4 oz. of lcoholic beverages, or 4 ox. of alcoholic perfume.* If any article brought with you is subject to duty or tax, of if the total value exceeds $10, no article may be exempted from duty or tax.

Automobiles, boats, planes, etc., taken our of the country for noncommercial use may be returned duty-free by proving to the customs officer they were taken out of the country; however, dutiable repairs or accessories acquired abroad must be declared.

Foreign-made personal articles taken abroad (watches, cameras, etc.) identifiable by serial number of other markings may be registered before departure. All foreign-made articles are dutiable each time they are brought into the country unless you have acceptable proof of prior possession (a customs certificate of registration, bill of sale, insurance policy, repair receipt).

Gifts of not more than $10 in retail value where shipped can be received by friends and relations in United States duty-free if the same person does not receive more than $10 in gift shipments in one day. Write "Unsolicited Gift—Value Under $10" on ourside of package. Alcoholic beverages and tobacco products are not included in this privilege, nor are alcoholic perfumes valued at more than $1. A gift mailed to friends is not declared on your return but a "gift" mailed by the traveler to himself is subject to duty. Gifts given you or intended as gifts for others, as long as they are not intended for business or promotional use, may be included within your exemption.

Household effects and tools of trade or occupation taken out of the United States are free of duty if properly declared. Items such as wearing apparel, jewelry, photographic equipment, tape recorders, stereo equipment, vehicles, and consumable articles cannot be passed duty-free as household effects.

Prohibited and Restricted Articles

Articles considered injurious or detrimental to the general welfare of the United States and prohibited are: absinthe, lottery tickets, narcotics and dangerous drugs, obscene articles and publications, seditious and treasonable materials, hazardous articles (fireworks, dangerous toys, toxic or poisonous substances), and switchblade knives. Books protected by American copyright cannot be brought to the United States if they are unauthorized foreign reprints.

If taking *firearms* and ammunition out of the country, register them before departing at any customs office; however, not more than three nonautomatic firearms and 1,000 cartridges will be registered for any one person. For more information write: Bureau of Alcohol, Tobacco and Firearms, U.S. Department of the Treasury, Washington, D.C. 20224.

Fruits, plants, vegetables, cuttings, seeds, and unprocessed plant products are either prohibited from entering the United States or require an import permit. Every single plant, plant product, fruit, or vegetable must be declared and presented for inspection. Canned or processed items are admissible, as well as bakery products. For more information or for import permits, write to Quarantines, U.S. Department of Agriculture, Federal Center Bldg., Hyattsville, Md. 20782.

Meats, livestock, poultry, and their byproducts are either prohibited or restricted: fresh, chilled, frozen, dried, cured and cooked meats, poultry, game, livestock, or any products or byproducts from wild or domesticated animals or fowl. Commercially canned meats and those not requiring refrigeration are permitted. For more specific information write: Quarantines, U.S. Department of Agriculture, Federal Center Bldg., Hyattsville, Md. 20782.

A traveler requiring *medicines* containing habit-forming drugs or narcotics (cough medicines, diuretics, heart drugs, tranquilizers, sleeping pills, depressants, stimulants, and so on) should: have all drugs properly identified; carry only the needed quantity; have either a prescription or written statement from physician indicating they are being used under a doctor's direction and are necessary for the traveler's physical well-being while traveling. (We have known Europeans entering the United States who have had both meats and medicines confiscated at considerable inconvenience.)

If you plan to take your *pet* abroad, or wish to import one, request the leaflet *So You Want to Import a Pet* from the nearest customs office or from Foreign Quarantine Program, Center for Disease Control, Atlanta, Ga. 30333. Strict regulations have been imposed on birds and are best obtained from Veterinary Services, Animal and Plant Health Inspection Service, U.S. Department of Agriculture, Federal Center Bldg., Hyattsville, Md. 20782. A rabies vaccination is generally not required for cats, but a dog does need one at least one month before but not more than 12 months prior to arrival. A valid rabies certificate identifies the dog, is signed by a licensed veterinarian, and specifies that the dog was vaccinated with nervous tissue vaccine or with chicken embryo vaccine within the time limits required. If an animal arrives without a valid certificate, the owner will be required to arrange for and bear the expense of vaccination. The dog must then be placed in confinement for at least 30 days following vaccination. Pets acquired out of the country are subject to customs duty, but if they are imported for personal use and not intended for sale they may be included in your exemption.

Trademarked articles that are foreign-made (cameras, perfumes, watches, musical instruments) cannot be brought in without the consent of the trademark owner if he has recorded his trademark with the Department of Treasury. Many trademark owners have consented to importation, but usually in limited quantities and in the possession of arriving travelers. If a trademark has been completely removed—not covered over—there is no restriction.

Federal regulations do not authorize the importation of any *wildlife or fish* into any state if they are prohibited or restricted by the state of destination, nor is wildlife taken or killed in violation of the law of their native country allowed entry. Ports designated for entry of fish and wildlife are Chicago, Los Angeles, New York,

San Francisco, and Seattle. A Declaration for Importation of Fish and Wildlife must be filed at the time of entry. Write for more information: Bureau of Sport Fisheries and Wildlife, U.S. Department of Interior, Washington, D.C. 20240. That agency also publishes the limits on migratory game birds prior to each hunting season.

Traveling Back and Forth Across the Border

You may lose your customs exemption, unless you meet certain requirements, when you swing back and forth across the border at various locations on one trip. Ask the nearest customs official *before* you cross. Articles bought in duty-free shops in foreign countries are subject to U.S. customs exemptions and restrictions. Articles purchased in duty-free shops in the United States are subject to U.S. customs if re-entered into the United States. Developed or undeveloped U.S. film exposed abroad may enter free of duty and need not be included in your customs exemption; however, foreign film purchased abroad and prints made abroad are dutiable but may be included in your customs exemption.

Rates of Duty

The customs officer examining your baggage will determine the rates of duty if you have dutiable articles; however, this may be of some usefulness in your decision making:

Alcoholic Beverages

	Int. Rev. Tax	Customs Duty
beer	$ 9 bbl. (31 gal.)	6¢ per gal.
brandy	10.50*	50¢ to $5*
gin	10.50*	50¢*
liqueurs	10.50*	50¢
rum	10.50*	$1.75*
whisky*		
Scotch	10.50*	51¢
Irish	10.50*	51¢
other	10.50*	62¢
wine		
sparkling	2.40-3.40	$1.17
still	.17-2.25	1-1/2¢-$1

*Per U.S. gal. (128 fl. oz.) if under 100 proof.
Duty and tax are based on proof gallon if 100 proof or over.

Antiques produced prior to 100 years before the date of entry are admitted free, but you must have proof of antiquity from seller.

Books by foreign author or in a foreign language are admitted free.

Cameras	
Motion picture, over $50 each	6%
still, over $10 each	7-1/2%
cases, leather	8-1/2-10%
Lenses	12-1/2%
Candy	
sweetened chocolate bars	5%
other	7%
Chess sets	10%
China	
bone	17-1/2%
non-bone, other than	
tableware	2-1/2%
China tableware, non-bone, available	
in 77-piece sets	
valued over $56 per set	5¢ doz. plus 18%
valued not over $10 per set	10¢ doz. plus 48%
Dolls and parts	17-1/2%
Figurines, china	12-1/2-22-1/2%
Film, imported, not qualifying	
for free entry is dutiable:	
exposed or exposed and	
developed film is classified	
as photographs	4%
Fruit, prepared	35% or under
Fur	
wearing apparel	8-1/2-18-1/2%
other manufactures of	8-1/2-18-1/2%
Furniture	
wood, chairs	8-1/2%
wood, other than chairs	5%
Jade	
Cut, but not set and suitable	
for use in manufacture	2-1/2%
other articles of jade	21%
Leather	
pocketbooks, bags	8-1/2-10%
other manufactures of	4-14%
Paintings (works of art)	
original	free
copies, done by hand	
entirely	free

Perfume	8¢ lb. plus 7-1/2%
Slippers, leather	5%
Sweaters, of wool, over $5 per lb.	37-1/2¢ plus 20%
Wearing apparel	
embroidered or ornamented	21-42-1/2%
not embroidered , not ornamented	
cotton, knit	21%
cotton, not knit	8-16-1/2%
linen, not knit	7-1/2%
manmade fiber, knit	25¢/lb. plus 32-1/2%
manmade fiber, not knit	25¢/lb. plus 27-1/2%
silk, knit	10%
silk, not knit	16%
wool, knit	37-1/2¢/lb. plus 15-1/2-32%
wool, not knit	25 to 37-1/2¢/lb. plus 21%

The debt we owe to
The play of imagination
Is incalculable.
CARL GUSTAV JUNG

-6

DIFFERENT TOURS/
DIFFERENT PEOPLE

In the mid-1970s more people are seeking something unusual, or at least are doing something purposeful in their travels. This is especially true of the young traveler who expects to make a number of visits to Canada over a lifetime.

There are numerous possibilities in special-interest, do-it-yourself tours; a few are outlined on the following pages as suggestions of how special-interest tours might be developed. Perhaps the focus for your travels will be a lifelong interest. Then again the focus might be something you never before dreamed of doing. Whatever your choice, let it provide contrast with your normal routine, giving your life and your travels added dimension.

The tours within this chapter include a look at some ethnic groups: Starting the chapter, we discuss the history, communities, museums, and festivals of the Doukhobors, the Hutterites, the Mennonites; ending the chapter we take a look at where Indian and Eskimo communities are, how we might learn more about their cultures. Other tours take you through the botanical gardens and arboretums of Canada, with emphasis on Ontario, through the hot mineral spring areas, particularly in the Rockies, and through the handicraft centers of New Brunswick. Perhaps your preference is for a canoeing tour through the Ontario lakes or a ghost town tour of British Columbia. Whatever your interest, start planning early—we have as much fun preparing as we do traveling.

HANDICRAFTS OF NEW BRUNSWICK

New Brunswick is a rich blend of Indian, French, and English cultures to which individuals from a score of European and Oriental nations have added their contributions. Among the handicrafts, the province is perhaps best known for its weaving: near St. Andrews, descendants of Scottish settlers weave homespuns similar to the Harris tweeds of West Scotland and at the Convent of St. Louis in Kent County, excellent linen is woven from home-grown flax.

In Sackville, the looms established in connection with the art gallery of Mount Allison University are noted for the variety and fine quality of the woolen fabrics turned out from them. Artisans in metal and pottery at the university have reached a high degree of proficiency, also; the association of these handicrafts with the gallery of pictures and art school is an excellent combination and arouses the interest of visitors to the province.

In Moncton at the University of Moncton Museum, crafts are displayed in the Folk Museum along with furniture and other artifacts of Acadian history. For more contemporary crafts, visit the Moncton Handcraft and Tourist Information Center.

Arts and Crafts Schools

The province operates an arts and crafts school for adults and children at Fundy National Park each summer, usually from the first week of July through the third week in August. Each craft project is done on an individual basis, and one may select from a variety of crafts including woodturning, jewelry, leatherwork, weaving, macramé, raku pottery, and such textile work as batik, tie-dyeing, and rug hooking. To insure selection, advance registration is recommended; daily registration fees are about $2 for adults and $1 for children, plus cost of supplies. For more information write to the director of Handicrafts Branch, Department of Finance and Industry, Exhibition Court, Fredericton, New Brunswick.

Another craft school is operated in St. Andrews during July and August. Sanbury Shores Arts and Nature Centre, Inc., at 139 Water St. in St. Andrews has workshops for both adults and children in painting, pottery, weaving, natural science, and silver. They offer programs, lectures, exhibitions, field trips, films dealing with art, crafts, and natural history throughout much of the year.

Art Festivals

An exhibition and sale of New Brunswick crafts is held at the facilities of the Creative Craft Program in Fundy National Park in late July. Fifty or so craftsmen (weavers, potters, glass blowers, jewelers, woodturners) sell and demonstrate their crafts during the three-day festival.

Another handicraft festival is usually held over Labor Day weekend (early September) at Mactaquac Provincial Park, 15 miles north of Fredericton. For more information regarding this festival write: The Handcraft Branch, Department of Tourism, P.O. Box 1030, Hut No.3, Woodstock Rd., Fredericton, New Brunswick.

Other fairs and folk festivals in the province also occasionally display crafts: You might examine the listing of current events provided by the New Brunswick Department of Tourism or the partial listing of events included in the appendix of this guide. Also, at the end of this discussion of handicrafts in New Brunswick is a partial listing of crafts exhibitions throughout Canada.

Home Industries

Home industries were well-developed throughout the province, among both English and French inhabitants, as late as the third quarter of the 19th century, but gradually since then they dwindled until quite recently, mainly because of an awakening interest among tourists in the province, they have shown indications of revival. Some artisans can be seen at work in their homes, but more frequently their products are seen on display in tourist bureaus, art galleries, and gift shops. An annual directory of craftsmen and their addresses is prepared by the Department of Tourism, so if you are interested in making a concentrated study of these artisans, their techniques, and their products write to the Handcrafts Branch, C.P. Box 1030, Fredericton, New Brunswick, requesting the most recent *Directory of New Brunswick Craftsmen and Craft Shops;* also ask at local tourist bureaus for a listing of artisans in each area.

For your convenience, we have prepared a map that illustrates at a glance the better known handicraft centers. Accompanying the map is a partial listing of craftsmen and where their products can be viewed. Phone numbers are included so you can call to determine when shops are open, when craftsmen are available, sometimes by appointment. And finally, we offer a few recommendations of base camps from which you can seek out these handicrafts.

Alma (in Fundy National Park, on Rte. 114)
Chalet Shop, open June to mid-September
Cleveland Place Gift Shop, Tel.: 887-2493
Craeftiga, open June to September 30

Bathurst (in the north on Nepisiquit Bay, on Rte. 11)
Sunflower, 820 Murray Ave., Tel.: 546-4754,
open July through September
Bathurst Handcraft Shop, 175 Main St., Tel.: 546-6464,
open mid-June to mid-September

Caraquet (in north on Chaleur Bay, on Rte. 11)
Le Centre D'Artisanat Co-op Ltée, 15 Boulevard St. Pierre Est, Tel.: 727-3269,
open mid-May to mid-October

Cocagne (off Northumberland Strait, on Rte. 134)
George Labelle, on Rte. 530, 200 yd. off Rte. 134, Tel.: 532-3800,
makes wheel-thrown and handbuilt stoneware

Fredericton (on St. John River, on Rte. 2)
Beaverbrook Art Gallery, Queen St.
Aitkens Pewter, 824 Charlotte St., Tel.: 455-5921
The Craft House, 610 Queen St., Tel.: 455-5460,
specializes in glass
Robert B. Harvey, 168 Henry St., Tel.: 472-2478,
makes small wooden objects, tableware
Frank Horvath, 780 Montgomery, Apt. 106, Tel.: 454-9263,
makes lutes, guitars
Karen Jackson, 159 Saunders St., Tel.: 455-5069,
does weaving; is available May to Christmas
The Pewtersmith Studio, 344 Albert St., Tel.: 455-8606
Thomas R. Smith, 224 Westmorland St., Tel.: 455-5844,
works in pottery, sculpture
Trojan Toys, George St., at the Market every Saturday morning,
wooden toys
The Works of Whalen, 328 Woodstock Rd., Tel.: 455-7679,
wooden and soft toys
Woolastook Wildlife Park Gift Shop, 18 miles west of Fredericton, on Rte. 6,
Tel.: 363-2352, open mid-May to mid-October

Gagetown (east of Fredericton, on Rte. 102)
Loomcrofters, Tel.: 488-2400

Kingsclear Indian Reservation (10 miles north of Fredericton, on Rte. 6)
Mrs. Veronica Atwin, on the Reserve, Tel.: 363-2256,   specializes in baskets
Mn'gwon Indian Crafts, opposite the Reserve, Tel.: 363-2256,
    has baskets, beadwork, leather, carvings
Sacobies Indian Handcrafts, on the Reserve, Tel.: 363-2544,
    has baskets, leather, beadwork; repairs cane chairs also

Nashwaak Bridge 22 miles north of Fredericton, on Rte. 8)
Mrs. Frank MacKinnon, Tel.: 367-2675
Mrs. Ernest Walton, Tel.: 367-2547,   both women specialize in quilts

Nashwaak Village (13 miles north of Fredericton, on Rte. 8)
Barbara Buck, Tel.: 472-2995, open mid-June to mid-September,
    specializes in weaving, batik

Oromocto (east of Fredericton, on Rte. 102)
Mrs. Fran Bezeau, 73 Dakota Dr., Tel.: 375-6456,
    does carving and sculpture in clay, wood, stone
Lyman R. Coleman, 39 Dakota Dr., Tel.: 357-5557,
    makes jewelry, candleholders

Paquetville (in north, south of Caraquet, on Rt. 135)
Le Bois Coti, Tel.: 764-2168
Studio Legére Cie Ltée, Tel.: 764-2168,
    weaving, pottery

Perth-Andover (in west, between Hartland and Grand Falls)
Abner Paul, Tobique Narrow, two miles north of Perth on Rte. 125, Tel.:
    273-2095
    open mid-May to mid-October,
    Indian crafts
Tobique Wigwam, in Andover on Trans-Canada Highway, Tel.: 273-2837,
    opens mid-May,
    Indian leatherwork, beadwork, paintings, carvings, moccasins

Richibucto (south of Kouchibouguac National Park, on Rte. 11)
Maritime Indian Arts and Crafts, Tel.: 523-4322

Sackville (near Nova Scotia border off Chignecto Bay, on Rt. 2)
Lorrie Bell, Jolicure, Rte. 3, Tel.: 536-0570,

open June 1 to October 31,
weaving, batik, jewelry
The Crofter, 17 Bridge St., Tel.: 536-1692
Owens Gallery, displays works of local artists
Tintamarre Crafts, Jolicure, off Rte. 16, Tel.: 536-0570
Ute Joerger, P.O. Box 1503, Tel.: 536-2404,
specializes in batik wall hangings, mobiles

St. Andrews (in the southwest on the ocean, Rte. 127)
La Baleine Boutique, 171 Water St., Tel.: 529-3839,
open June through October
Cottage Craft Ltd., 209 Water St., Tel.: 529-3190,
specializes in woolens
The Leather Shop, open May through October
St. Andrews Woolens, 22 Douglas St., Tel.: 529-3367,
tweeds, blankets, tailored garments
Sea Captains Loft, Tel.: 529-3300,
open May through Christmas

St. John (on Bay of Fundy, Rte. 1)
Handicraft Centre & Information Bureau, Admiral Beatty Hotel on King Square
Morrison Art Gallery Ltd., 221 Union St., Tel.: 657-6860
Candi Schedler, 42 Orchard La., on the old Rothesay Rd., Tel.: 847-8295,
makes earthenware pottery
Studio Arts Reg'd, Sand Cove Rd. at MacLarens Beach, Tel.: 672-6271,
has silk screening on textiles, other handicrafts
Clara J. Woodland, 28 Sydney St., Tel.: 657-2682, open afternoons,
has knitted and sewing crafts, toys

St. Leonard (in the northwest, east of Edmundston, on Rte. 2)
Madawaska Weavers, Main St., Tel.: 423-6341,
woven table accessories, clothing

St. Stephens (southwest corner of province, on Rte. 1)
Acadian Studios, 111 King St., Tel.: 466-4184,
open mid-May through October
Fundy Rocks and Minerals, 4 miles from St. Stephens on Rte. 1, Tel.: 466-1562
Vera and William Mosher, 4 miles south of St. Stephens, Tel.: 466-1562,
silver jewelry available May through mid-October

Shediac (northeast of Moncton on Northumberland Strait)
Villa Providence Craft Shop, 215 Main St., Tel.: 532-4484

Sussex (northwest of Fundy National Park, on Rte. 1)
Anne's Cottage, next to Valley Motel and Restaurant on Rte. 2, Tel.: 433-2557,
open May 1 to October 31
Beth and Peter Powning, 4 miles east of Rte. 111 from Hammondvale, Tel.:
433-4736,
specialize in stoneware
Kenneth Radcliff, 503 Main, Tel.: 433-2039,
does weaving
Lucy and Barth Wittewaall, 48 Arnold St., Tel.: 433-3779,
make sterling silver jewelry

Woodstock (on St. John River, west of Fredericton, on Rte. 103)
Clyde Dickinson, Meductive on Rte. 1, Tel.: 272-2163,
does woodworking
Woodstock Weavers, sell at Cozy Cabins Motel, Tel.: 328-3344

Campgrounds

While in the Alma-Sussex area one can do no better than to try one of the
four campgrounds within Fundy National Park. If you desire showers, require
hookups or wish to camp relatively close to the swimming pool, craft school, or
restaurant then you will prefer the headquarters for Fundy National Park, 5
miles west of Alma on Highway 114 or 37 miles east of Sussex. The campground
at Point Wolfe (6 miles east of headquarters) has a boat launch and flush
toilets; the campgrounds at Bennett and Wolfe Lakes (8 and 12 miles east of
Headquarters) both have boat rentals, but neither has flush toilets or showers.
Chignecto (2-1/2 miles east of headquarters, on Route 114, like the two previous
campgrounds) does have flush toilets but no showers. In peak season headquarters is
usually full: Do not be surprised even in peak season to have night visitors (bear,
raccoon), particularly in the outer campgrounds; also, do not be surprised even in
peak season if getting from the change house to the heated swimming pool offers a
chilling challenge.

The Moncton area has several good campgrounds. The ones recommended are
most scenically located: Kimarie Ocean Kamping, northeast of Shediac on
Route 530, not far from Cocagne, is on the ocean and has a semi-wooded setting
with hookups, showers, and boating; Stonehurst Trailer Park (on Route 2,

northwest of Moncton, between Route 126 and Berry Mills) also has family camping on a scenic slope overlooking a strawberry farm, with the usual amenities plus a recreation hall, golf, and playground; and Ocean Trailer and Tent Park (1½ miles east of Shediac on Route 15), although large with over 300 sites, is usually full in peak season, has ocean swimming, mini-golf, fishing as well as a recreational hall, laundry, and hot showers. Fine location as long as you don't require privacy.

The Newcastle-Chatham area on the Southwest Miramichi River, because of its central location, is perhaps best for serving as home base while visiting the Bathurst region. The Enclosure Provincial Park (3 miles southwest of Newcastle on Route 8) does not have showers but does have flush toilets, electric hookups, swimming, and a boat launch; Clarks Camping (1 mile north of Chatham on Route 8) has water and electric hookups, showers, flush toilets, and golf nearby. Another alternative is to camp at Youghall Trailer Park on Youghall Drive, overlooking Nepisiquit Bay in Bathurst where you will find hookups, showers, laundry, fishing, a swimming pool, and waterskiing, all in a semi-wooded setting.

In the St. Leonard area there are several possibilities: the provincial park, 3 miles north of St. Leonard on Route 17, has fishing and swimming but few comforts; if comfort is what you desire then Grande River Campground (2 miles north of St. Leonard on Route 2) will provide them as well as fishing and swimming in the river. Connell Park (on Connell St., 3/4 mile west of Woodstock) also provides showers and flush toilets; golf, a boat launch, and fishing are nearby. If a more central base camp is preferred, Dutch Trailer Park (3 miles north of Florenceville on Route 2) will take care of your needs: hookups, showers, and flush toilets are available, and fishing is possible within a short distance.

Two provincial parks in the Fredericton area are nicely situated on lakes and offer the usual amenities and recreational possibilities: Grand Lake PP (19 miles east of Fredericton on Route 2 and 15 miles northeast of Route 690) is the larger of the two and has slightly better recreational possibilities; Sunbury-Oromocto PP (on French Lake, 18 miles southeast of Fredericton, off Route 7) is the other. If you prefer something closer to Fredericton, you might check the KOA (4 miles west on Route 2)—it should be completed by now—or Grant's Tent and Trailer Site (10 miles east of Fredericton) if you would like camping in a rural setting on Maugerville Island. In addition to showers and hookups they have a dock and boat launch.

Passamaquoddy Park (on Water St. in St. Andrews) has a pleasant ocean setting and plenty of comfort and recreational possibilities. Although a large campground, you may have difficulty getting a site—or privacy—and would prefer to try Skippers Tent and Trailer Park (5 miles east of St. Stephens on Route 1, then right for 2,000 yards) having the usual comforts plus fishing, boat launch, and boat rentals, or to try Oak Bay Provincial Park (5 miles east of St. Stephens on Route 1) with electrical hookups, flush toilets, salt water swimming, and boat launch.

Craft Happenings Elsewhere in Canada

En route you may like to visit one or more of the following art fairs   outside the province of New Brunswick. A more complete list of such fairs might be obtained from the Canadian Government Travel Bureau in Ottawa or by scanning the events bulletins of the individual provinces you plan to visit.

July and August in N. Vancouver, House British Columbia	Textile Arts: Northwest Handicraft
Early July in Neepawa, Manitoba	Festival of the Arts with workshops in ceramics, sculpture, painting
August in Gimli, Manitoba	Creative Arts Week
August in Vancouver, British Columbia	Shawnigan Lake Summer School of Arts
Early August in Charlottetown, Prince Edward Island	A Crafts Fair is part of Old Home Week

Early-mid-August in Banff,
  Alberta
mer
	Banff Festival of the Arts; various
	  workshops are held during the sum-

Mid-August in Dawson City, Yukon	Discovery Days Celebration includes handicraft displays
Late Augusp in Halifax, Nova Scotia	Nova Scotia Festival of the Arts

Early October in Halifax, Nova
  Scotia
	Joseph Howe Festival includes a
	  Craft Market

Early-mid-December in Montreal,
  Quebec
	Exhibition of Quebec Arts and Crafts at
	  Place Bonaventure*

Mid-December in Quebec, Quebec	Quebec's Craftsman's Show at the Convention Center

*Some claim the Quebec handcrafts are the best developed in Canada. There are now 12,000 known artisans in Quebec partially because of the Canadian Handicrafts Guild in Montreal with its encouragement in keeping up old handicrafts, with its shop and annual exhibition. Although it is the artisans working with pottery and wood carving that have won distinction, others are working with ceramics, batik, tapestry, binding, jewelry, enameling, weaving, metal crafts, hooked rugs, and Indians beadwork and basketry. Visit Saint-Jean-Port-Joli, the woodcarvers' town on the south shore of the St. Lawrence , LaMalbaie, and Pointe-au-Pic where weaving is done with remarkable skill. State stores known as Centrales d'artisan also serve as outlets for Quebec artisans. There are four of these stores in Montreal, one in the city of Quebec.

HOT SPRINGS TOUR

Not as a main focus of a vacation but perhaps as a secondary or adjunct interest, a family may wish to visit a few of the 14 hot mineral springs of Canada: British Columbia and Alberta have by far the greatest number, but they can also be experienced in the Northwest Territories, the Yukon, Saskatchewan, and Ontario.

It was the discovery of thermal springs by Canadian Pacific railmen on the south side of the Bow River and the ensuing legal conflict over ownership that came to the attention of public-minded Canadians, who succeeded in having the springs set aside as a public reserve. This ten-square-mile area became the birthplace of the National Park System of Canada, now numbering 28 parks and encompassing 29,000 square miles.

With the thermal springs of Banff, Alberta, having this historic significance, we have chosen to concentrate just a little on the specifics of their geology before listing the locations of other hot springs and suggesting a few campgrounds in their vicinities.

Banff Hot Springs

Five of the six thermal springs in the Banff area are situated on the northeast side of Sulphur Mountain: Upper Hot Springs, the Kidney Springs, Middle Springs, Cave Springs, and Basin Springs. The sixth apparently is an unrelated spring and is located on the north shore of Third Vermilion Lake.

The volume of water flowing from the many springs differ considerably. The Cave, enclosing one of the original springs, is the largest with a 250-gal. flow per minute; the Kidney Spring with a flow of about 20 gal. a minute is the smallest.

The water from the five springs on Sulphur Mountain is believed to originate from Sundance Creek on the west side of the mountain. "Water from the Creek apparently percolates down along a fault plane (where two masses of rock have broken and slipped against each other) to a depth in excess of 15,000 feet below sea level...The water is heated by the internal heat of the earth encountered at such depths. It then rises along another plane to emerge as springs on the flank of Sulphur Mountain. The exit points of the water are of course lower in elevation than the entrance points. As the water rises from the depths it is diluted with varying amounts of colder ground water causing the temperature of the various springs to differ. The Upper Spring is the warmest with a temperature of about 115^0 F. while the Cave Spring is some 30^0 cooler.

During its circulation the water dissolves lime and sulphur compounds from the rocks. The lime is deposited as tufa around the spring mouths and the sulphur gives the water its characteristic odor."

The quotes in the preceding paragraphs were taken from the Natural History Notes leaflet entitled, *The Mineral Springs of Banff National Parks*, published by the National Parks of Canada. You might also wish to read "Banff Thermal Springs, a Fascinating Problem," by T. Binnert Haites, in the *Alberta Soc. Petrol. Geol.* Vol. 7, No. 2, 1959.

The following is a list of the other hot mineral springs of Canada.

Alberta: Banff Hot Springs—Banff National Park
Canada's first National Park was established following the discovery in 1885 of hot springs bubbling from the slopes of Sulphur Mountain. The Cave encloses one of the original springs. These hot sulphur springs, with a daily flow of 575,000 gal., feed a natural sulphur water pool at a temperature of 88^0 F and a fresh water pool at a temperature of 80^0 F.

Banff: Upper Hot Springs
About 2½ miles from Banff, on the slopes of Sulphur Mountain. The outdoor pool is open year round. This pool, fed by sulphur springs at 100° F, is popular with winter skiers as well as summer visitors.

Miette: Hot Springs
37 miles north of Jasper, 10 miles from Pocohontas. Four mineral springs, among the hottest in the continent, reaching 129° F are piped to a fully serviced pool and the water cooled to 90° F for comfort.

British Columbia: Ainsworth Hot Springs
30 miles north of Nelson in Kootenay area. Swimming pool, steam-baths, showers in caves, hydro-kinetic mineral whirlpool baths, dining and accommodation at resort. Besides the main spring, there is a hot lithia water spring. Mineral content: sodium carbonate, potassium and lithium chlorides, silica, and iron.

Canyon Hot Springs
On Trans-Canada Dhe in Rogers Pass at Albert Canyon, British Columbia. In a rain forest setting are two mineral pools, 102° F. and 86° F. Swim suits and towels can be rented.

Fairmont Hot Springs
One mile off Rte. 95, 24 miles south of Radium Hot Springs and 80 miles north of Cranbrook. Odorless sulphur hot mineral baths 96°-110° F; indoor and outdoor swimming and health pools.

Harrison Hot Springs
80 miles from Vancouver on Rte. 7 to Agassiz, then 4 miles north. The Harrison Hotel open year round had three pools ca. 100° F (one public) fe: ʋy ɩʋotast and sulphur hot springs. Mineral content: chloride of otassium, of sodium; sulfate of sodium, of magnesium, of lime; bicarbonate of lime, or iron; sulfurated hydrogen.

Liard Hot Springs
Near mile 496 on the Alaska Highway (Rte. 97) near the British Columbia-Yukon border, with developed bathing facilities. Temperature of the water is approximately 115° F.

Lakelse Hot Springs
Two large lithia (nonsulphur) mineral pools (one sheltered outdoor, 85° F; one indoor, 100° F) are located at Lakelse Hot Springs Resort on Highway 25, 12 miles south of Terrace on Highway 16 to Prince Rupert. Open year-round. Water analysis: calcium, magnesium, sodium calculated, bicarbonate, carbonate sulphate, chloride,

silica, dissolved solids, penolphthalien alkaline, iron, phosphorous, lithium, flouride.

Radium Hot Springs—Kootneay National Park
65 miles south of the Trans-Canada Highway (Rte. 1) on Rte. 93, or 67 miles south of Golden on Rte. 95. Open year-round. Two pools supplied by odorless hot mineral water from 114⁰ F to 85⁰ F. Mineral content: calcium sulphate, magnesium sulphate (epsom salt), sodium sulphate (Glauber's salt), and calcium barcarbonate, variable small amounts of iron, manganese, aluminum, boron, silica, and potassium. Principal gases are nitrogen, carbon dioxide, argon, helium, and radon.

Toad Springs
Northeast off the Alaska Highway, at junction of Racing River and the Toad River. There are about 15 pools; the water is very hot; access by foot or horse.

Northwest Territories: Nahanni River Hot Springs
Accessible only by chartered plane from Fort Nelson, British Columbia, or Fort Simpson, Northwest Territories; there are three hot mineral springs with a temperature of about 98⁰ F.

Ontario: Hespeler Hot Springs
Hot mineral springs may be found at Kress, just east of Hespeler near Kitchener.

Saskatchewan: Moose Jaw Hot Springs
Hot mineral water from a deep well, originally bored for gas, is piped into the MosseJaw Natatorium, a large city-owned swimming pool. The water is cooled to 80⁰-90⁰ F.

Yukon: Takhini Hot Springs
Situated 11 miles north of Whitehorse (6 miles off the Dawson-Mayo Rd.) There is a swimming pool fed by hot mineral springs and accommodation facilities.

Campgrounds near Hot Springs

Alberta: Banff National Park
There are at least ten campgrounds within the park, and all are comparable in terms of facilities, but the campgrounds at Tunnel Mountain have a store and laundry nearby, so they may be your choice if you have needs along those lines. These campgrounds are located 1 and ½ miles east from Banff on Highway 1A. Note the trailer campground (#1) charges twice as much as TM #2 and TM Village because of hookup facilities. If interested in nearby fishing you might prefer staying at Two

Jack Lake Campground, 9 miles northeast of Banff on Highway 1 at Minnewanka Loop, where all amenities are possible including hookups, playground, boat rental, and boat launch.

Miette Hot Springs National Park
Many opportunities for primitive camping are available in the region around Jasper; the same can be said for "civilization" camping. If wishing to stay as close as possible to the hot springs, drive northeast from Jasper for 27 miles on Highway 16, then turn east onto Miette Rd. and continue another 11 miles to the campground. Although you will not find showers, horseback riding, a store, and a snack bar are nearby.

British Columbia
Canyon Hot Springs camping offers tables, firewood, showers, flush toilets, and a snack bar plus swimming, fishing, and playground facilities. The campground is on Trans-Canada One at Albert Canyon between Mt. Revelstoke and Glacier National Parks. The Albert Canyon "Ghost town" is a short distance south of the present pool site.

Fairmont Hot Springs
The resort at the site makes it possible to live indoors (lodge, motel, cabins) or outside at the trailer court and campground. The recreational facilities are also varied: 18-hole golf course, trail rides, a roller rink, fishing streams, hiking trails, mountain climbing, boating on nearby Columbia and Windermere Lakes, and, of course, three pools with water temperature ranging from 96° F winter and summer. (There is a charge for using the pools.) The campground has all the usual amenities at a usual campground price; however, even though the resort is open year-round, the campground is only open April through November. If driving on Trans-Canada One, take Highway 95, driving 90 miles south of Golden; if on Highway 3, take 93/95 and the campground is 70 miles north of Cranbrook.

Harrison Hot Springs
Here, too, is a hotel-resort atmosphere if you wish to take part, but reservations are usually necessary. There is no high-quality campground nearby to our knowledge. The closest area where you might camp is one-half mile from Harrison Hot Springs at the Pines Motel. Tables and flush toilets are available, and a store is nearby. Possibilities for boating, golfing, and horseback riding are there as well as swimming at the public Harrison Hot Springs pool.

Liard Hot Springs

Camping is possible year-round at the small liard River campground. Table and firewood are provided, fishing and swimming are possible. If driving in British Columbia on Highway 97 near the Yukon border, the hot springs are near mile 496. The Lower Liard River Lodge is about one mile from the springs.

Lakelse Hot Springs

You have a choice of staying at the resort at the hot springs, primitive camping, or staying at either the Exchamsiks River campground (36 miles west of Terrace on Highway 16) or at the Timberland Trailer Park in Terrace (2 and 1/2 miles southwest of the Skeena River bridge on Queensway). The former is open year-round and is free; fishing is nearby, but no drinking water is available. The latter has showers, a laundromat, and a public golf course within 5 miles. Take your pick.

Radium Hot Springs

You can choose from at least four camping areas in Kootenay National Park alone; however, we suggest Redstreak Campground, since it has nearby shower facilities and a store as well as fishing and swimming in the adjacent area. Redstreak is located 3 miles northeast of Radium Hot Springs on Highway 93. At a slightly lower elevation and with many more amenities (showers, hookups, and store in camp), you could stay at Canyon Camp on Highway 95, 1/4 mile north of the 93/95 junction.

Toad Springs

You have a choice of at least four campgrounds in the vicinity of the Toad River on the Alaskan Highway or BC 97. The nearest camping areas are provincial parks at mile 405 and mile 420: no charge, open year-round, no drinking water. For more comfort, continue North to Muncho Lake, mile 463, where there is boat launch and rental, showers, flush toilets. Wiebe's Wilderness Motel has a laundromat and is considerably cheaper than Muncho Lake Lodge, which has pull-through sites, but no laundry facility.

Ontario: Hespeler Hot Springs

The closest camping area as best we can determine is Bingeman Park, 1 mile east of Kitchener, on Bingeman Park Road, off of Highway 7. You will find it open year-round and with all the amenities plus swimming pool and opportunities for golfing, snowmobiling, and skiing within a short distance.

Saskatchewan: Moose Jaw

Two campgrounds are in or near Moose Jaw. River Park Campground, city-operated, has showers, electricity, and water hookups all for about $2 a night. Prairie Oasis is about 2 miles west of Moose Jaw on TC 1, and for about $3.50, you can get all the comforts, including the use of a recreational hall.

Yukon: Takhini Hot Springs
At Jackson Lake Rest Stop, mile 15 on Fish Lake Road, west of Whitehorse (mile 918), you will find stream water, privies, tables, and firewood as well as lunchroom facility nearby.

BOTANICAL GARDEN TOUR

To demonstrate our openmindedness, and to draw your attention to one of Canada's lesser known cultivated wonders, we are including a list of botanical gardens and flower festivals around which an extensive tour of the provinces might be planned. If you wish to concentrate in one central province, we offer a comprehensive listing of gardens and conservatories in Ontario.

We have not gone out of our way to see any of these, except for the benefit of others who happened to be with us—always at the wrong time. So for flower lovers, accept this bouquet:

Botanical Gardens, Arboretums, and Herbariums of Canada

Calgary Zoological Gardens	Calgary, Alberta
Nikka Yuko Centennial Garden	Lethbridge, Alberta
Cowichan Valley Forest Museum	Duncan, British Columbia
Crown Zellerback Canada Arboretum and Museum	Ladysmith, British Columbia
Queen Elizabeth Arboretum	Vancouver, British Columbia
Stanley Park Botanical Gardens	Vancouver, British Columbia
University of British Columbia: Herbarium Museum Nitobe Memorial Japanese Garden Rose Test Garden	Vancouver, British Columbia
Butchart Gardens	6 ictoria, British Columbia
Assiniboine Park	Winnipeg, Manitoba
Royal Botanical Gardens	Hamilton, Ontario
Storybook Gardens in Springbank Park	London, Ontario
School of Horticulture Niagara Parks Commission	Niagara Falls, Ontario
Museum of Natural Sciences	Ottawa, Ontario
Plant Research Institute	Ottawa, Ontario
James Gardens	Toronto, Ontario
Centre Culturel	Amqui, Quebec
C.I.P. Company Nature Centre, Centre de la Nature—C.I.P.	Harrington, Quebec
Botanical Garden of Montreal	Montreal, Quebec
MacDonald College Morgan Arboretum	Sainte-Anne-de-Bellevue, Quebec
Mendal Art Gallery and Conservatory	Saskatoon, Saskatchewan
W.P. Fraser Herbarium, University of Saskatchewan	Saskatoon, Saskatchewan

Flower Festivals of Canada

Last two weeks of May: Tulip Festival in Ottawa, Ontario
End of May-early June: Annapolis Valley Blossom Festival in Windsor, Nova Scotia
August: International Flower Show in Winnipeg, Manitoba
Mid-August: Horticultural Show in Saskatoon, Saskatchewan

Gardens and Conservatories of Ontario

Brantford, Glenhyrst Gardens: This is a 16-acre estate, overlooking the Grand River containing formal gardens and a nature trail through a wildflower garden. The fine old mansion, the home of the Art Gallery of Brantford has excellen gallery shows at all times. (Located at 20 Ava Rd., 1 mile north via Highways 2 and 24.)

Dundas, Veldhuis Greenhouses: These wholesale growers, with 80,000 sq ft. of greenhouses are world-famous for cacti and African violets. (Located at 154 King St., E., Dundas.)

Goderich, Floral Clock: The clock, about 12 ft. in diameter, is located on the grounds of Huron County Pioneer Museum, 104 North St. and operates by 1/4 H.P motor. Sixty plants represent seconds on the border of the clock and are called Santolinda. The "325" are Red Alternanthera; the rest of the clock is planted in Hens and Chickens.

Guelph, Floral Clock: The largest floral display of its kind, the clock is 44 ft. in diameter and contains between 6,000 and 7,000 flowers of 14 varieties. Minute and hour hands are filled with flowers. The clock also has a flower calender which is changed daily. (Located in Riverside Park, Woolwich St. near junction of Highways 6 and 7, beside Sir Adam Beck Power Plant.)

Hamilton, Gage Park: This 70-acre park is one of Hamilton's showplace parks, noted for its floral displays and summer open-air musical concerts. (Located on Main St. E. at Gage Ave.)

Hamilton, Royal Botanical Gardens: The gardens cover 2,000 acres of forest, marshland, and meadows within the municipalities of Hamilton, Burlington, Dundas, and West Flamboro. Topographically, the gardens comprise large open-water areas, ravine lands, tablelands, stream valleys, and over 2 miles of the face of the Niagara Escarpment with a falls at Rock Chapel over 75 ft. high.

Hamilton, The Rock Garden: An internationally famed garden transformed from abandoned gravel pits has three main seasonal displays against a backdrop rich in horticultural interest. Open May to October. Other gardens at Hamilton: Spring Garden, Children's Garden, Arboretum, Henrie Park. (Accessible from the Queen Elizabeth Way and from the west by Highway 2, from the north by Highway 6.)

Kingsville, Colasanti Tropical Greenhouses: A 3-acre site filled with almost every type of temperate and tropical vegetables and fruit. The Tropical Greenhouse features bananas, oranges, lemons, grapefruit, tangerines, tangelos, date palms, figs. Located 3 miles east of the Jack Miner Bird Sanctuary on the 3rd Concession, or 1/4 mile west of Highway 3, near Ruthven.)

Kitchener, Rockway Gardens: The gardens contain beautiful illuminated fountains, flower gardens, and rockeries. (Located at the eastern entrance of the city, on King St. E., formerly called Jantzen Gardens.)

London, Victoria Park: This is a pleasant park with its formal gardens and lily ponds and open-air concerts at the bandshell. (The park is bounded on the north by Piccadilly St., east by Wellington St., south by Dufferin St., and west by Clarence St.)

Niagara Falls, Niagara Parks Commission Greenhouse: Many of the Niagara parks flowers are grown here: Common and exotic plants can be seen. Special seasonal shows are held. (Located half mile south of Horseshoe Falls. Outdoor displays are at Queen Victoria Park, Oakes Garden Theatre, and the School of Horticulture.)

Niagara Falls, Oakes Garden Theatre: Formal gardens in the style of an ancient Greek theater. The Rainbow Gardens are adjacent to this area. (Both gardens are situated between Falls St., and the Niagara Parkway, near the Rainbow Bridge.)

Niagara Falls, Queen Victoria Park: Landscape Illumination at night; gardens, greenhouse, conservatory, fountain; Dufferin Islands; band concerts in summer. (Located on the Niagara Parkway, adjacent to the Falls area.)

Niagara-on-the-Lake, Floral Clock: This unusual floral clock was designed and built by the Ontario Hydro's regional staff. It is three times larger than the original floral clock in Edinburgh. The dial is composed of some 24,000 carpet plants, interwoven into a new design each summer. The overall diameter is 40 ft. The hands of the clock are constructed of stainless steel tubing. The hour hand is 14 ft. 6 in. long, and the minute hand, 17 ft. 6 in. long; they have a combined weight of half a ton, while the 21-ft. long sweep second hand weighs 250 lb. The clock's Westminster chimes ring every quarter hour. The illuminated water garden at the clock's base is stocked with fish. (Located near the Sir Adam Beck Generating Station.)

New Hamburg, Waterloo County Arboretum: A 6-acre area on the eastern edge of New Hamburg provides an opportunity for the study of native and introduced tree species. Seventy-one species of native and exotic trees are alongside windbreaks of Carolina poplar, Norway spruce, Scotch pine, and a hedge of white cedar.

Oshawa, Parkwood (McLaughlin Estate): This is the estate of the late Col. R.S. McLaughlin, which consists of a stately 55-room residence on a 12-acre, parklike setting of unbelievable beauty. The grounds are a planned landscape of mature trees, shrubberies, plantings, and pools. The spectacular sunken garden and its unique 225-ft. pool with five fountains offers exceptional interest and beauty. Another highlight of Parkwood grounds is the Italian garden. A huge greenhouse, adjacent to the residence, offers a wide variety of native and exotic plants and flowers that would rival those of many commercial greenhouses. In the winter months, tours are limited to house and conservatory only. (Located at 270 Simcoe St., N.)

Ottawa, Central Experimental Farm: Headquarters of the system of Dominion experimental farms comprises nearly 1,200 acres. Research experiments are conducted in plant breeding, soil and fertility tests, orchard management, the development of better crops, and raising livestock and poultry under practical conditions. There are beautiful flower gardens, spacious lawns, and a 65-acre arboretum containing 2,500 different kinds of trees and shrubs. (Located on the Driveway, off Carling St.)

St. Catharines, Stokes Seeds Flower Trial Gardens: This is the headquarters of a huge mailorder seed firm and proving grounds, which are open to the public. Their gardens, extending along both sides of Martindale Rd., are a scene of horticultural beauty during the summer months. This is one of the official sites of the All-American Trials.

St. Thomas, Waterworks Park: The park contains tiny islands and lagoons filled with goldfish and waterlilies, rustic bridges, and gardens. (Located on Balaclava St.)

Thunder Bay, Botanical Garden Conservatory: The conservatory offers a world-wide variety of plant life, including an unusually attractive display of exotic tropical plants and cacti. Special shows are arranged during the year such as the Easter Lily Show, the Christmas Poinsetta Show, and the Summer Rose Show. (Located just behind Chapples Park.)

Thunder Bay, Chapples Recreation Centre: The grounds feature the International Friendship Gardens in which organized ethnic groups have, on a designated plot of land, designed and developed their own floral and mini-architectural displays. These are clustered around beautiful Reflection Lake, which has a bridge crossing over the narrows. (Located on Victoria Ave. at corner of Tarbutt St.)

Thunder Bay, Hillcrest Park: Sunken gardens are situated adjacent to this park. (Located on S. High St., just off Highway 17A).

Toronto, Allan Gardens: Here are located the indoor and outdoor botanical display gardens which feature seasonal horticultural exhibits and tropical plants. (Located in downtown Toronto, west side of Sherbourne St. to Jarvis St., between Carlton St. and Gerrard St. E.)

Toronto, Edwards Gardens: This was originally a private estate and is now a metropolitan park. It contains a Civic Garden Centre in addition to rock gardens, shady arbors surrounding running streams and pools in the floor of a wooded valley.

Toronto, High Park: High Park's 353 acres feature Hillside Gardens overlooking Grenadier Pond, plus sunken and overhanging gardens, nature trails, duck ponds, animal paddocks, picnic areas, and boating. Summer concerts are presented by barge-based bands upon Grenadier Pond. (Located in west Toronto at Bloor St. W. and Parkside Dr.)

Toronto, James Gardens: The park consists of formal gardens covering 10 acres. The gardens are particularly noted for well laidout flower beds and are a favorite spot for summer trips. The area is adjacent to one of the few wildflower reserves in North America.

Toronto, Toronto Islands Park: One of the features of this series of islands is a formal mall extending from Manitou Bridge to Lake Ontario, with the Pier at the southern end. (Located on the Avenue of the Islands on Centre Island reached by a ten-minute ferry ride.) Most recreational activities are available on the Islands in Toronto Bay.

Windsor, Jackson Park Sunken Garden: The natural beauty of the Sunken Garden is superb during the day. The evening visitor will find himself transposed into another world, for over 400 custom-designed ornamental lights have been installed among the numerous flower beds and shrubs. The fountains, by underwater lights, are further enhanced by interesting sculpture. The Memorial Rose Garden, with approximately 12,000 roses of different varieties, is situated in the park adjacent to the Sunken Garden. (Located at Tecumseh Rd. and Highway 401 overpass.)

INDIANS

What is life?
It is the flash of a firefly in the night.
It is the breath of a buffalo in the winter time.
It is the little shadow which runs across the grass and
Loses itself in the sunset.
—CROWFOOT

One tour of Canada could not begin to touch upon the many facets of Indian life; any in-depth exploration would require extensive research, a life-time of study. We assume, however, that yours is a causual interest, that you simply hope to learn a little of the history, cultural values, life, and livelihood of the Indians of Canada—and perhaps the meaning of *pemmican* and *yo-ho*, from what wampum was made and why, which tribes were responsible for inventing lacrosse and sunglasses, why the Beothuks vanished. We assume you will use your local library's card catalog, your local bookstore, the book list in the appendix of this book, and the literature provided by Information Canada (address in appendix) and the Information Service of the Department of Indian and Northern Affairs (Ottawa, Ontario K1A OH4).

Tawow, a handsomely illustrated quarterly magazine, publishes Indian legends and stories written by contemporary Indians, describes the accomplishments of Indian notables, and informs about forthcoming Indian events. Subscriptions ($4) are available through Information Canada (121 Slater St., Ottawa K1A 0S9).

Two excellent booklets written for elementary-school use, as a part of Concepts/A Series in Canadian Studies, are *Nestum Asa: The Way It Was in the Beginning* b, Kent Gooderham (Griffin Press Ltd., 455 King St. W., Toronto 135) and *The Days of the Treaties*, b, the same author and publisher. Both were written in the early 1970s; the first is especially well-illustrated, informative, and appreciated by all ages.

The Historical Guide to New Brunswick, published by the New Brunswick Travel Bureau (pp. 66-70), provides some insight into the former life of the MicMacs and the Passamaquoddies of that province. *Historic Newfoundland* (from the Newfoundland Department of Tourism) includes a piece (p. 7) on the Beothucks, the vanished Indian race. When you have completed the article you will probably keep right on reading about the folk medicines, folk songs, weather lore, even the superstitions.

A New York establishment we only recently learned about may also provide you with additional literature: Books Canada, Inc., 35 E. 67th St., New York, N.Y. 10021. Perhaps they can help you secure a copy of Alma Green's *Forbidden Voice*, a Canadian bestseller written by a descendent of the Mohawk chieftans.

Restored Villages

In addition to seeking out some of the pictographs (Sioux Narrows, Ontario, and elsewhere) and archeological diggings (Whiteshell Provincial Park, Manitoba, and elsewhere) you will undoubtedly try to visit at least one of the re-created Indian villages. Our search has not been extensive, so there may be more. We did locate one on Prince Edward Island—a 16th-century MicMac village at Rocky Point. This re-creation, on route 19, has birchbark wigwams and canoes, fishing and hunting implements, and lifelike sculptures of Indians and animals, all arranged in a natural setting. An artifacts museum and a unique craft shop with bark and leather handicrafts can also be visited daily from mid-June to mid-October.

In Ontario, southwest of Hamilton in the city of Brantford, an authentic reproduction of an ancient Iroquois village is open Sundays from June to September. And in central Ontario, northwest of Barrie, the city of Midland has a replica of a 17th-century Huron village that is open daily from mid-May to mid-October.

On the west coast, at the junction of the Skeena and Bulkley Rivers in west central British Columbia (northwest of Prince George and northeast of Prince Rupert), is the authentic Gitksan village in the town of Hazelton. 'Ksan, as it is called, was built in 1969 with the hope of perpetuating the history and culture of the Gitksan people—and to bolster their economy as well. This attraction on Highway 16 includes five buildings, four communal longhouses, and a carving shed. The Frog House of the Distant Past illustrates the old ways of the tribe, the slender branched fish traps, the wood-carved feast pot, the bent cedar cooking and eating vessels, the cures of the medicine man. The Fireweed Clan's House of Treasures is a showplace of arts and crafts and houses the artifacts of the Gitksan culture. The Wolf House of the Grandfathers includes representations of the present-day tribe made from plaster-of-paris. A feastlike setting includes birchbark dishes and animal skins. Kitchen wares, blankets, muskets, and iron pots from the fur traders are also displayed. A totem pole under construction is featured in the Carver's House of All Times (the carving shed). The fifth building, Today House of the Arts, houses the village office and displays products made for sale by Gitksan and Carrier artisans. While there you might ask about seeing an example of the carved wooden masks that have brought 'Ksan's Freda Deising well-deserved recognition. The 'Ksan trademark found on all handicrafts sold at the village guarantees them to be of genuine Indian craftsmanship.

'Ksan trademark.

If lucky, while at the village you will witness an Indian ceremony or special event; if not so lucky, you will at least see the Gitksan at work on their carvings and crafts, see their canoes and totem poles, their brightly decorated house paintings of the classical west coast Indian style.

Adjacent to the village is a modern campground and trailer park. Hot showers, flush toilets, drinking water, sewer and electrical hookups are available.

Museums

An Indian Hall of Fame was established by a group of Indian people and the Indian Eskimo Association in 1967 to honor Indians of the past and present. As far was we know a physical structure does not yet exist but there is consideration of a traveling exhibit. If you would like to learn about those who have been chosen for inclusion in the Hall of Fame, we are providing their names to get you started.

Indian Hall of Fame

Poundmaker	Cree; buffalo hunter
Joseph Brant	Mohawk; war leader
Thunderchild	Cree; last of life chiefs
Tecumse	Shawenese; statesman, war chief
Louis Riel	Metis; freedom leader
Big Bear	Plains Cree; leader against tyranny and injustice
Corporal Frances Pegamagabow	Ojibway; soldier of valor
Oronyatekha (Dr. Peter Martin)	Mohawk; fraternal organization leader
Dr. Elmer Jamieson	Cayuga; teacher of science
James Gladstone	Blood tribe of Blackfeet; first of race in Canadian Senate
George Armstrong	Irish-Scot father, Objibway mother; leader in hockey
Crowfoot	Blackfeet; tribal chief and leader of confederacy
Chief Pequis	Objibway; protecyed settlers of Manitoba
Saulteaux Chief Oozawekwun	Yellow Quill; led fight for reserves
Emily Pauline Johnson	Mohawk; poet, leader in race relations
Cameron Dee Brant	Mohawk; first Indian to give his life in World War I
George Clutesi	Distinguished artist and writer
Chief Dan George	Popular actor
Joseph Benjamin Keeper, Sr.	Cree; athlete
Oliver Milton Martin	Mohawk; brigadier and magistrate
Dr. Gilbert Monture, O.B.E.	Mohawk; authority on mining economics
Thomas Longboat	Onondaga; noted long-distance runner
Ethel Brant Monture	Mohawk; author and teacher
Andrew Tonahokate Delisle	Mohawk; director and curator of the Indians of Canada Pavilion in the permanent exhibition "Man and His World" in Montreal
Frank Calker, L.Th.	Nishgas of Nass River; political leader and first Indian representative in Canadian legislature

A partial list of museums containing material on the Indians follows:

Alberta
Luxton Museum, P.O. Box 850, Banff

British Columbia
Public Library and Museum, and Kwakwala Arts and Crafts Ass'n., P.O. Box 245, Alert Bay
Centennial Museum, Tyee Plaze, P.O. Box 601, Campbell River
NA WA LA GWA TSI, Simoom Scount, P.O. Box 177, Gilford Island
'Ksan Indian Village, Hazelton
Indian Village, P.O. Box 1, Okanagan Mission
Lipsett Indian Museum, Hastings Park, Vancouver
Provincial Museum and Thunderbird Park, Belleville and Douglas St., Victoria

Manitoba
Eskimo Museum, Roman Catholic Church, Churchill

Nova Scotia
MicMac Museum, R.R. #1, Pictou

Quebec
Indians of Canada Pavilion at "Man and His World," Montreal

Ontario
Public Library Museum, 363 Church St., Fort Frances
Huron Indian Village, Little Lake Park, Midland

Indian-Operated Campgrounds and Outfitters

Tourists are invited to acquaint themselves with the Indian way of life, to learn the secrets of nature they respect. The directory *Canadian Indian Tourist Outfitting and Outdoor Recreation Facilities* is available to tourists from the Department of Indian Affairs and Northern Development. Nine provinces from New Brunswick to the Yukon are included, with notes on each campground's facilities, the recreational possibilities in the surrounding area, and its mailing address. For example, we learn Stoney Indian Park, in Alberta, is owned and operated by members of the Stoney Indian Reserve. Situated in a wilderness setting with the Rockies nearby, it is just 5 miles off Trans-Canada Highway 1A, 45 miles west of Calgary, 35 miles east of Banff, and 8 miles west of Morley. Ten teepees are ready for those who wish to rent a new experience. Buffalo Paddock, Teepee Village, and archeological excavations at Old Bow Fort offer diversions in the area. Opened in 1970, this tent and trailer park now has 150 tent sites, drinking water, a store, outdoor toilets, garbage service, fireplace—plus horses, guides, trail rides, firewood, and handicrafts. A children's playground, a riding stable, nature trails, and a baseball diamond are found nearby. Whitefish and trout keep fishing exciting at Broken Lake or Bow River and moose, elk, deer, bear, bighornsheep, and goat are both observable and huntable. We haven't been there yet-would like to!

Friendship Centers

Friendship centers in areas where there are good-sized Indian populations, such as Thunder Bay, Kenora, Winnipeg, Regina, Vancouver, Whitehorse, provide a variety of services. You might inquire about their locations in specific communities, may enjoy stopping in and getting acquainted—perhaps even offer to sew on a button, write a letter, or make some other donation of time or money as seems appropriate or as suggested by the director.

Festivals

Attending festivals is another way of observing, getting acquainted, developing understanding. Beautiful beaded outfits, tall feathered headdresses, spectacular dances, reenactment of historical events—and all in a natural setting! The most current listing during the months of May to September showed Indian festivals taking place in these communities:

Alberta:	*Brocket, Cardston,* Blood Reserve, Morley, Gleichen, Banff, Hobbema
British Columbia:	Terrace, Kamloops, Mt. Currie, *Cultus Lake,* Squamish Band, *North Vancouver,* Williams Lake, Vancouver, False Creek, Anahim Lake, Victoria
Manitoba:	Brandon, The Pas, *Griswold,* Selkirk, St. Theresa Point, Long Plains (Portage La Prairie), Norway House
New Brunswick:	Campbellton
Northwest Territories:	Yellowknife
Nova Scotia:	MicMac P.O. (Hants County)
Ontario:	*Deseronto,* Native Canadian Center (Toronto), Sarnia, Walpole Island, *Ohsweken,* Sault Ste. Marie, Curve Lake, Chippewa Hill, Thamesville
Prince Edward Island:	Lennox Island
Saskatchewan:	Cupar, Punnichy, *Kamsack,* Alingly, Balcarres Turtleford, Regina Beach, Duck Lake, Onion Lake, Broadview (10 miles north), Ft. Qu'Appelle
Quebec:	Kanesatake, Oka, Village Huron, Restigouche
Yukon:	Whitehorse

NOTE: Italicized cities had more than one Indian festival during the summer months.

Indian
Fine Crafts

Handicrafts

If you hope to take home a reminder of your encounter with the Indian community, whether aesthetic or practical, you will probably find that most of the festivals, pow wows, and rodeos have a handicraft sale as part of the affair. If you have an interest in their handicrafts, you might want to locate the two-page, illustrated article by Dorothy Francis, "Indian Crafts," in the July/August, 1973, issue of *Canadian Antiques Collector*. A deeper treatment of a particular handicraft is provided us by Oliver N. Wells, *Salish Weaving, Primitive and Modern*. You may obtain a copy of the book or inquire about custom-made articles by writing to Salish Weavers, Box 307, Chilliwack, British Columbia. Outlets in British Columbia exhibiting and selling Salish belts, sashes, handbags, ponchos, chair covers, table runners, saddle blankets, rugs, and tapestries include:

Salish Weavers' Headquarters, Coqualeetza Project, Sardis
Hand Loom, Victoria
Provincial Museum Gift Shop, Victoria
Sam Hill Saddle Shop, Sardis
Tempo Canadian Crafts, Vancouver
Vancouver Art Gallery Gift Shop, Vancouver
Vancouver Planetarium Gift Shop, Vancouver
Woodward's Coggery, Vancouver

Salish tribes along the lower Fraser River and on Vancouver Island in British Columbia were early known for their weaving of cedar bark, mountain goat's wool, and dog's hair into blankets, pack straps, dancing aprons, and mats. With the coming of the Hudson Bay Company in the 1830s, however, it became easier to trade fresh salmon for a Hudson Bay blanket then to make a blanket, so gradually the ancient craft of loom-weaving was abandoned.

In the 1960s through the efforts of people like Oliver Wells, the Salish returned to their traditional method of weaving, using warm natural dyes made from lichen, flowers, bark, and tree roots, and with wool washed, carded, and spun by hand on simple equipment, they reproduced ancient Salish designs combining symbolic birds, mountains, lightning and mammals.

If on the east coast, you can seek out the MicMac crafts, of which the potato baskets have received most attention. Some of the shops in Nova Scotia handling Indian arts and crafts are:

Cape Breton	Megmow Crafts, Whycocmagh
	Eddie Goo Goo Craft Shop, Whycocomagh
	Ulnoo Crafts, P.O. Box 112, Shycocomagh
	Michael Goo Goo Craft Shop, Whycocomagh
Truro	Glooscap Trading Post, Highway 102, Millbrook Indian Reserve
	Goo Goo's Indian Handcraft Shop, Highway 102,
Millbrook	Indian Reserve

Shubenacadie, Hants County   MicMac Handcraft Shop, Highway 102

For specific information you can write to the Union of Nova Scotia Indians (117 Membertou St., Sydney, Nova Scotia) or to the Handcraft Centre (P.O. Box 2147, Halifax). The most current directory from the Handcraft Centre lists the addresses of these artisans:

Mr. and Mrs. Noel Michael, MicMac P.O. Shubenacadie, Hants County, Nova Scotia, Indian baskets

Edith Baxil Peter, Highway 102, Millbrook, Truro, S.S. 1, Colchester County, Nova Scotia, Indian baskets.

Indian crafts, of course, are found in many tourist shops—particularly in areas where there are concentrations of Indians—and in metropolitan area department stores and museum gift shops, but not all are authentic. Check out the following shops if in the vicinity:

Alberta	The Indian Trading Post, Banff
	Tipi Shope, 8th Ave. N.W., Calgary
	The Team Products Store, Jasper Ave., Edmonton

British Columbia	Besides the shops selling Salish wovens try: The Cowichan Trading Company, Victoria
Manitoba	Indian Handicrafts of Manitoba, 470 Portage Ave., Winnipeg Crafts Guild of Manitoba, 183 Kennedy St., Winnipeg
New Brunswick	Refer to those shops and artisans mentioned in the New Brunswick Handicrafts Tour
Newfoundland	Nonia, Water St., St. John's Cog Jigger, Duckworth St., St. John's
Nova Scotia	Refer to shops and artisans already mentioned and: The Tartan House, Halifax
Ontario	Refer to gift shops at Indian villages and museums, and Shops and homes in the Sioux Narrows area (Rte. 71), east of Kenora and in the Thunder Bay area
Quebec	Refer to the suggestions at the end of the New Brunswick Handicrafts Tour, and: Quebec Handicraft Centres at: 1450 St. Denis St., Montreal Queen Elizabeth Hotel, 900 Dorchester Blvd. W., Montreal 403 St. Catherine E., Montreal 1474 Peel St., Montreal Place Laurier, St. Foy (Quebec suburb)
Saskatchewan	The Trading Post, Saskatoon The Sioux Handicraft Co-operative, Fort Qu'Appelle The Buffalo Craft Shop, Regina Northern Handicraft Centre, Lac La Ronge Grassroots Arts and Crafts Center, Regina
Yukon	The Yukon Indian Craft Shop, Main St., Whitehorse

Among the handicraft items you will see are beaded, fur, and leather moccasins, gloves, jackets, and mukluks—principally from the northern and nonagricultural areas. On the west coast, the items seen most frequently are totem carvings, carved masks, fire baskets, Cowichan sweaters, and Salish woven items, and in the Maritime region potato baskets are most popular.

Eskimos

Eskimos are mainly coastal dwellers in arctic regions of Quebec, Labrador, and Manitoba, and in the Northwest Territories, where we find the greatest concentration. Although some still live in remote camps, snowmobiles have replaced dog sleds.

One of the best reference lists we have seen for studying Eskimos is near the end of *Explorers' Guide,* most complete travel brochure for the Northwest Territories. You might like to check our own book list or see if you can get your hands on the Nov. 2, 1974, issue of *Saturday Review/World,* in which the article "Burning Issue at 60 Below" tells the plight of today's Eskimo. (p. 22). Robert Trumbull, the author, describes how their economic resources are increasing at fantastic rates, and life is becoming more comfortable with improved housing and medical care, yet "the transition to town life has been accomplished by alcoholism of catastrophic proportions. The suicide rate has tripled in the last 15 years. Increasing violence, family disruption, and mental breakdowns, all related to alcohol abuse more often than not, have become a cause of grave concern to the government as well as to the churches." Less personal pride and independence is reported along with poorer family and community relations. Another magazine article of possible interest is "The Canadian North, Emerging Giant" in the July, 1968, *National Geographic.*

Although an increasing number of books are published about the culture and life of the 17,000 or so Eskimos of Canada, it is extremely difficult and expensive for the ordinary tourist to visit an Eskimo community. For the well-heeled it is possible to make arrangements with outfitters (get address from the provincial travel bureaus) or to fly in for special occasions such as the Northern Games—a king of arctic Olympics, where competitions are in duck plucking, fish cutting, harpoon throwing, and animal skinning, where traditional dress and handicrafts are exhibited and judged as well as dancing, fiddle playing, and drumming.

A more popular way to see an Eskimo community is achieved on the Polar Bear Express, a five-hour rail ride from Cochrane to Moosonee, Ontario. Although the countryside en route cannot be called picturesque, the trip does enable tourists to catch a glimpse of the Hudson Bay, to see the frontier settlement of Moosonee, and to visit the historical museum at Moose Factory. Three times a week from June to September, the Ontario Northland Railway makes the tour.

Museums

Several museums of the Northwest Territories and Manitoba display historic artifacts of the Eskimos:

Cultural Centre
Igloolik, Northwest Territories

Northern Life Museum
Fort Smith, Northwest Territories

Eskimo Museum
Churchill, Manitoba

Museum of the North
Yellowknife, Northwest Territories

Other than in these distant cities we know of no museum specializing in Eskimo artifacts, although the Art Gallery of Windsor, Ontario, situated in Willistead Park, has a fairly notable exhibit of Eskimo sculpture. One of the finest collections of Eskimo carvings anywhere, is on the top floor of one of the towers of the Toronto-Dominion Centre in Toronto. Also in Ontario, at the National Gallery of Canada, Eskimo graphics are part of the permanent collection. (The Museum of Modern Art in New York City has Eskimo graphics, too.) Eskimo exhibits heard about most frequently, however, are the traveling exhibits. Their current locations may be learned through the Canadian Government Tourist Bureau or the Department of Indian and Northern Affairs in Ottawa.

Handicrafts

Cooperatives are engaged in commercial fishing, logging, boat building, crafts, graphic arts, and sculpture, but it is Eskimo soapstone carvings and stone-cut prints that have won world attention.

Gifts shops in the tourist centers of Quebec, Ontario, Alberta, and British Columbia display a variety of Eskimo handicrafts made from seal, muskrat and arctic hare skins, from raw quills, bone, stone, and ivory, often providing an insight into a way of life that is physically harsh yet sensitive to the beauty and harmony of nature. How do we identify Eskimo and Indian sculptures, prints, slippers, wall hangings, so we are certain our purchase is authentic rather than a

Japanese or Chinese adaptation? Look for these indications of authenticity.

Eskimo
Carvings

Conclusion

If learning about any culture turns you on—or if you have a special personal interest in the Indians and Eskimos of North America—you may be interested in knowing that a Native American Centre for Living Arts has been proposed to coordinate all existing information on arts among native people and to help develop other projects involving drama, books, crafts, tapes, a recording library, a museum, a restaurant, a film workshop, and an ecology program. Professionals in their fields are asked to serve as consultants and other Native Americans from the United States and Canada are encouraged to involve themselves. This can be done by writing: Delia Opekokew, Native American Center for Living Arts, 325 E. 57th St., New York, N.Y. 10022.

Who first perceived the need for this center? Buffy Sainte Marie, the Cree folk-singer of international fame. Early in 1971 the center's research and development office was opened in New York, born out of frustration and exploitation. The center is founded in the interest of accurately portraying the history of Native Americans, developing Native American artists, and presenting Native American arts and artists to the rest of the world. The Center for Native Canadians in Toronto may have a similar though broader goal—we just don't know enough about the center yet.

And so we conclude our brief—and we hope, useful—attempt at pulling together a few resources and events where you might become more familiar with Native Americans as you seek to make travel and life more purposeful.

The air nimbly and
Sweetly recommends itself
Unto our gentle senses.
—SHAKESPEARE

-7

SELECTED
CAMPGROUNDS

A mixture of advice, ideas to ponder, a few hard facts, and recommendations on the better camping areas and selected campgrounds comprise this chapter. The provinces are first discussed in a general way. Then we make recommendations on campgrounds in the most visited areas. The sequence of presentation within a province follows a route you might take, from south to north, or east to west. Outline maps are included, along with our recommendations, for these provinces: British Columbia, Alberta, Saskatchewan, Manitoba, Ontario, Quebec, and the Maritimes. We do not make suggestions for the Yukon, the Northwest Territory, or Newfoundland, since we have not visited these provinces.

While the recommended campgrounds are among the best in the immediate city or area under discussion, do not hestitate to stop at any other campground you come upon that seems satisfactory. On occasion you may take us too literally and pass up a fine campground in order to locate the one we recommend, only to be disappointed. New campgrounds are appearing almost overnight; old ones are improved or sometimes mismanaged; new facilities are added; roads are built to destroy what may have been a quiet refuge; and so on.

By *best* campgrounds, we usually mean those that have hot showers, a store in camp or nearby, and flush toilets. In addition, the recommended campground, with few exceptions, will have many sites so it is unlikely to be full, will be shaded for day use, and will be quiet at night. Quiet at night is sometimes the most difficult quality to have, especially in the western provinces along Trans One, because the Canadian Pacific and Canadian National Railroads seem to be everywhere.

We try to pinpoint the location of the campgrounds, but their location occasionally defies easy description. In these cases, rather than give complicated directions, it is clearer to say, "Follow the signs," which are usually well-placed, or merely, "Ask for directions," when on-the-spot directions are simple. A good map is required in addition to our maps, as the directions to campgrounds are usually given only in reference to nearby towns or the main highway.

Even if you should be looking for a campground we recommend, and instead find yourself at another, the chances are very good that you will be in a pleasant place, because, next to Europe (where the best camping in the world is available), Canada's public campgrounds are the finest, better on the average than those found in the United States. The sites in the public campgrounds are usually larger than their counterparts in the United States, the grounds are cleaner and generally less crowded, the bath and laundry facilities—due to their newness—are usually better, and their placement is planned to provide maximum accommodations both for campers in transit and at points of destination. Even the private campgrounds generally provide better accommodations. For example the KOA chain in the United States operates many roadside campgrounds that do not provide much beyond a level site and the usual concession-office building; the typical Canadian KOA, however, offers the same level site and the familiar concession-office building, plus a location that is often farther from the road noises, is well treed, has more tables, and is more often appropriate for a place of destination rather than just a place simply to stop in transit.

BRITISH COLUMBIA

British Columbia is big. Montana will fit into British Columbia, and there will still be room for Oregon, Washington, and much of Idaho. British Columbia is beautiful. There is a coastal range of mountains known as the Coast Mountains, snow-covered year-round. And the Rockies help form the province's eastern border. Mountains, forests, rushing rivers, and ruggedly magnificent wilderness—that's British Columbia.

British Columbia is *the* inland passage route to Alaska. Vancouver has been compared with San Francisco and Rio de Janeiro because it is scenic and cosmopolitan. Victoria is compared with London, because it is most certainly British. Lake Osoyoos borders on Canada's only authentic desert, a pocket of aridity with an average rainfall of only eight inches. The Columbia and Fraser Rivers drain a high heartland. Like the rest of Canada, British Columbia is more than a kind of vast hunting preserve convenient to the United States.

As in the rest of Canada, good provincial planning means there are campgrounds everywhere, from Vancouver Island to the Alberta border, and from the border with the United States well into the far northern border with the Yukon. Most of the campgrounds are in the south and southeast (where the scenic grandeur is) and along the highways to Alaska and Prince Rupert (where they are needed to serve the long-distance traveler).

Vancouver

This cosmopolitan city is Canada's third largest, so it is big and busy, and, unfortunately, not well provided for in campgrounds. The closest public campground is at Golden Ears Park (1), 30 miles east on Highway 7 to Haney. At Haney turn north toward the park following the well-placed signs for about eight miles. This is an all-year campground with over 200 sites. One of the nice things about the park is that horeseback riding is available; one of the bad things is that it is almost always full during the summer.

Some people make the mistake of driving north of Vancouver to Garibaldi Provincial Park (2), only 50 miles, to discover that all the camping there is the hike-in variety, so it is not good for visiting the city. Garibaldi is excellent, however, for the wilderness hiking camper—glaciers, alpine lakes, meadows, rivers, and streams.

There are at least three private camping possibilities (4) in Surrey, just south of Vancouver, and North Surrey. Unfortunately, all have the same problems: small, crowded, and too near urban transit; however, for a brief visit to the city, they at least offer convenience. Aldon Bungalows and the Plaza Motel and Trailer Court are both just off Rte. 99, the Plaza is closer to Vancouver. The other private campground is the Dogwood Trailer Park, close to Trans One in North Surrey .

Skihist Provincial Park

Two of the smallest provincial park camping areas are ideally located for those traveling Trans One either to or from Vancouver: Skihist and Gold Pan Campgrounds are between the towns of Lytton and Spence's Bridge. The Skihist (5) campground is the larger of the two campgrounds, with about 70 sites; it is located at the base of a mountain about five miles east of Lytton, in a forest of Douglas firs. Despite the trees, there is an excellent view of the Fraser River Canyon. As is true of all the British Columbia Provincial Parks, there are no hookups; but the usual clean washrooms, without showers, add to your comfort. Gold Pan, an even smaller campground, is farther to the east from Skihist, about six miles south of Spence's Bridge.

Tweedsmuir Provincial Park

If you are oriented to getting away from it all, Tweedsmuir Provincial Park (6), on the road to Bella Coola, 300 air miles north of Vancouver, is made to order. While this is a large park, it has two of the smallest camping grounds (Tweedsmuir Park and Atnarko River campgrounds) found in any of Canada's provincial parks. Combined, the sites number under 50; but then, there are few people who want to go to Bella Coola. En route to Tweedsmuir, a fine small private campground-resort is near Redstone, on Puntzi Lake. The focus of this campground is the lake, so fishing, boating, and swimming are popular pastimes; there is also horseback riding. Ask for directions in either Redstone or Chilanko Forks, or follow the signs to Eagle Lodge Resort

Manning Provincial Park

Only 150 miles southeast of Vancouver, the complex of five campgrounds in this Cascade Mountain district is one of the most popular vacation areas for British Columbians in the metropolitan area. The campgrounds are along Highway 3 (sometimes called the Southern Trans-Canada), and the combined capacity consists of about 300 sites.

Vancouver Island

Almost in the center of Vancouver Island is the rugged mountain wilderness marked by Strathcona Provincial Park (9), the oldest provincial park in British Columbia. There are several easily accessible and well-marked campgrounds in the park. There are convenient sites all over the island; and because most tourists stop in their westward travels at either Vancouver or Victoria (both of which get very crowded), finding a good site on the island usually is not a problem.

Victoria

The city is essentially on a level, open field; but the campground is conveniently located at the north edge of Victoria, two miles from the center of the city. The Inn-City Camper Trailer Park is *almost* strictly for trailers and RVs; but, if there is room, tenters can be accommodated. Fortunately, the site is away from the main roads, so road noise is not a major problem. It is likely to be full almost all the time because of its location, so it may be desirable to call first (Tel.: 382-4322). Also useful for the visitor to Victoria is the Goldstream Provincial Park, 12 miles west of town on Highway 1. The stream running through the picnic area may still contain some gold, and in season will contain a few spawning salmon. And, finally, for the beachcomber there is a KOA at Saanichton, ten miles north of Victoria, overlooking the Strait of Georgia.

Shuswap Lake District

Shuswap Lake and the surrounding region are a relatively undiscovered vacationer's delight. It seems most people are either heading for the area around Banff or the Pacific Coast, so they overlook this halfway spot. Compared with the areas to the east and the west, Shuswap is gentle. It is an area with hundreds of miles of shoreline, coves, sandy beaches (although not everywhere, as most of the lake has a rocky shoreline), gentle hills, and farms. The region almost seems out-of-place, more like the Finger Lake district of New York, northern Minnesota, or Ontario. There are two fine choices for camping on the lake: one is the Shuswap Lake Provincial Campground (11) on the north shore of the lake, west of Celista, taking the turnoff at Squilax Bridge; the other choice is one of the best KOA campgrounds we have had the pleasure of visiting. Like many other KOAs, this is a family enterprise with everyone helping cut wood, cleaning the small beach, fixing roads, and so on. The Shuswap KOA Campground is on Brind Bay about two miles off Trans One, 15 miles north of Salmon

Arm. If you are fond of swimming, you should know the water in Blind Bay is about 8⁰ warmer than at the government park.

Wells Gray Provincial Park

This is the park for the wildlife buff. Mule deer, caribou, and moose are common. Mountain goats and grizzly bear are found in the northern reaches of the park, while black bear roam everywhere. The park entrance is 25 miles north of Clearwater; the road is gravel all the way. Clearwater is on Highway 5, about 25 miles north of Kamloops. The first small campground is five miles beyond the park entrance at Dawson Falls (13), while a large campground at Clearwater Lake is an additional 15 miles past that.

Hope

Hope is one of the small, historic, and scenic towns that has an important location: near to Vancouver (about 95 miles) and at the junction of Trans One and Highway 3. Fortunately, Hope has one of the best private campgrounds we have to recommend: Hope KOA is designed, built, and owned by Gerry de Vries (from Holland) and members of his family. This KOA is located about four miles west of Hope on the south side of Trans One, at the foot of a mountain, in a forest of tall hemlocks. Despite the forest, there is some road noise, except for the sites that are far back and well into the woods. Some of the sites are also a bit too close to one another, despite the care the son took in laying out the camping areas; and there are no grills, only stone pits. The grounds are well-maintained.

Cranbrook

It is not unusual for towns to maintain a small tourist park with camping; but these are usually not first-rate camping stops, right? Cranbrook is *the* exception. Cranbrook's Municipal Tourist Park on the south edge of town is an out-standing example of what a community can do. This is one of the most attractive city campgrounds outside of Europe: grassy sites, shaded or open, small store, brook running through the campground, trails and foot bridges, full hookups, flush toilets, with a caretaker living on the grounds. It is not quite perfect, however. There are too few tables, and no grills. And one side of the campground is bounded by a fairly busy street. Even if you do not stay overnight, it is a perfect picnic stop. If you have children, you might like to stop at the children's playground at the center of Cranbrook: grass, benches, flowers, swings, wading pool, slide, merry-go-round.

There is another in-town campground that may be useful if the Municipal Trailer Park is full. A & B camping at the east end of the town, south side of Highway 3, has large marked sites, well graveled, with tables; but the area is congested, and very dusty in dry weather. We think the best alternative is the Jim Smith Lake Park (you can't say it fast), which is southwest of Cranbrook; take Highway 3 south for about one mile, then turn right (follow signs) onto a paved road for a three-mile drive to the park.

Creston

Creston is hard to believe because of the tremendous fruit-growing area on the *east* side of town, where you will also find all the fruit markets (open in season) and most of the private campgrounds. From among the choice of perhaps five, our suggestion is to look for the Sherwood Forest Campground (18) near the river and Little John's fruit stand. It is in a most pleasant setting on a deeply forested hillside. A second choice is a campground we cannot find in any of the usual government publications, but it *is* located about five miles west of Creston (on Highway 3), in a wooded river valley just to the north of the road. You can only see it when you approach from the east. This is the only public campground in the area; and because it is adjacent to a recreation area, it is crowded on weekends. It is the Summit Creek Recreation Area Campground

Yahk

We wouldn't even bother to mention Yahk (silent "h"), except it is a rather interesting and played-out mining region full of hillsides with small drift tunnels; there are some remains of ghost towns, good fishing, and a pleasant valley. The area has three small campgrounds. Only one campground is public. It is quite small, with about two dozen sites. The other two campgrounds are private and also small. The railroad is too close to all the campgrounds. Maybe it isn't worth mentioning.

Fernie

Mt. Fernie Provincial Park Campground is not large but the terraced sites are; and it is quiet and deeply forested. This is a particularly restful campground, high on a hillside about one mile north of Highway 3. The entrance is about two miles west of Fernie. There is a small stream and waterfall nearby for pleasant fishing and a hike. There are both flush and pit toilets. Excellent grills and heavy, well-varnished tables. Oh, yes, and bear! We really like the down-to-earth qualities of this small campground.

Yoho National Park

Because of the crowded conditions around Banff, many campers stay in either of the two large roadside campgrounds in the Yoho National Park   . When we say *roadside* here, we do not suggest they are so close to the road that road noise is a problem; both campgrounds are far enough from Trans One that sleep will not be disturbed. The camp south of the highway (known as the Hoodoo Creek Campground) is well back from the road in a heavily treed forest; while across the road (on the north), you have the opportunity of camping alongside the Kicking Horse River. Both camps are in the shadow of 11,000-ft. Chancellor Peak.

Yard Creek Park

Yard Creek tumbles down from the local, snow-topped mountain; *cold* and clear, it runs through the Yard Creek Campground. This is one of the cleanest, quietest, newest, and most bear-infested public campgrounds along Trans One (37 miles west of Revelstoke). The last time we were there (1974), a bear trap occupied site 3, just to the left as you enter the campground. We could have had any site in the place, if we had stayed.

There is another campground across the road (north side) that might easily be confused with the public campground because the name is almost the same, Yard Creek Campgrounds. This is also a fine campground and should be examined before deciding on a place to stay. Bud and Barb Seney, your hosts, are developing a western resort-style campground on the bank of Eagle River. There is a small canoe pond with canoes to rent, as well as the opportunity to fish via canoe down the river for five miles, where you can be picked up to try again.

Alaska Highway

There are a series of camping places (25) along the Alaskan Highway, most of which are primarily free wayside rest areas with a limited number of sites (one or two dozen). In addition to the public camping places, there are about a half-dozen private campgrounds, with primitive facilities.

ALBERTA

Many Americans are not sure if the famed Banff is in British Columbia or Alberta, and assume it must be in British Columbia since Alberta is flat. Yes, Alberta is comparatively flat; but Banff, Lake Louise, *and* Jasper National Park are all in Alberta. Yes, the Rocky Mountains dominate the attractions of Alberta; and Banff and Jasper National Park dominate the mountains.

Competing with the mountains are two man-made wonders, Calgary and Edmonton; the latter is the capital, but the former acts as though it is. Calgary has its annual Stampede, which Edmonton attempts to outdo with its Klondike Days; Calgary has cattle, Edmonton oil.

Alberta has the most uniformly placed camping grounds of any western province; and unlike British Columbia, which has most of its camping grounds in the southern regions, Alberta has most located in the central regions, with additional concentrations in the two national parks. One of the reasons for the even distribution of campgrounds is because the Alberta Highway Department maintains over 200 free roadside sites. Most of these occupy two or three acres near road intersections, have a wooden shelter with broken screened windows, a few tables, a pit toilet, and a supply of wood. If you want to camp free every night, it is only necessary to get used to the road noise. This is a wealthy province and, except for the Highway Department sites, the campgrounds reflect this wealth in newness and quality. It is hard to find a really poor campground in Canada; in Alberta it is almost impossible.

Banff National Park

Although we have not seen a confirming statement, Tunnel Mountain Campground   must be the largest campground in Canada, perhaps the largest in North America. It is the premier campground of Canada's national parks with over 800 campsites, *and* an additional 300 plus sites for trailers—over 1,000 sites altogether. And they are needed. The facilities are complete, too, from hot showers to stores. The campground is easily located about a mile and a half east of town; follow the signs uphill. There are about a dozen other public campgrounds in excellent locations throughout the park. The next largest camp is the Two Jack Lake Campground, about nine miles east of Banff; look for the Lake Minnewanka loop road, north off Trans One. While both of the largest camps are off Trans One, most of the smaller, usually quieter sites are along alternate Rte. 1 (the old highway).

Unfortunately, all the campgrounds near Banff and Lake Louise are also near enough to one of the trans-Canadian railways so that you never forget this is not far from civilization. To get away from the railroads as well as some of the touring tourists, camp along Rte. 93   which links Banff National Park to Jasper National Park to the north.

Before leaving this discussion of Banff-Lake Louise, we must inject a warning so you will not be disappointed: Lake Louise has become commercialized, like all good places that appeal to the mind and eye of the artist and writer; the wealthy with good taste came to enjoy nature and comfortable surroundings. They in turn were followed by the wealthy with bad taste, who were followed by the middle classes who want to go where the wealthy congregate. Finally, everybody goes. The lakes and trails get crowded, and the motel and concession operators get rich. It is the 20th century. If you go a few miles into the backwoods, however, it is still possible to recapture the original natural setting.

Jasper National Park

The campgrounds around Jasper are located to the south and the northeast. The two largest campgrounds are both about three miles south of the town, located on either side of the road. Although these are the largest campgrounds in the area, and as a rule we avoid the bigger places, you have a choice of large size and no railroad, or small-sized campgrounds (to the northeast) and the roar of the locomotive. Like Highway 93 north of Lake Louise, Highway 93 south of Jasper has a string of campgrounds that are convenient for the north-south traveler

Coleman-Blairmore-Bellevue

The mining buffs will enjoy this corner of Alberta, for both its operating and closed mines. There are also many small campgrounds with a good choice of either free public camps (at Island Lake, Frank, and Lundbreck Falls) or private camps with amenities like hot showers. Among the private campgrounds, we recommend the Lost Lemon in Blairmore (it has complete facilities including a heated swimming pool), and the Sleepy Teepy Camp at the Travel Alberta booth near Frank. Sleepy Teepy, because it is easy to find, not because of amenities. All the camps here are supplied with locomotives 24 hours a day.

Rocky Mountain Forestry Trunk Road

Most visitors to the Banff and Jasper Parks coming from the south will drive up Highways 2 or 23 (assuring themselves of seeing nothing) and then take Trans One into the mountains. If you want to be in the mountains all the way, then consider an unnumbered, unpaved, but very good mountain road that links Coleman in the south with Seebe (on Trans One) in the north. Most of the time the road follows river valleys, so it is not really a mountain road as such; and there are campgrounds which do not show on most maps about every 10 to 25 miles for the entire 150 miles.

Calgary

Inside the city of Calgary, next to the zoo is a municipal park with camping: St. Patrick Island is small, about 40 acres, on a well-wooded island; it has a small store, laundry, showers, and is almost always full. There is a good public alternative, however, if you do not mind being about 25 miles from town; beyond Bragg Creek (southwest of Calgary), following the gravel road along Elbow River, are a half-dozen small campgrounds, with pit toilets, tables, and firewood—and nothing more. But why complain?—it's free camping. The first site you come to is only a picnic area, so keep going for the campgrounds.

West of Calgary, about a half mile from the city limits is a nearly roadside KOA with the usual facilities. The only problem with this campground is the lack of trees; it gets plenty hot in the summer, so this camp is not recommended in hot, sunny weather. The place is not well-marked either.

Fort Macleod

Fort Macleod is probably at the second most important road junction in the province (main north-south and east-west trunk highways), so it is unfortunate that the camping in this area is not better, even for overnight stays. About 15 miles south of the town on Highway 2 at the Waterton River   , there is a small provincial park campground (pit toilets, firewood, and a few tables on eight acres); and two miles northwest of Fort Macleod with access roads from both Highways 2 and 3, there is another provincial park campground of the same size with the same minimal facilities, Old Man River Campground   In town, at the northwest corner of the city and visible from Highway 3 in an open field, is the private Daisy May Campground, with its attractive whitewashed tables and posts. Daisy May is well off the road, so road noise is minimal; there is a large building for showers and laundry, so this may be the best option, unless you want to wash up in one of the local rivers. Daisy May's sites are smallish, and because there are few trees, there is no privacy.

Lethbridge

At the west end of town on Highway 3 in a valley on the west bank of a scenic turn of the Oldman River is a free municipal campground with minimum facilities: wood, pit toilets, wooden table shelters, and a few trees. It is far enough from the road to be reasonably quiet. It is well-marked as you leave the city.

Brooks

No one, as far as we know, cares much about seeing the town of Brooks; but the town is near one of the fine highway campgrounds that have been built by the province to accommodate campers in transit. Tillebrook Park is about five miles east of Brooks on Trans One. This is a 200-acre site—an oasis—in the midst of the oil and gas fields of the prairie. It has been planted with poplar trees, so there is some shade, and the sites are grassy. Modern camp buildings provide showers and a laundry. The only problem, and it is small, is that there are too few fireplaces to accommodate all the campsites. If you want a fire, you might ask if the lost and found has an hibachi to loan; we asked, and they had one. It might still be there.

Edmonton

The city of Edmonton has provided a nice combination of camping options for visitors who want to stay in or very near the city. On the southern end of the city (inside the city limits) follow the well-placed signs to the Edmonton Tourist Trailer Park, for trailers only. Here you will find complete facilities with shade. To the north   follow Highway 2 to 45th Ave., turn left (west), and follow the signs about three miles to the Rainbow Valley Campground (tents and RVs only). Neither campground is large, about 50 sites, and both are surrounded by the city, but you cannot beat the convenience.

If you want to stay outside the city, take Highway 14 to the southwest, and you enter the Battle River tourist area. There are many public and private campgrounds   along Highway 14 within a short drive to Edmonton. About 20 miles northeast of Edmonton, there is the Elk Islands National Park with a good campground (although not large) at Sandy Beach   . The Sandy Beach campground is about ten miles inside the park.

Cypress Hills Provincial Park

There is a surprising group of hills rising from the otherwise flat prairies in southeastern Alberta. The area has a long history of Indian trouble, bandits, and illegal whisky trading. All this probably resulted in the early establishment of the Northwest Mounted Police Headquarters at nearby Fort Walsh. (The police are now headquartered in Saskatchewan.) This is also an unusual region for shrubs, small animals, fossils, and early stone writing. One of the best campgrounds in Alberta is also here, with the same name as the park: Cypress Hills. This campground has all the facilities you expect of the best parks, except shade in the trailer section: full hookups, showers, store. More of a resort than a smoky, get-away-from-it-all campground. Best for a short vacation stop.

SASKATCHEWAN

Frankly, it is difficult to get excited about Saskatchewan. The highways across all but the northern third of the country cover flat country with few trees over a few feet in height. Much of the land is not even good enough for crops. There are few signs of water, and when there is water, there is also mud.   If there isn't enough water, and usually there isn't, then there is dust. Only the little farming towns with their cathedrals of the plains—grain elevators—interrupt the flat horizon. One of the best aspects of this province for the camper, however, is few campers. Except along Trans One in the summer, the camper will seldom find the campgrounds more than a third full. This can be especially rewarding in the northern areas where it is easily possible to have whole small campgrounds to oneself. And each of these campgrounds is a camper's dream, since it is almost impossible to find a northern campground that is not on either a lake or a river.

Trans One

The province has provided the traveler with four fine campgrounds along the main east-west road. Moosomin Campground, near the border with Manitoba, is not typical of the others because it is set in a dense, if not tall, forest, which features a substantial variety of unusual birds. (Since we are birdwatchers, this is important). There are grills at every site and plenty of wood. The camp has complete facilities: full hookups, showers, shelters, fireplaces. We said "not typical" above because the remainder of the Trans One sites are relatively free of trees, although saplings are planted at each stop. Maple Creek   ʃ on the border with Alberta is especially worth a stop because of the main building, which houses a display telling of the area's history in an architectural award winning building. You should also remember the Maple Creek Campground on any day the wind is blowing hard, since part of the campground is in a small valley. The McLean Campground   ) is best for visiting Regina, since it is only about 25 miles to the east of the capital. The Besant Campground   , four miles east of Mortlach, should be avoided on weekends, as it serves as a resort for Canadians from Moose Jaw and Regina who want to picnic, fish, and play baseball, while their children are making the most of the playground equipment or are paddling in the pools.

Gull Lake

There is a quaint little municipal campground in Gull Lake, which is 20 miles west of Swift Current. Except in wet weather, when it will be muddy and have too many pesky flies, this will be a good overnight. It is clearly marked from town, quiet, with showers, playground, homemade grills, grass, choice of shade or sun.

Regina

There are at least four private trailer camps as you enter the city from the south   and several more along Trans One within 12 miles of Regina to the east   None of them seems adequate to us, since they are virtually without trees, on perfectly flat land (of course, there is no choice), and too close to the main highways. The best of the bunch close in is probably the Highlander, which is easy to locate because it is next to the CKCK television and radio towers.

Nipawin Provincial Park

This is a large, heavily wooded wilderness with few campers and only a few, little-used campgrounds; like almost all campgrounds in the northern parts of the province, the camp at Lower Fishing Lake allows the camper to tent within a few feet of the lake on large private sites. This is the perfect setting for canoeing, fishing, berry picking, and campfires. And the days are surprisingly warm and dry during the summer, with the nights refreshingly cool.

Highway 106, Prince Albert to Flin Flon

Anyone who cannot take the time to drive into the far north country and cannot afford to fly in, owes himself a drive along Highway 106—of gravel, dusty, but smooth. There are a few outfitting stores, some canoe rental places, and occasional small restaurants associated with private campgrounds along the way, but not much else to remind you of human encroachment, not even a phone system. The campgrounds whether private or public tend to be primitive, usually not much more than a small clearing prepared as a campsite, and, as we mentioned earlier, almost always on a lake or a river. There are campgrounds every 20 or 30 miles along the entire route. Of course, with an RV, it is possible to camp almost anywhere. Bring your canoe.

MANITOBA

Half of Manitoba is Winnipeg, *at least* half the population lives in Winnipeg, and at least 80% of the rest of Manitoba has hardly any population. First of all, a large part of the province is water; Lake Winnipeg itself is larger than Lake Ontario and combining Lakes Manitoba, Cedar, and Winnipegosis gives another body of water about the size of Lake Ontario. Another large part of the province borders on the Hudson Bay, and hardly anyone lives up there. In fact, hardly anyone lives north of a line drawn from Swan River to Selkirk. The southern one-fourth of the province is flat; the northern three-fourths is even flatter, except when the wind whips the waves. With over 100,000 lakes, this should be called the Great Lake Province.

Camping here, except for a few places along Trans One and in Winnipeg is, of course, water-oriented. The great Whiteshell Park in the southeast is representative of the water-based camping that tends to dominate the scene. With a campground on almost every one of the 131 lakes and canoeing waterways, canoes, rubber boats, and motorboats are as common as tents and RVs. In addition to the water, there is one other characteristic of Manitoba's campgrounds, which sets them apart from those in the other provinces: Almost all are like resorts, with shopping centers, motels, restaurants, riding stables, marinas, tennis courts, golf courses, and more. Different, isn't it? But, of course, if you want solitude, that is available too.

Whiteshell Provincial Park

The camping in the southeastern corner of the province is dominated by Whiteshell Provincial Park's 600,000 plus acres; and the Fulcon Beach Campground   is the park's largest campground, with about 600 sites close to restaurants, snack bars, supermarkets, and anything else one would need in a complete recreational community. Fulcon Beach Campground along with the park headquarters is on Trans One.

The whole area north of Trans One and Highway 44 is sprinkled with camping places   , many of which can only be reached by water through a maze of interconnected lakes. We do not recommend this for an overnight stop—it is simply too like a city park. It is, of course, great if you want to spend your vacation time in one of nature's playgrounds. Outside the park, Manitoba maintains a roadside information building. A fine campground that is operated in conjunction with this service is best for a simple overnight stop only.

Sandilands Provincial Forest

There aren't many camping places east of Winnipeg until you get to the Whiteshell area; but there is one that is easy to miss if you're not careful. Pine Grove Halt is about ten miles west of Hadashville; but the easier way to recognize this otherwise not-well-marked Forest Department-operated campground is to look carefully for the entrance when you arrive at the *first* tall stand of tall evergreens as you travel east, or the *last* tall evergreens before coming to the prairies when going west.

Brandon

One of the best camping places to seek out for an overnight or a longer stay in southwestern Manitoba is west of Brandon at the junction of Trans One and Highway 1A. It is almost impossible to see south from Trans One if you are traveling west, but is worth a careful search. The entire camping area is on a fairly steep hillside with terraced sites overlooking a gentle valley. Some of the sites have large brick fireplaces, and all have sturdy grills. There are flush toilets, a playground, a wading pool, laundry facilities, even a snack bar, but no showers. The campground is part of the Grand Valley Recreation Area.

Portage La Prairie

About six miles east of Portage La Prairie is the Norquay Beach Campground. There is no better campground along Trans One for either an overnight or for visiting Winnipeg. The park is set in a forest of mixed hardwoods, and the sites are large. There are a series of ponds around the campground for fishing and swimming; and the campground is fully equipped with laundry, showers, firewood (although few places to burn it), kitchen shelter, and tables. It is likely to be crowded on weekends.

Grand Beach   on Lake Winnipeg

North of Winnipeg at the edge of the Precambrian rock shield that separates the plain from the rocky, northern, uninhabited regions lies Grand Beach Provincial Park. Small as parks go, its main feature is a shallow sand beach that allows great latitude for waders and young children to go from one shallow sand bar to the next. In fact, the enormous lake is unusually shallow everywhere, with its deepest spot only 65 ft. There is a large campground behind the sand dunes with places for about 400 tents and trailers. Like the other resort camping grounds of Manitoba, there are motels and restaurants on the grounds; and by the time this book is available, there may be a golf course and riding stables. Grand Beach is about 60 miles north and east of Winnipeg.

Winnipeg

Public parks close to Winnipeg are nonexistent, and we do not feel comfortable recommending any of the private campgrounds; but since Winnipeg is such an important city, we will share our impressions. There are two Jellystone Park Campgrounds   serving Winnipeg:

Jellystone-East is at the southwest corner of the city near the intersection of Trans One and the Bypass Route 100. It is in an open field, but the management is trying to plant some trees; it is near two main roads, but far enough from each so sound is minimized. There is a pool, mini-golf course, game rooms, and playground; kids and teenagers would probably enjoy the experience.

Jellystone-West is on Trans One (about ten miles west of Winnipeg) and has about the same features as Jellystone-East, except the pool is larger and this is a heavily treed area. The major problem is that the ground is too wet and soft; at least management had not solved the drainage problem yet in the summer of 1974.

Near Jellystone-East, there is also a standard KOA   sharing a section of the same open prairie.

And a final mention is the Sunny Harbor Resort about eight miles west of Winnipeg, and just south of Trans One. Look for the signs. The campground is situated on a wooded loop of the Assimiboine River, has full hookups, a large swimming pool, game areas, the ubiquitous mini-golf course (which always turns us away from a camping place), showers, store—everything.

Grass River Provincial Park

This is the park for you if the camping and canoeing possibilities at Whiteshell are too well-developed. Grass River Provincial Park offers more primitive camping and will challenge the skilled canoeist in its 154 lakes, most of which are only reachable by canoe, as are the park's many campgrounds.

Riding Mountain National Park

The park got its name because canoeists going west could no longer use their canoes when they reached the high grounds here and had to ride horses—at least that is the way the story goes. In any case, this park is supposed to be a naturalist's dream because of the combinations of animal and plant life to be seen everywhere: 60 species of four-legged animals, 230 species of birds, grassland, conifers, hardwoods, trout, bass, pike, and so it goes. There are many fine wilderness camping places throughout the park, as well as in the town of Wasagaming at the park's south entrance.

ONTARIO

It is an impossible task to summarize Ontario in a few sentences, a few paragraphs, a book, or even several books. Ontario is the urban complex around Toronto, the agricultural region north of Lakes Erie and Ontario, the automotive center of Windsor, the government of Ottawa, the Great Lakes region, the far north of Hudson Bay, and more.

It even seems impossible to do an adequate summary of the camping prospects. We will, nevertheless, present some information on the more important camping regions, and highlight a few places that are unique. One of the important regions is north of Lake Superior, so we will start there; one of the unique features is a campground owned and operated by the Ojibway Indians, so we will discuss that, too. First, about the north shore of Lake Superior.

North Shore of Lake Superior

The first opportunity to camp near, not on Lake Superior, at the far western border of the province, where it intersects the lake, is at the smallish Middle Falls Provincial Park   36 miles south of Thunder Bay on Highway 61 at Pigeon River. This is a small park with a small campground (only about two dozen sites) and is a popular day-use facility for people from Thunder Bay, so it is likely to be crowded. It is, however, a specially good stop for children because of a supervised swimming and wading pool; there is also a playground, store, and snack bar. Most campers in this area go to Kakabeka Falls Campground on Route 17 west from Thunder Bay; this is also a day-use style campground, so the emphasis is on picnicking, swimming, and visiting the 128-ft. waterfalls on the Kemistiqua River, but the campground is much larger.

This is a great area for waterfalls, so the next park we recommend is also noted for its waterfalls: Rainbow Falls Provincial Park   . Located just east of Rossport, at the Selim River, it has secluded campsites, in a large campground setting. Good swimming in warm weather. Even better for access to Lake Superior, however, is the campground at Neys Provincial Park   where you can camp *on* the lake (if you get there early!) and have a choice of open or wooded sites. This is also a good park for hikers. The Neys campground is on Rte. 17 about 15 miles west of Marathon.

The next truly good campground, on the lake as you travel east, is at the south end of Lake Superior Provincial Park, near the tiny town of Frater (really not much more than a railroad stop): the Agawa Bay Camping and Picnic Grounds   This is a particularly good area for scenic drives and hikes, although it is seldom comfortably warm here because of the prevailing westerly wind off the lake. If this campground is full—and it has been known to happen in the summer—there is another campground *in the park* closer to the south entrance and still another (and larger) campground *on the lake* at the Pancake Bay Provincial Park   . This is a terrible name for a provincial park, but its two miles of sandy beach make up for it. Pancake Bay is about 50 miles north of Sault Saint Marie (pronounce *Sault* "sue"). .

Lake of the Woods

There are a lot of public and private camping possibilities around and on the Lake of the Woods; but the one that stands out from the rest is the Rushing

River Campground, about 15 miles south and east of Kenora. This campground is on Dogtooth Lake and the Rushing River. Anyone coming out of the prairie provinces will especially appreciate the sandy and grassy sites (no more mud!). This is one of those camps where campers stay several days to a week; some may even stay the legal limit of two weeks. We know of few campgrounds having the aesthetic charm provided by the particular mix of trees and land formations found throughout the camping area. While it is close to the road, it is also far enough away so there is no road noise. There is a tiny lake with rocky islands and with lifeguards near the entrance—a particular favorite with small children. The only drawback is the lack of underbrush between sites, so there is little privacy.

North of Lake Superior

If you want to get away from the usual camping and tourist traffic that goes around the Lake, go a little farther north along Highway 11, known simply as the Northern Route. There are a series of evenly spaced, good campgrounds where the focus is less on the pleasures of swimming and hiking and more on wilderness and fishing. North of the town of Nipigon on Lake Nipigon is Blacksand Provincial Park   , providing the only campground on this lake. There is, of course, a sandy beach (black sand, too); but the more important feature of this area is the long history of the Indians who have lived along the shores. Some of these Indians are now doing well for themselves economically, as the value of furs has increased rapidly in recent years. Park visitors are encouraged to learn about the Indians from the archeological study teams who are often in the park throughout the summer.

The next important campground driving east along Rte. 11 is one in which the focus moves from Indians to rocks. Just beyond the turnoff to Hardrock Mines is Macleod Provincial Park and its campground on the south shore of Keno-gamisis Lake. This is a good lake for family swimming, fishing, and boating. It is also a good area for the rockhound, since there were some active gold mines in the area that uncovered jasper and agate rock. One of the smaller, and least used campgrounds, is even farther to the east on Klotz Lake. The Klotz Lake Provincial Park   is oriented to the fisherman and serves as a base camp for people to fish the many small lakes in this area. There is no town nearby, so get provisions before deciding to stay at Klotz Lake.

North of North Bay

The true north country from the standpoint of the people of Ontario is supposed to begin on the other side of North Bay and terminate at the Hudson Bay. Well, it is still a bit crowded with both people and cars until well north of North Bay; but you certainly are in north country by the time you get to the Moosonee Campground   in Tidewater Provincial Park on the Hudson Bay.

Going north from North Bay, the first campground of any significance is at the intersection of Rte. 11 and 64, about 35 miles north of North Bay. This is the Marten River Provincial Park   \ with over 200 sites. While there are a lot of sites, because they are spread out along the banks of the river, it does not seem crowded. Just 30 more miles will find you in an even more attractive park, but this one is more likely to be full on the busy summer weekends: Finlayson Provincial Park   at Finlayson Point.

North of here the crowded conditions end and you sense the northern landscape. One of the best places to enjoy the wilderness setting is at the Kap-Kig-Iwan Provincial Park   , which is easy to reach by road, yet is a natural wilderness with an emphasis on the Englehart River and its waterfalls and rapids. Kap-Kig-Iwan is just off Highway 11 at the town of Englehart. Still a bit more wilderness in character and off the main roads, is the provincial park in the Esker Lakes Natural Environment Park   \ located north of the town of Kirkland Lake.

Still farther north, but with less natural wilderness, is the Kettle Lakes Provincial Park   \ recreation area, with emphasis on day-use, swimming, fishing, and hiking among the low-lying hills. And finally there is the Moosonee Campground   , which can only be reached by taking the Ontario Northland Railway to the end of the line near the Hudson Bay. For details, write to the Manager, Tidewater Provincial Park, 140 Fourth Ave., Cochrane, Ontario.

Crown Land Camping

One of the features of camping in northwest Ontario is the availability of free camping on the Crown Lands (public lands). Some of these sites are accessible by road but most are only reached by foot or canoe. There is no directory of such places, and, understandably, campers who know of places where a camp may be set up outside the organized campgrounds seldom reveal its location. In fact, even by mentioning location, we may be giving the impression that the Crown Land camping is somehow organized. Not so. The spots are simply chosen and developed for camping by anyone, as long as they are at least a mile from a paved road. After camping is done for that time, the next camper may use, and in fact improve upon, the crude shelter or facility that may be left by the first camper, and so it goes.

The only problem is that some of these casual camping sites are becoming better known, and consequently may become overused so their condition worsens. Since we are visitors, it is understandable if the Canadians sometimes are concerned to find foreigners camping in their special places. The problem is lessened, of course, if we do more than others to keep these places in respectable condition, so the generosity of our host is not abused.

SOUTHEASTERN ONTARIO

Ojibway Indian Campground on Georgian Bay

Elsewhere, we described the possibilities of learning more about the original North Americans; but nowhere else are we aware of a completely Indian-owned and operated campground like the one on Georgian Bay named by the Nawash Indians: the Cape Croker Indian Park   . The park and campground are reached by taking Rte. 6 to Wiarton, going about a mile beyond town to the north, then turning right on the road to Colopy Bay; after making the turn, it is only necessary to follow the colorful signs directly to the park. The setting at the entrance to the park is all Indian—and unique. There are rustic timber arches, teepees, carved Indian heads, and brightly painted signs everywhere. In keeping with the rugged character of the Indian's life before and since the paleface, the campgrounds are for roughing it: no electricity, few marked sites, carry your water from springs. One of the major attractions is the beach area on Sydney Bay, where you may also camp. The scenery is excellent everywhere. They rent canoes. There is a choice of wooded and unwooded sites.

Lake Erie

For some reason that we cannot explain, most of the camping possibilities along the shoreline of The Great Lakes are on the north shore of Lake Erie. We cannot explain it because this, of course, is the most polluted of the lakes. The better camping prospects start in the west at the Holiday Beach Provincial Park south of Windsor and extend as far east as the Rock Point Provincial Park near Dunnville. Swimming is available at all the parks, and the water is not as polluted as it is on the American side. In fact, the swimming off Point Pelee, which is near Wheatly Provincial Park   , is quite good. In addition to swimming, a major attraction of the parks, especially those at Rondeau (173), Long Point   , and Point Pelee   , is the variety of birds, especially at times of migration, where they rest either before (fall) or after (spring) crossing Lake Erie. The campground at Turkey Point   has a special attraction, as the nearby fish hatchery at Normandale has built an underwater viewing facility for observing fish and turtles in their environment, but you should know this "turkey" is not on the lake. The new, but small campground at Iroquois Beach (174) is not on most maps yet.

Alliston

One of the largest and best located campgrounds for travelers heading north out of Toronto—or, of course, heading toward Toronto—is west of Alliston: Eral Rowe Provincial Park   has well over 500 sites and complete facilities, everything for all types of camping. If this park is too large for your taste and you can get along with fewer facilities, there are several other smaller campgrounds in the area on the Boyne and Nottawasga Rivers.

St. Lawrence River

The parks along the St. Lawrence River are well-known and usually crowded, especially around Upper Canada village. A new park is available to take some of the pressure off the Thousand Island area and is still not on most maps. It is not on the waterway either. It is located about 35 miles northwest of Kingston on Charleston Lake. This is not a day-use facility, so it is a good place to stay if you are anticipating staying in the area several days or a week. From this relatively secluded area, it is only a short drive to the major east-west expressways, so it is easy to move about and explore. The name is the Charleston Lake Provincial Park

One of the densest concentrations of small campgrounds is found near Inglewide (about ten miles west of Cornwall). These are in a good location to enjoy both the beauty and shipping on the river. They are close to the Upper Canada village, too. They are all operated as part of the St. Lawrence Parks Commission. The best way to find them is simply to go to Ingleside (191) and turn east. The first camp is one mile beyond town.

Presqu'ile Provincial Park

On the north shore of Lake Ontario, south of Brighton, is located one of the largest and modestly well-equipped parks serving the north shore. Over 500 sites are here, with a store, laundry, full hookups, fishing, and boating. This is a particularly good park for the marsh, meadow, and sand dune enthusiast.

Algonquin Provincial Park

Algonquin is the most famous of Ontario's provincial parks and the first destination of many Canadians on their early camping trips. The park is large, with most of the interior inaccessible by car. It is famous probably because it is large and near a heavily populated region, not because it is particularly unusual in any way. The hills are modest, as are the lakes and rivers. The vegetation is not unusual, nor is the animal life. This is a good, all-purpose, family park, emphasizing labeled nature trails, conducted tours, evening movies by the park naturalists, museum, preserved logging camps, and so on. There are many campgrounds, almost all of which are along Rte. 60 through the southern corner of the park; and they are well-equipped for everyone from the tenter with a bike to the group arriving by bus, and there are lots of the latter kind.

Emily Provincial Park

In the heart of the Kawartha Lakes tourist area, Emily Provincial Park offers about 300 sites, flush toilets, store, laundry, and the O-me-mee River (Pigeon, in English). The main attraction in this area is the fishing in the many lakes. The park is ten miles west of Peterborough.

A Wild River Park

The drive from North Bay to Ottawa (via Rte. 17) is not rewarding for views of the river or other scenery. But it is rewarding if you are willing to do some white water canoeing in a wild river park. One of these trips is between North Bay, where you can rent canoes, to Mattawa, where the 25-mile trip usually ends. This stretch of water, including portages, roughly parallels the Mattawa Provincial Wild River Park, established to maintain the character of the original use of the water in this area. Camping in the provincial park is essentially a two- or three-day canoe trip. For details, write to the Mattawa Provincial Park, Wild River Division, Box 147, Mattawa, Ontario.

Pinery Provincial Park

You won't care, but this is the first Canadian park we camped in. It is beautifully situated on the shore of Lake Huron in a pine forest. You get to the park from the north entrance at Grand Bend. The park has over 1,000 sites and all facilities, and is open year-around. We still like it.

Restoule Provincial Park

This is really one of those places that should be kept secret. Almost everyone going north goes up Rte. 69 or 11 and passes right by this most out-of-the-way, undeveloped camping area. Its special attraction for the canoeing vacationist are the opportunities for river and lake canoeing, as well as fishing the nearly untapped wilderness south of the more famous Lake Nipissing. The personnel at the park will provide campers with brochures on the main canoe routes and give advice on fishing. The campground is at the end of a gravel road north from Restoule, which is west of Powassan (Rte. 11.)

Mara and McRae Provincial Parks

These parks are located on the east shore of Lake Simcoe near Atherley. Mara is a small park with all types of camping facilities, but the emphasis is on the needs of the recreation vehicle and tenter; whereas McRae (opened in 1972, and still not on most maps) is oriented toward trailers and any water activity. Stephen Leacock's home is nearby.

QUEBEC

Take a land twice the size of Texas, with an attractive geography like New England, the food of New Orleans, and the people of France, and you have Quebec. Quebec, like Mexico, is a foreign experience, a trip to Europe without the castles. Montreal and its suburbs contain half the 4,000,000 people of the province, so you know the remainder is not overcrowded. About 80% of the people speak French. Sometimes it seems like 99%, because, surprising as it may seem, French is *the* language for large proportions, perhaps the majority, of the residents. It is difficult at times to find *anyone* who can speak English, sometimes impossible. Note the basic French vocabulary provided

Unlike the other provinces, most of the camping in Quebec is provided by private operators—there simply are far fewer provincial parks. And the parks that are operated by the province are a bit different in that they less often have the wilderness orientation found in other places. Their more "civilized" approach is largely exhibited by the restaurants in camping areas, which provide a sense of gastronomic haven rather than wilderness haven. Like the other provisions, Quebec is well served by *les parcs du Quebec*, and our recommendations will concentrate on them.

Gaspé Peninsula

Unless Montreal is the sole objective, there are few visitors t Quebec who do not go out to the Gaspé Peninsula to see the fishing villages, the beaches, and the most celebrated feature, Perce Rock. And fortunately the pennisula is especially well-provided for both by large provincial park campgrounds (in the interior) and small provincial campgrounds near the water. The water-related campgrounds begin at Beaumont   where the St. Lawrence River outlet begins and swing around the peninsula to Carleton   where you can see across the bay to New Brunswick. The campgrounds around the peninsula are fairly standardized in their offering: They are either on the water or have direct access to it, usually have hookups, seldom are well-treed, have stores in camp or nearby, have one to two hundred sites, and are in scenic locations. Those along the north shore tend to be associated with resort districts, as at Trois-Pistoles   whereas others (on the south shore), such as the campground at Carleton   , are oriented toward the natural setting. Carleton is actually developed on a sandbar that stretched into the bay, so camping is available directly on the water. The water at Carleton is the same warm water that surrounds Prince Edward Island, so it is excellent for swimming.

Most campers make a mistake by driving around the peninsula without visiting the inland Gaspesie Provincial Park and its campground at Mont-Albert (230). This is a heavily wooded campground located along the banks of a river, without any hookups, at the foot of Mont Albert. The reason you might visit the campground is the Le Gite, a gourmet's delight. The restaurant is across from the campground and was built by the government to provide the average person with a high-class dining facility in the wilderness. The restaurant and adjoining facilities are used to train chefs for service at other provincial parks. The food is worth the high prices. The park and campground are reached by taking Rte. 299 inland from St. Anne des Monts. The Gaspé campgrounds are at Beaumont

Montreal

Most of the public camping is south and west of the city. Except for the provincial park at Côte St. Catherine   south, across the river, near the junction with Highway 90, the close-in prospects are private. The best of the private are two KOAs: Montreal-South and Montreal-West   ). South is closer to the center of the city, in the suburb of St. Phillipe, while West is just off Rte. 20 in the suburb of Coteau du Lac. Both are well marked with signs and easy to find. One of Quebec's largest and best-known public campgrounds can also be used for visiting Montreal. In the town of Oka is the campground named Paul-Suave   with over 1,000 sites. Most people simply know this as "Oka Campground."

Laurentides Provincial Park

The Laurentians are the northern extension of the Appalachians, so the land forms are almost identical. The areas set aside to preserve this wilderness include several large parks; the best known, of course, is the Laurentides Provincial Park   There are, however, two other northern extensions of the mountain parks: Chibougamau   and Mistassini   These parks are a fisherman's delight, with scores of lakes and streams among the oldest rock formations known to man. Moose, caribou, wolf, and black bear are common in the northern parks. Mistassine reaches into the almost treeless north, with its sparse forest cover giving way to bogs and the Precambrian bedrock. Each of the parks is served by large campgrounds oriented to outdoor enthusiasts rather than resort campers. The combined size of the three provincial parks equals two Switzerlands!

Park du Mont Orford

This is a remarkably small and equally attractive park with one of the prime campgrounds of Canada near its northern border on Lake Stuckely (where you can fish without a license). The southern part of the park is day-use oriented with a fine golf course and in the winter a ski center. Because of the expressway south of the park, it can be used as a base for visiting the urban areas throughout southern Quebec.

De La Verendyre Park

This park is not noted for high land forms; rather it is noted for its lakes and streams. Thus, its orientation is to fishing and canoe camping. It is also great country for viewing moose. There are several campgrounds in the park, each of which is the base camp for several well-marked canoe circuits. There are over 1,000 miles of canoe-camping circuits; maps are available free; boats can be rented, but are in short supply, so it is advisable to bring your own.

MARITIME PROVINCES: New Brunswick, Nova Scotia, Prince Edward Island

These provinces share the Atlantic and about there the similarity ends. New Brunswick is distinctly an extension of Maine—woodsy. Nova Scotia is more varied—Arcadian French in the south, British at Halifax, Scottish in the north, Welsh and Cornish near Sydney. Prince Edward Island is cosy and pastoral. All three are relatively unspoiled by the holiday throngs.

Camping is excellent everywhere. It is resort like on parts of Prince Edward Island—that is, lots of comforts for staying for days and weeks. Most of New Brunswick offers wilderness orientation, with good facilities throughout. Bob still remembers the night with the bear pawing outside the tent and him trying to get out of the sleeping bag with the zipper stuck! Nova Scotia's campgrounds tend not to provide the luxury of the campgrounds in the other provinces, stressing instead the back-to-nature aspects of the out-of-doors.

Nova Scotia

Nearly everyone goes to Nova Scotia to visit the Cape Breton Highlands National Park, and the campgrounds are well-spaced for touring. In fact, because the park is not large, it is possible to drive entirely around it in one day and not stay in any of the park campgrounds. People who do this—and many do—will simply come away with a blurred image of an ocean far below and undulating, deep greenery above. But because the park is not large and most of it is accessible by the ring road, it is really only necessary to select one camp as a base from which to explore the highlands. The two busiest campgrounds are at the entrance to the park at Cheticamp in the west   and Ingonish Beach in the east   '; the two best equipped (full hookups) are Cheticamp and Broad Cove   Our favorite is at Black Brook Cove   because it is the least busy, less developed, more natural. We also like Black Brook Cove because it is possible to tour north to the little fishing villages of Neil's Harbour, New Haven, and White Point. These are remarkably unspoiled, natural settlements, where many of the inhabitants seem to speak an unrecognizable language (at least to these ears). The only provincial camp we definitely cannot recommend is Cheticamp; it reminds us of Coney Island.

At the south end of Nova Scotia near Shelburne and Yarmouth (where the ferry *Bluenose* from Maine lands), there are two parks off Rte. 340; one is on the ocean and the other on a freshwater lake. The closest to Yarmouth is the Ellenwood Park Campground, (one mile south of Deerfield (toward Digby) on a small lake. The ocean site is just south of Shelburne at the Islands Park ; this is on a long, sheltered bay that is good for swimming, fishing, and boating.

Halifax

There is no problem is finding a camping place for visiting Halifax, as there are a substantial number of public and private campgrounds surrounding the city and well-marked on every approach. On Rte. 3 we suggest Graves Island Park (281), which is on the ocean two miles east of Chester; off Highway 2 at Grand Lake, there is Laurie Provincial Park ; on the main highway into Halifax from Annapolis Valley is Smiley's Park ; and in from the east through Dartmouth is Porter's Lake Park on the shore near Mosquodobit. In fact, the number and quality of public parks serving the urban areas of Nova Scotia suggests the private campground association lobby is weak.

It is possible to sample the famous inland sea, the Bras d'Or at the Whycocomagh Park near the town by the same name on Rte. 105. This is also a good park for hiking, swimming, and fishing; a good location from which to reach the Cape Breton National Park, too.

Those taking the ferry to Prince Edward Island will want to stay at the Caribou Park Campground It is just south of where the ferry docks. There are nearly 100 sites on the Northumberland Strait.

New Brunswick

Many of the camping possibilities in New Brunswick have already been commented upon in the section on the handicrafts of New Brunswick, so you are referred to the discussion

The only additional place to mention is the Mactaquac Provincial Park about 15 miles north of Fredericton, the provincial capital, and only five miles off Trans One. This is the location of many annual festivals in addition to the Annual Handcrafts Festival mentioned earlier. This is a showpiece campground with two beaches, an 18-hole golf course, a marina, an amphitheater, a grocery store, and, of course, complete hookups. There are about 300 campsites in three separate campgrounds.

Prince Edward Island

Prince Edward Island is at the same time the least and the most. It is the least, because it is the smallest of the provinces. Yet, it is the most in a leisured pace of life. It is the "Garden in the Gulf."

Even this small island province has 20 provincial park campgrounds—all lovely. Yet we offer only one recommendation, and that campground is in the Prince Edward Island National Park rather than one of the provincial parks. We do this because it is one of the superlative campgrounds, providing just the right kind of place to end our recommendations. In closing this chapter, we would like to quote what the author of the *Two-Ton Albatross* had to say about the Stanhope Beach Campground

"Each trailer stall is located in a cove of trees, complete with full hookup, a picnic table, and a stone barbeque. Piles of firewood are immaculate and well maintained. Canadian National Parks are by far the nicest trailer parks either government or privately owned on this continent....Canada goes greatly out of its way to provide accommodations for the camper, as though this beautiful country were meant to be enjoyed in a very personal relationship. Nowhere is there more splendid scenery, better fishing, hunting, boating or swimming than in this nature lover's paradise and nowhere is the camper more enthusiastically welcomed."

Who doth ambition shun,
And loves to live i' the sun,
Seeking the food he eats,
And pleas'd with what he gets.
SHAKESPEARE

-8
COPING WITH CAMP COOKING

To eat or not to eat: If that were only the question. The question, however, is how to make camp cooking enjoyable –for even the cook! Good nutrition, an essential ingredient in a camping diet, joined by variety, pizzaz, and simplicity makes campground eating pleasurable in all respects. How do we achieve variety, simplicity, and pizzaz?

Variety

Cooking need not be a bore or a chore. Variety is the trick variety in technique (cooking) and kind (foods) adds zest and surprise to camping life.

Let's examine how to achieve variety through technique. The inexperienced camper may think only of grilling, frying, or toasting on a stick. With a little more imagination and thought, however, we might expand our choices to include one-pot meals, aluminum-foil cooking, planking, in-the-ground cooking, pressure cooker cooking, on-the-stick roasting, and steaming. If you want to employ variety and creativity in your camp cooking but are still unsure of some of the techniques mentioned, perhaps the following illustrated descriptions of each will be helpful.

Grilling or Broiling (Direct Exposure to Heat)

If you are traveling by car or RV, a hibachi, portable grill, or just a grid is a must. You will find many campgrounds in Canada do not have barbecue grills. If a campsite is not the clipped-lawn variety, a small hole dug into a sandy area (away from all flammable materials, roots, and limbs) or three or four rocks on a rocky outcropping *plus* your grid (about four inches above the coals) will serve you well. If traveling by foot or canoe, you may resort to cutting a green branch and weaving your own grid. If possible carry metal skewers for toasting(a slow process of turning frequently over ash-colored coals) rather than denuding trees at each site.

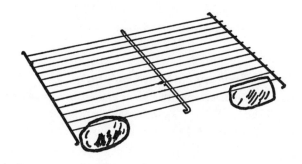

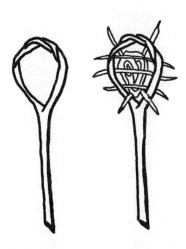

Foods grilled, broiled, and toasted require little help but a few seasonings. An exception are kabobs, where the meat is first marinated in a salad dressing or wine, the vegetables seasoned with sauces and sesame seeds, while cooking. If using a lean meat, a strip of bacon woven in and out amongst the tomato, green pepper, lamb, mushroom, and onion adds additional flavor and moistness. (See recipe section at end of chapter for more kabob suggestions.)

A long, slender strip of cheese inserted into one side of a hot dog, then wrapped with bacon is a delicious way of "dressing" the dog before skewering. Cheese sandwiches, buttered well on the outside, toast well on a skewer, also.

A toasting meal might be ended with the popular "some-mores" sandwich (toasted marshmallow placed between thin layers of sweet chocolate, covered by graham crackers) or a "delightful angel" (slice of angelfood cake, spread with sweetened condensed milk, coated with coconut, and toasted on a skewer). Have you tried a toasted banana?

Aluminum-Foil Cookery (Steam Cooking)

Although foil is an indisputable time saver in no-pan, no-wash cooking, since it does not disintegrate, it does require toting out when no garbage pickup is available. Its uses are varied: (1) Wrap heavy-duty foil around a forked stick, thus making a griddle on which eggs and bacon can be fried. (2) Place your food in a square of heavy-duty foil, close ends securely, and lay package on coals. Corn, for instance, with silk and husks intact and wrapped in foil, are delicious in about ten minutes if coals are placed all around and on top of them. (A little water sprinkled on the corn before wrapping keeps it moist.) Other vegetables are steamed similarly. We prefer two layers of heavy-duty foil and no water, however, for our 45-minute potatoes. (Wash and prick potatoes before wrapping securely.) Potatoes could be coated with mud or clay instead of foil. Have you tried an egg after 20 minutes in the coals using mud or foil as a wrapper? (3) Take a double square of foil, and place your whole meal aboard before wrapping. In Scouts we called it "pocket stew": some ground beef plus sliced potato, carrot, onion, and seasonings. After about 15 minutes on the coals, it is a tasty, nutritious, no-pot-to-wash meal. (4) A hot dog wrapped with biscuit dough or pie crust, then wrapped in foil is another 15-minute meal.

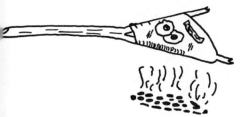

Other combinations for cooking in aluminum foil might include:
Pork chop, onion, apple, sugar, and seasonings

Cheese, zucchini, tomato, garlic, and onion

Hamburger, bacon, onion, and tomato

Lamb chop, carrots, potato, and beans

Canned luncheon meat, potato, carrot, and onion

Ham, peas, pineapple, and yams

Sliced apple, sugar, and cinnamon, or sliced banana and sugar

Sliced peach, nectarine, or apricot plus sugar and cinnamon, topped with
biscuit batter. Berries or cherries might also be used in this cobbler.

Stewing or Boiling (Cooking in Water)
If all of the meal is prepared in one pot, then this method, too, is a good way
of providing a simple, hot, nutritious meal. Begin by browning meat in fat with
onion and seasonings; add water and cook until almost tender before adding
vegetables. A metal or aluminum foil cover speeds cooking time; slow cooking,
however, provides a better flavor, but requires careful watching that it does not
boil dry.

Planking (Cooking on a Board, Generally by Reflected Heat)
The meat or fish filet are attached by nail to the flat side of a heavy plank or
piece of wood (fish head and tail are already removed, of course). Place the
wood alongside but not in the flames. Slices of bacon attached at intervals over
the fish add flavor and moistness. Expect a two-inch filet to require about two
hours of slow cooking.

If preparing Indian-style salmon, use green or water-soaked alder kindling, allowing the smoke to flavor the fish while cooking. Prepare wild rice (purchased perhaps from Indians in the Ontario-Manitoba region) as suggested in an earlier chapter. This almost authentic Indian meal appropriately concludes a day of examining Indian rock paintings, Indian artifacts, Indian totem poles, or long-houses.

In-the-Ground Cooking

Though seldom used by most of us, this is another method of steaming. Great for the beach! Line a hole with rocks; build a fire in the hole; when coals and rocks are hot, put in seaweed, clams, ears of corn—whatever; cover with aluminum foil and sand; steam for about an hour. If skeptical about this method, attend an authentic New England or Maritime clam bake before trying it on your own.

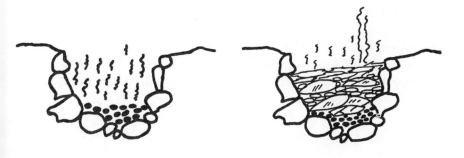

Pressure Cooker Cooking (Steaming Under Pressure)

Although too heavy to carry on foot, the pressure cooker is an efficient method of preparing foods when traveling in high country. Since the higher the altitude, the lower the air pressure, even though water boils at lower tem-peratures, foods require longer cooking time. Below 2,000 ft. there is no significant difference in cooking time, but some experts claim as much as a 50%

increase in required cooking time at 6,000 ft. Percentages are not for us, but efficiency is, so whether camping in mountains or in desert, when we have the space, we have the pressure cooker. Instructions accompanying the cooker MUST be followed, and the cooker MUST be kept in good repair. Enough said, except to say there is nothing like a pot roast with vegetables when you've been "on the road for a spell." And, in my opinion, the only efficient way to prepare a pot roast in the campground is to pressure cook it. Never use the pressure cooker over the campfire, however, for the heat is too difficult to regulate; better to use a gas burner. Ham, stews, spareribs –even some soups and desserts—may be prepared in the cooker. Check the cooker's instruction booklet for recipes.

Pan Broiling (Frying in Pan Without Grease)

Tender meats are frequently prepared in this manner if a grill is not ready or if the efficiency of gas is preferred. Heat pan before putting meat in; turn meat often; pour off grease as it accumulates or you'll fry instead of pan broiling.

Cooking-on-a-Stick

This technique ranges from preparing biscuits on the end of a green stick (a slower process than toasting) to preparing a roast or chicken on a spit, possibly using a sauce for additional flavor.

Baking

Cooking slowly on a stick is a form of baking, like the more elaborate reflector oven. Another way to bake is in the dutch oven. Our family has not made that acquisition yet, but we remember the day while camping with friends when a chocolate cake (using a box mix and Hershey bar) produced one of the best aromas you can imagine in a campground. While the cake was mixed, the dutch oven was warmed over the coals, then oiled generously. (We decided later a layer of foil lining the inside of the cast iron would have simplified removal of the baked cake.) The batter was poured in, the cover was fastened securely, the coals were placed all around and on top, and the wait was begun. Neighboring campsites emptied—into ours. Need I say more? Hardly was the chocolate spread over the cake and it was gone.

Another method of campground baking is done at the side of the fire as illustrated, with a rock—or better yet, a foil-covered rock—as a reflector, a straight stick, a forked stick, and a nonburning cord or rust-proof wire.

Wishing to amuse the children you might experiment by covering a plate-sized rock with foil and placing it on the coals. When hot, brown your bacon, fry your eggs. Another method appealing to kids makes use of a large can. Remove one end and cut away a door on one side; place over coals, adding more fuel through the door when needed. When the can is hot, it is ready for frying; however, we suggest avoiding bacon or sausage because it becomes hazardous as grease collects. Better to add a little oil to top of can and fry your eggs, sunny side up, or fry eggs in foil liner on top of can and use liner as plate when eating.

Undoubtedly there are methods we have overlooked; if you have favorites and care to share, let us know for future editions.

Variety in Technique, Yes! But Kind, How?

Variety in cooking technique usually leads to variety in foods, menus. Although meals built around Hamburger Helper and similar prepackaged meals simplify your packing problems, pan-washing concerns arise. If browning is not part of the preparation, they you *might* try lining the suucepan with foil and ever so gently stirring when necessary. A few combinations with canned soups and vegetables are suggested at chapter's end for your convenience in one-pot cooking.

Getting sufficient variety of fresh fruit and vegetables—particularly green, leafy ones—is a common camping problem. Cabbage keeps well and is one solution. A couple of recipes requiring cabbage are included for your convenience in the in-camp section of this chapter. You might also consider growing alfalfa or cress sprouts, so when lettuce, then cabbage, is gone, your sprouts can provide the needed lunchtime crunch.

Growing sprouts requires a one- or two-auart jar with a strainer top. Cheesecloth or nonrusting wire mesh secured with a rubber jar ring will do fine if you don't wish to purchase a regular top in a health food store. Measure one or two teaspoons (depending whether you are using a one- or two-quart jar) of alfalfa seed into the jar, and with just enough water to cover, set aside for the night. In the morning drain off unabsorbed water, shake the seeds to the side of the jar, and allow the jar to remain on its side in filtered light. Continue to rince the seeds twice a day; drain well each time and allow strainer top to remain in place. As soon as leaves appear, give sprouts more light, but not direct light, and after four- to six-days, when most sprouts have at least two fully open green leaves, they are ready to use. Remove strainer top, and replace with an airtight cover. If they are kept cool, you'll have sprouts for eating raw in salads or sandwiches, for sauteing and adding to eggs or vegetables, or for simmering in cheese, potato, or legume soups. (If you want additional information on growing alfalfa or cress sprouts, read *Sunset's Western Campsites*, pp. 44-49 in the 1973 edition.)

Local fruit stand offerings are supplemented with dried fruits, such as (apples, pears, apricots, prunes, raisins, and dates. Fruit soups, packaged in aluminum foil and imported from Scandinavia, may be obtained in gourmet departments and health food stores, which carry several flavors, including vitamin C-rich rose hip soup. Because of their sweetness these prepared soups are best used as dessert. You can make your own soup using dried and fresh fruits, a little honey, lemon juice, cinnamon, and cloves. With a toasted cheese sandwich this makes a super Swedish supper.

Prepackaged and freeze-dried foods offer efficiency and variety in camp food, but probably are best considered only as back-up food for those times when the fish don't bite or you decide to remain in camp an extra day or two. Freeze-dried food, although ideal considering weight, seldom satisfies in taste, quantity, or price. With few exceptions—one is powdered fruit drinks—our advice is to talk with hiking friends and learn of their brand favorites; then experiment before buying in family-sized quantities. Also worth mentioning are the quantity notations: a package advertized as serving four more frequently, serves two.

A list of some freeze-dried food producers and their addresses is provided in the appendix if you don't have a local distributor and would like to receive a listing of what is available from the manufacturer.

Dried vegetables are available in Canada (imported from England under the Surprise label) and are worth trying if only about half the quantity of water suggested for reconstctution is used. The dried soups (also imported from Europe) such as onion, oxtail, shrimp, leek are excellent and worth finding in the gourmet department or supermarket.

Savory, Special, and Simple

Vacationing is a blast—to the system! For this reason, even though a camping diet includes daily portions of meat, vegetables, fruits, bread, and dairy products, a daily multi-vitamin is added health insurance.

To add dash to your food, keep plastic containers filled with slivered almonds, lemon juice, cooking wine, cloves of garlic, bouillon crystals, parsley, onion, bay leaves, basil, pepper flakes, and so on.

Making camping meals special includes eating with candlelight, using plastic stemware for the wine, decorating with a centerpiece of wild flowers or weeds as well as adding gourmet touches to the food. Why not civilize camping to include a before dinner cocktail with hors d'oeuvres if that's your pleasure? (Little ingenuity is required to pack tiny tins of artichokes, caviar, sardines, a pate.) Corn chips dipped in melted jack cheese with canned chilis added are a zesty meal starter—and permit easy cleanup, too, if a throw-away aluminum foil pie plate is used as the frypan liner.

Or why not an after-dinner cordial for variety? Some campgrounds prohibit drinking alcohol in public, but generally consumption of alcohol in moderate amounts within the confines of your own campsite is now acceptable. (Provincial restrictions regarding alcohol are included in the appendix.)

Simplicity begins with organization from menu planning, to packing meal-size quantities, to everything having its own storage place.

Simplicity is setting out ingredients and everyone making his own sandwich.

Simplicity is dirtying as few pans as possible, using foil liners, everyone wiping his plate clean with a napkin at meal end, and filling pans with water immediately after food is removed.

Simplicity is everyone having his own clearly marked cup, avoiding confusion—and extra dirty dishes.

Simplicity is boiling dishwater *while* eating, drip- or sun-drying, *not* towel-drying.

Simplicity is everyone sharing responsibilities.

Thus, begin with simplicity inspired by variety; add large doses of savor with a dash of pizzaz, and you'll have it—*everyone's* pleasure!

RECIPE SECTION

In our family, vacationing *is* camping. Thus, camping is special with us and our sharing of family camping recipes becomes more than a gesture of friendship—it's a bit of us.

Ready-for-the-Road Favorites

Before leaving home *everyone* helps to bake bread and cookies, to mix the "house" dressing and cereal. No Cope camping venture is off to a good start without them.

Granola

3 cups instant oatmeal
½ cup wheat germ
¼ cup sesame seeds
½ cup flaked coconut
⅓ cup brown sugar
½ tsp. salt
1 tsp. vanilla
1 cup raisins

Mix all except raisins. Bake at 275° F oven for 50 min., or until coconut is brown, stirring occasionally. Cool; mix in raisins. Substitutions: Honey, dry-roasted peanuts, dried apricots, soy bean granules.

Russian Tea

1 cup instant tea
1 cup sugar
1 package (3 oz.) powdered
  lemonade mix
1-½ cups Tang
1 tsp. ground cloves
1 tsp. ground cinnamon

Mix 1 tblsp. of mixture to 1 cup boiling water, and you have one hot, nutritious, spicy drink!

Camper's Casserole

1 pkg. (8 oz.) elbow macaroni	2 tblsp. parsley, chopped
1 medium onion, chopped	2 tsp. monosodium glutamate
1 tbslp. margarine	2 tsp. chili powder
2 lb. ground beef	1-¼ tsp. salt
3 cans (8 oz. each) tomato sauce	1 tsp. hot pepper sauce
1 can (12 oz.) whole kernel corn	½ tsp. sugar
1 green papper, chopped	½ tsp. oregano leaves
1 clove garlic, minced	¼ lb. sharp cheddar cheesj, grated

Cook macaroni according to package directions. Drain and reserve. In large skillet cook onion in margarine until golden; add meat, stirring occasionally.

Add remaining ingredients, except cheese. Simmer 30 min. stirring frequently. Mix in drained macaroni and grated cheese.

Pour into oiled aluminum foil meat loaf pan or similar disposable, meal-sized container. Wrap with foil and freeze for travel; feeds 8 heartily. (At a campground several days later when food has thawed, place a small amount of water in bottom of large saucepan; use the same foil container as pan liner when heating food. After the meal, throw liner away, drip dry saucepan, and meal is done.)

l   Bean Salad

1 No. 2 can whole green beans	1 large green pepper, sliced thin
1 No. 2 small wax beans	1 cup vinegar
1 No. 2 can kidney beans	1 cup sugar
1 large sweet onion, sliced thin	¼ to ⅓ cup salad oil

Drain beans; add onion rings and green pepper. Mix vinegar, sugar, and salad oil. Pour over beans and refrigerate. (Alternate method: mix everything *except* canned vegetables at home; open cans, drain, and mix in campground.)

n   Cabbage Salad

1 qt. chopped cabbage	2 medium carrots, grated fine
2 stalks celery, cut fine	2 tsp. salt

Combine these four ingredients and allow to stand for 1 hour in 1 cup of cold water. Drain well, and press water out.

Syrup mix:

½ cup water	1 cup sugar
½ cup vinegar	

Boil this and cool. Pour over cabbage mixture, and refrigerate, if you can.

Sweet and Sour Salad Dressing

½ cup sugar	½ cup vinegar
½ cup salad oil	½ cup catsup
1 clove garlic, cut in half	4-5 dashes tobasco sauce
¼ tsp. celery salt	1 tbsp. chives, chopped fine
Salt and pepper to taste	

Mix ingredients and allow to stand overnight before removing garlic pieces. The longer it stands, the better it gets.

Italian Spaghetti Sauce

1 onion, chopped
1 lb. ground beef

1 lb. ground pork

Brown the meats and onion in fry pan with a small quantity of olive oil. When nicely browned, add the following:

2 cans tomato paste, rinsed
  with 5 cans water
1 large can tomatoes
2 tblsp. sugar
Salt and pepper to taste

1 tsp. oregano
1 tsp. sweet basil
½tsp. anise seed
1 green pepper, chopped
1 clove garlic, minced

Simmer sauce and meat mixture for 3 to 4 hours before freezing for trip in disposable or plastic container.

Smoked Salmon

Filet salmon, leaving skin on but removing all blood and bones. Soak cleaned fish in following brine mixture 8 to 10 hours:

1 cup table salt
1 cup sugar

2 qt. water
¼ jar seafood or poultry seasoning

Rinse in cool water, and allow to air-dry for 1 to 2 hours. Note a shiny coating appears.

Using alder or other hardwood and keeping fire low, smoke for 8 to 12 hours if you intend to use salmon within a week or two. If you intend to keep salmon longer, smoke it longer; a heavy cure requires 5-6 days of smoking. Brush occasionally with vegetable oil during smoking process. (We have used both Japanese kamado and a smoker fashioned out of an old breadbox. Both work well as long as heat is kept low.)

Beef Jerky

4 lbs. flank steak, or hanging tender
3 cups Burgandy wine
¼ cup salt
1 tbsp. garlic powder

1 tbsp. black pepper
1 tbsp. Tobasco sauce
2 tbsp. Worcestershire sauce
1 tbsp. onion powder

Remove fat, and slice meat into ⅛-¼-in. strips, cutting *with* the grain. Mix wine and seasonings, and pour over meat until well covered. Refrigerate for 1-1-½ days, turning meat occasuonally. Pour off marinade, and pat meat dry with towel.

Set oven at 150° F or less, and with door propped open slightly, allow beef to dehydrate on the oven or on cooling racks. Two or three days of this drying process may be required before meat is chewy and flexible, yet not brittle.

Package in sterile, unbreakable containers.

Biscuit Mix

16 cups all-purpose,
  unbleached flour
4 tsp. salt

½ cup baking powder
2 cups powdered milk
3 cups vegetable shortening

Mix the dry ingredients thoroughly; cut in the shortening with pastry blender or two knives until shortening is the size of small peas; store in airtight containers.

When ready to make biscuits, use 1 cup mix to ⅓ cup water; when making dumplings, use 2 cups mix to ¾ cup water.

You may wish to use this mix for pancakes, too, with the addition of an egg, adjusting water to desired thinness.

Camper's Log Candy

¼ cup dry-roasted cashews
1-¼ cup walnuts
6 dried figs
½ cup raisins

¼ cup dried apples
½ tsp. lemon juice
1 tblsp. orange juice
confectioner's sugar or
    flaked coconut

Grind nuts and fruit together in meat grinder or food chopper. Add fruit juices, and mix thoroughly.

Make small logs, using about 1 tblsp. mixture for each log. Roll in either sugar or coconut and allow to dry (uncovered) for 24 hours or so. Wrap in plastic film or foil, and refrigerate until ready to depart.

Gorp

Mix equal parts of salted peanuts, M & Ms, and raisins, or if you prefer no chocolate and more fruit, mix: 2 parts raisins to 2 parts other dried fruits (apricots, apples, pears, prunes, dates) to 1 part nuts (almonds, brazils, hazelnuts).

Package in small plastic bags ready for quick energy snacking.

In-Camp Cooking

Since our family while camping prefers spending as little time as possible during the day around stove and table, we use gas for heating hot drinks to accompany breakfast granola and lunchtime cheeses, sausage, crackers, and fruit. However, come dinner we enjoy lingering around the campfire, experimenting with this and that. A few recipes simple both in preparation and cleanup, we now offer.

Pork en Brochette

(Several years ago a friend in Yugoslavia prepared what became this family favorite.)

Slice 1-½ lb. of pork tenderloin, and mix with 2 sliced onions and 2 or 3 sliced cloves of garlic. Cover tightly and keep cool overnight. Next day when charcoal is ash-colored, skewer pork and onions; cook until pork is well-done, brushing with oil or barbecue sauce if desired.

Delicious with applesaue, rice, and salad!

Sesame Beef Kabobs

2 lb. beef, sirloin, or flank
½ cup soy sauce
½ cup cooking wine
½ cup sesame oil

1 clove garlic, minced
1 tblsp. chopped onion
¼ tsp. ground ginger (optional)
¼ cup sesame seeds

Cut beef into strips, ⅛ in. thick. Combine all ingredients except sesame seeds, and allow meat to marinate in mixture for at least 2 hours before skewering, coating with sesame seeds and cooking. Coals are best. Meat is ready in about 3 minutes and will serve 6-8.

Chicken Liver Kabobs

1 lb. chicken livers, absolutely fresh
½ lb. sliced bacon
Cherry tomatoes
Medium-sized mushrooms
Small onions, fresh or canned

¼ cup olive oil
¼ cup flour
½ tsp. salt
¼ tsp. black pepper

Alternate chicken livers with bacon, tomato, mushroom, and onion on skewer; brush with oil; dust with flour and seasonings. Hold skewer about 3 in. from coals, turning frequently, until browned on all sides. You may brush occastionally with oil.

Fruit Kabobs

Brush cubed fruit with a honey and lemon juice mixture; hold filled skewer over coals until fruit is nicely browned. For appetizer or dessert, make it!

Pork and Sauerkraut

4 pork chops
1 can potatoes, sliced
1 can sauerkraut

1 can applesauce or
    2 apples, sliced
1 onion, sliced

Brown chops and onion in heavy skillet; remove from skillet and put in sauerkraut, applesauce, then pork chops, and onion; cover tightly. Simmer for about 40 min., adding a little water if needed, until pork is well-done.

Chicken-Flavored Cabbage

Using chicken bouillon crystals or canned chicken broth, heat about 2 cups of broth while slicing cabbage. Bring broth to boiling again after cabbage is added; then cover and simmer for 10 min.

The broth might be served in cups, the boiled cabbage with the main course.

Bannock

2 cups whole-wheat or
    all-purpose flour
2 tsp. baking powder

½ tsp. salt
⅔ cup whole milk

Preheat skillet over coals, then distribute oil around sides and bottom. Mix dry ingredients and milk, making a stiff dough. Pat dough into a shapre, about 1 in.

Dush the dough lightly with flour, then drop into hot, oileu skillet; cook over coals; turn occasionally to brown both sides. As in all breadmaking, if bannock sounds hollow when knocked by knuckles, it is ready for butter and jam. Expect the baking process to take about 15 min. (We haven't tried it yet, but we are told a greased coffee can or even aluminum foil can be substituted for the skillet.) If a richer bread is preferred, a teaspoon or so of melted butter, oil, or bacon drippings can be added to the liquid; if a solid margarine is used, cut it into the dry ingredients with the aid of two knives until the margarine pieces are about the size of large peas. Add liquid, stir, and shape to size of skillet.

Alternate method: We suggest mixing a double or triple batch of bannock *at home*, substituting 2 tblsp. plus ½ tsp. dried milk for the whole milk required for *each* batch. Put half the batch (half the recipe above) into each of several sturdy plastic bags. Then in camp, when mixing bannock, merely take out one plastic bag, containing the half quantity, add ¼ cup water—and presto! the bannock is ready to shape for skillet.

Manomin Rice

2 cups wild rice
8 cups water
2 tsp. salt
1 green pepper, chopped

1 clove garlic, minced
1 onion, chopped
½ cup vegetable oil
1 cup almonds, chopped and blanched

While salted water is heating to a boil, rinse rice several times in cold water. Drain rice well, and add to water when it reaches a rolling boil; allow rice to simmer covered for about 30 min. before draining.

Heat oiled skillet before adding nuts. When brown, remove nuts to paper towel to absorb excess oil; sprinkle with salt.

Add more oil to skillet and brown chopped onion, green pepper, and garlic; stir frequently. Combine cooked rice with vegetables and stir until rice is warmed again; salt and pepper to taste, and garnish with browned almonds.

Substitution: Using onion, garlic powders, and dried pepper flakes would simplify campground preparation of this recipe.

Camper's Chowder

1 onion, chopped
1 tblsp. margarine
1 can cream of celery soup, condensed

1 can clam chowder, condensed
1 can shrimp, drained
Parsley, basil, sherry to taste
1 soup can of water

Brown onion in margarine in heavy saucepan; add remaining ingredients and mix well. Simmer for 5-10 min.; add a little milk before serving, if desired. Browned bacon pieces, mushrooms, corn, potatoes might be added for greater flavor and heartiness.

Quick Chili

1-½ lb. ground beef
1 large onion, chopped
1 large can stewed tomatoes
1 can (8 oz.) tomato sauce
1-½ tsp. salt

¼ tsp. garlic powder
2 tsp. chili powder
1 can red kidney beans, drained
2 cups cooked macaroni

Brown meat and onions in heavy saucepan; add remaining ingredients *except* beans and macaroni; cover and simmer for ½ hour. Cook macaroni in boiling, salted water until tender; drain. Add macaroni and beans to beef mixture; stir gently and serve.

Tuna and Rice

1 can cream of celery or cream
  of mushroom soup condensed
1 can (6½oz.) tuna, drained

1 small onion
1 tblsp. margarine
Chopped celery or green pepper

Brown onion and green pepper in margarine; add soup, tuna, and a little water. Stir occasionally as mixture heats. Serve on bed of rice or on toasted hamburger buns, topped with canned french fried onion rings, if you like.

Chicken Fricassee

2 cans boned chicken
1 can cream of celery soup,
  condensed

1 can potatoes, drained
1 can peas

Mix chicken and undiluted soup before adding vegetables. Heat and season to taste.

Chicken Stew and Dumplings

1 large can chicken fricassee
1 can mixed vegetables

Salt and pepper, to taste

Open cans and heat fricassee, seasonings, vegetables, and vegetable juice. Mix dumplings and drop onto slowly bubbling stew; cook for 10 min., cover and cook another 10 min. before serving.

Camper's Casserole

1 lb. ground beef or 1 can
  meatballs or canned corned beef
2 cans spaghetti with tomato sauce
1 can mushrooms, drained
1 can corn, whole kernel

1 can stewed tomatoes
1 small onion or 1 tblsp. dried
  minced onion
1 cup grated cheese

Brown meat and onion, if canned meats are not used; combine all ingredients except cheese and heat. Garnish with cheese.

Franks au Gratin

1 lb. skinless franks, sliced

into ½-in. pieces
3-4 slices bacon, quartered,
  or imitation bacon bits

1 can 5-⅓ oz.) evaporated milk

2 cups water
1 can peas, undrained
1 pk. (5-½ oz.) au gratin potatoes

Brown bacon in skillet; add frankfurters and brown lightly. Stir in potatoes, water, and milk; heat. Add peas and cook covered, until potatoes are tender (15-20 min.).

The recipes were suggested in part, to demonstrate how a variety of canned and partially prepared foods need only by combined, seasoned to your taste, and heated. Quantities were suggested with a four-member family in mind unless otherwise indicated; and many gourmet touches were omitted to avoid stunting your creativity. (Doesn't that sound like a cop out?) Additional simple meal suggestions follow for the inexperienced camper, the cook's helper, the liberated cook's replacement:

Eggs are the perfect traveling companion and needn't become a bore. Vary them by adding one or more of the following: green peppers, tomatoes, mushrooms, capers, chopped meats, cheese, onions, garlic, parsley, asparagus, spinach, green beans.

Rice, too, can form the basis for a number of meals. Brown meat in hot oil; add onion, garlic, celery, or green pepper and cook until browned; add stewed tomatoes, tomato sauce, seasonings, precooked rice; heat and serve. Vary the meat and vegetables.

Hearty soup or stew serves well in the campground. (1) Chicken and vegetable soup is started by opening a can of whole stewed chicken or by placing a whole stewing chicken in boiling water with onion and garlic; simmer until meat falls away from bones. With skin, bones, and fat removed, add canned or fresh vegetables, precooked rice or noodles. (2) A simple stew is begun by browning beef or veal in oil and cooking in a covered pan with water, salt, pepper, and onion until meat is almost tender. For extra flavor, add a can of consomme or bouillon crystals. Then combine sliced potatoes, carrots, and celery, and cook until tender. (3) A simple borscht is made by following the stew directions and adding canned beets, sliced raw cabbage, and a dash of lemon juice or vinegar 10-15 min. before serving.

Before frying fish, rinse, dry, and toss pieces in a bag with flour and seasonings. Fry fish in hot oil or butter for 5 min. per side or until lightly brown. Drizzle with a little white wine, a little lemon juice, a few browned almonds, and you'll know you're living right.

When preparing live crab or lobster, fill a large pot with sea water and when water reaches a rolling boil (you may prefer to close your eyes) drop it in. When water again reaches a rolling boil, start timing. After 15-18 min., remove from shell and enjoy with lemon, butter, bean salad, French bread, and white wine.

Continue to steam clams, mussels, and oysters until shells pop open. Serve with lemon butter or add to your casserole of the day.

Tips—Perhaps Useful

Cook for two meals at one time. Tomorrow's eggs hard-boil nicely in today's potato or spaghetti water; today's vegetables add heartiness to tomorrow's soup.

Hard-boiled eggs do not require refrigeration as long as shells remain free of cracks. If long-term wilderness camping is planned, grease egg shells with salad oil.

Margarine keeps better than butter; store in a covered plastic container. Oils keep best of all and transport well in polytubes from your local sporting goods store.

Use canned mushroom soup in creamed dishes; if there is no cream soup in the larder, melt 2 tblsp. margarine and blend with 2 tblsp. flour before slowly stirring in 1 cup reconstituted milk. Add salt and pepper to taste, stirring frequently until heated.

Sour cream is improvised by adding lemon juice or vinegar to evaporated milk. With the addition of salt it serves as a cabbage slaw dressing.

Dry milk is made tastier by adding a little sugar, vanilla, or chocolate; mix ahead and cool in stream. (⅓ cup dried milk plus ⅞ cup water makes 1 cup reconstituted milk.)

Use dried soup mixes and bouillon crystals, powdered fruit drinks, powdered milk, etc., instead of troubling with weight and space requirements of cans. Individual packages of instant coffee and hot chocolate further simplify.

To sweeten water in camper or trailer tank, add 1 tsp. baking soda to 1 cup hot water. When soda is dissolved, add mixture to rest of tank water.

If plastic containers have absorbed foul odors, soak in a strong detergent and very hot water solution.

Drawstring bags of assorted colors and sizes made from denim or other sturdy fabric are useful in keeping clothing and supplies clean and organized. Nylon mosquito netting drawstring bags are handy for drip-drying tableware, for hanging food from tree limbs.

A good supply of plastic bags in assorted sizes is essential.

Salt-cured meats in large pieces rather than thinly sliced ones keep best, for less surface is exposed to the air; thus, buy hard salami, Thuringer, bacon by the chunk. Slice later, as needed. Although bacon molds, if kept cool—even without refrigeration—it will keep for months if it has been rinsed in water when purchased, patted dry, and then rinsed in a salty vinegar solution (1 tsp. salt to 1 cup vinegar). Pat dry a second time and wrap in several layers of cheesecloth or toweling, allowing bacon to breathe.

If it is only bacon flavor you desire, consider using imitation bacon bits, which are texturized soya protein with bacon flavor.

Cheese is a great traveler. Buy small packages and those encased in wax, and cheese care is simplified. They must not get moist, but then will lose palatability if completely dried out. Flat plastic (Tupperware) boxes for cheese and sausage storage work well. A little sugar in the container helps to absorb moisture.

For cleaning ease, coat exterior of pots and pans with soap before placing over open fire.

Mayonnaise, organ meats, ground meat, fish, and seafoods spoil very quickly. To prolong life of fresh fruits and vegetables, allow air to circulate around them.

Start a lengthy trip with frozen casserole, frozen ground beef, frozen bread, frozen spaghetti sauce in various-sized-containers—some thick, some thin—in order that some will thaw more quickly than others as you go.

Keeping fires small and using only dead limbs helps preserve forests for future generations. Have you, too, seen campfires ablaze long after families have snuggled into their sleeping bags?

If in doubt about water purity, boil water for 5 min. (and add a little salt to improve flavor) or use water purification tablets as directed.

Are you guilty, as we have been occasionally, of scraping griddle drippings or dumping dishwater into a nearby bush—thoughtlessly attracting insects and animals?

If you have tips you would like to share, let us know for future editions.

FOODS CHECKLIST

We hope this checklist will jog your mind and will save you time when planning and packing. You will not use all items included on the list, you will wish to include others. On each line cross out what you don't wish to take, circle what you need to purchase, and check when packed. When the first and third columns have the same number of checks, you are ready. Go!

Take	Purchase	Packed	
	Will Did		
			Fruit drinks (dried, canned, concentrated syrups)
			Milk (fresh, dried, canned), nondairy creamer
			Coffee (regular, instant), tea (Russian, instant, bags)
			Instant cocoa
			Cereal (mixes, instants, dry)
			Biscuit, muffin, pancake, cornbread mixes
			Eggs (fresh, dried)

Cheeses (sliced/individually wrapped, grated, block)
Soups (dried, canned concentrates)
Salt-cured meats (bacon, ham, hard salamis, Thuringer, jerky,
    salmon), sun-dried seafoods/fish
Canned fish and meats (Vienna sausage, tuna, salmon,
    shrimp, crab, sardines, luncheon meats, ham, patés, corned
    beef, chicken, sandwich spreads)
Fresh meats (pork, hot dogs, ground beef, lamb, sausages,
beef steak)
Homemade: frozen casserole, spaghetti sauce, etc.

Tomato sauce, tomato paste, stewed tomatoes
Canned stew, spaghetti, chop suey, hash, french fried onions,
    pork and beans
Packages dinners (premeasured, freeze-dried)
Legumes (dried, canned), other canned vegetables
Potatoes, onions (fresh, dried)
Fresh vegetables (carrots, cauliflower, cabbage, cucumbers)
Instant rice, spaghetti, macaroni, noodles

Fresh fruits (oranges, lemons, apples, melons), canned Dried
    fruits, fruit soup mixes (dried)
Cake and frosting mixes, puddings, gelatins
Nuts, gorp, hard candy, pretzels, potato chips
Crackers, canned Boston brown bread, breads
Marshmallows, popcorn, chocolate bars for "some-mores"
Dinner wine, cocktail mixes, hors d'oeuvres
Vinegar, lemon juice concentrate
Salad oil, margarine
Salt/pepper, favorite spices, herbs, tenderizers, tantalizers
Sugar, flour, baking powder, baking soda
Syrup, honey, jelly, peanut butter
Catsup, mustard, pickles, Worcestershire sauce, Tobasco
    sauce
Vinegar-and-oil salad dressings
Gravy, sauce mixes (canned, dried)
Bouillon crystals
Alfalfa seeds, cress seeds
Baby foods

APPENDICES

Contents

Canadian Government Travel Offices
Other Canadian Government Agency Addresses
Information Canada Addresses
Provincial Travel Bureau Addresses and
    Other Agencies Within Provinces
Selected Travel Literature List from
    Federal and Provincial Governments
Book List
Holidays
Leading Artists, Architects, and Writers
Art Galleries, Art Museums, and Cultural Centers
Natural History and Historical Museums
Historical Chronology
Camping Organizations
Selected Sporting Organizations
Nature Federation Affiliates
Ethnic Groups: Selected Organizations
Regional Foods
Freeze-Dried Food Companies
Events
Farm Vacations/Guest Ranches
Language

CANADIAN GOVERNMENT TRAVEL OFFICES

Canada
Canadian Government Travel Bureau (CGTB)
150 Kent St.
Ottawa, Ontario, Canada K1A OH6

England
CGTB   Tel. 01-930-0731
19 Cockspur St.
London, England SW1Y 5BP

France
CGTB or Office National du Tourisme Canadian   Tel. RIC 22-50
4 rue Scribe
Paris 9, France

Germany
CGTB or Kanadisches Fremdenverkehrsamt   Tel. 28-01-57
6 Frankfurt
Biebergasse 6-10
Frankfurt, West Germany

United States

California
510 W. 6th St.   Tel. 213-622-1029
Los Angeles, Cal. 90014

600 Market St.   Tel. 415-981-8515
San Francisco, Cal. 94104

District of Columbia
1771 N St., N.W.   Tel. 202-223-2855
Washington, D.C. 20036

Georgia
260 Peachtree St. N.W.   Tel. 404-577-6810
Atlanta, Ga. 30303

Illinois
332 S. Michigan Ave.   Tel. 312-782-3760
Chicago, Ill. 60604

Massachusetts
The Prudential Center   Tel. 617-536-1730
263 Plaza
Boston, Mass. 02199

Michigan
1257-1259 Washington Blvd.   Tel. 313-963-8686
Detroit, Mich. 48226

Minnesota
Northstar Center   Tel. 612-332-4314
124 S. 7th St.
Minneapolis, Minn. 55402

New York
680 5th Ave.   Tel. 212-757-4917
New York, N.Y. 10019

1417 Main Pl.   Tel. 716-852-7369
Buffalo, N.Y. 14202

Ohio
Room 1010, Enquirer Bldg.   Tel. 513-421-5445
617 Vine St.
Cincinnati, Ohio 45202

Winous-Point Bldg.   Tel. 216-861-2559
1250 Euclid Ave.
Cleveland, Ohio 44115

Pennsylvania
Suite 1309   Tel. 215-563-1708
3 Benjamin Franklin Pkwy.
Philadelphia, Pa. 19102

Four Gateway Center   Tel. 412-391-4747
Pittsburgh, Pa. 15222

Washington
Suite 1117, Plaza 600   Tel. 206-447-3811
600 Stewart St.
Seattle, Wash. 98101

Other Federal Government Agencies Providing Tourist Aids

Information Services   National parks, hunting, and fishing
Conservation Group
National & Historic Parks Branch
Department of Indian Affairs and Northern Development
400 Laurier Ave. W.
Ottawa, Ontario K1A OH4

Canada Map Office   Indexes available free;
Department of Energy, Mines, and Resources   topographic and general
615 Booth St.   maps 25¢-$2.50; aeronautical
Ottawa, Ontario K1A OE9   charts $1.50

Publications Division   Geological maps and reports
Geological Survey of Canada   50¢; mining-minerals map
Department of Energy, Mines, and Resources   50¢
601 Booth St.
Ottawa, Ontario K1A OE8

Hydrographic Chart Distribution Office   Nautical charts 50¢-$4.00;
Department of the Environment, Room 230   free indexes available
615 Booth St.
Ottawa, Ontario K1A OE6

INFORMATION CANADA

(Distributor: Canadian Government Books)

Information Canada Center
  171 Slater St.
  Ottawa, Ontario K1A OS9

Information Canada Bookshops
  800 Granville St.
  Vancouver, British Columbia

  393 Portage Ave.
  Winnipeg, Manitoba

  1683 Barrington St.
  Halifax, Nova Scotia

  171 Slater St.
  Ottawa, Ontario

  221 Yonge St.
  Toronto, Ontario

  640 St. Catherine St. W.
  Montreal, Quebec

PROVINCIAL TRAVEL BUREAUS and Other Travel Literature Sources

Alberta

Travel Alberta   Tel. 403-424-0474
10255 - 104th St.
Edmonton, Alberta, Canada T5J 1B1

Lobby, Legislative Bldg.
109th St. and 97th Ave.
Edmonton

J. J. Bowlen Bldg., Room 907   Tel. 403-268-8539
620 7th Ave., S.W.
Calgary

501 Victoria Bldg.   Tel. 613-237-2615
Ottawa, Ontario

703-510 W. 6th St.   Tel. 213-624-6371
Los Angeles, Cal. 90014

37 Hill St.   Tel. 01-499-3061
London, W.1, England

Other Travel Alberta Information Centers

In Alberta: Banff, Canmore, Fort Macleod, Frank, Jasper, Lloydminster, Milk
    River, Provost, Wainwright, and Walsh

In British Columbia: Dawson Creek and Golden

In Saskatchewan: Alsask

In the United States: St. Mary, Mont.

Other Information Centers in Alberta

Bow Island, Calgary, Camrose, Drumheller, Edmonton, Edson, Grande Prairie,
Hinton, Jasper, Lacombe, Lethbridge, Medicine Hat, Red Deer, Viking, and
Wetaskiwin

Other Provincial Agencies Providing Tourist Aids

Department of Lands and Forests   Fishing and hunting information;
Natural Resources Bldg.   provincial and county maps;
109th St. and 99th Ave.   legal survey plans
Edmonton, Alberta T5K 2E1

Department of Indian and Northern Affairs
C.N. Tower, 27th Fl.
Edmonton, Alberta

British Columbia

Department of Travel Industry   Tel. 387-6417
1019 Wharf St.
Victoria, British Columbia, Canada V8W 2Z2

British Columbia Information Centre (BCIC) Tel. 681-5177
652 Burrard St.
Vancouver 1

BCIC   Tel. 351-4442
Douglas

BCIC   Tel. 859-9219
Box 155
Abbotsford   (open April 15-Nov. 15)

BCIC   Tel. 495-6052
Box 644
Osoyoos   (open May 15-Sept. 15)

BCIC
Trans-Canada Highway
Golden   (open May 15-Sept. 15)

BCIC   Tel. 424-5561
Yahk (open May 1-Sept. 30)

Other British Columbia Information Centers or Representatives

BCIC   Tel. 762-2221
Box 43
Banff Ave.
Banff, Alberta (open June 15-Sept. 3)

Jasper Chamber of Commerce
P.O. Box 98
412 Connaught Dr.
Jasper, Alberta

British Columbia Department of Travel Tel. 213-380-9171
 Industry
Suite 585, 3303 Wilshire Blvd.
Los Angeles, Cal. 90010

British Columbia Government Department Tel. 415-981-4780
 of Travel Industry
Suite 400, 100 Bush St.
San Francisco, Cal. 94104

British Columbia House   Tel. 01-930-6857
1-3 Regent St.
London, S.W.1, England

Other Provincial Agencies Providing Tourist Aids

Fish and Wildlife Branch   Fishing and hunting information
Department of Recreation and Conservation
Parliament Bldgs.
Victoria, British Columbia

The Lapidary Rock & Mineral Society of British Columbia
Box 194, Postal Station A
Vancouver, British Columbia

Director of Surveys and Mapping   Provincial and county maps
Department of Lands, Forests, and Water Resources
Parliament Bldgs.
Victoria, British Columbia

Manitoba

Department of Tourism, Recreation, and Cultural Affairs
Tourist Branch
491 Portage Ave.
Winnipeg, Manitoba R3B 2E7

Manitoba Government Travel
Norquay Bldg.
401 York Ave.
Winnipeg, Manitoba R3C OP8

Manitoba Government Visitor Reception Center (MGVRC)
Legislative Bldg.
Broadway and Osborne
Winnipeg, Manitoba R3C OV8

MGVRC
on Highway 75 at Canadian border

MGVRC
on Highway 1 at the Ontario-Manitoba border

MCVRC
on Highway 10 at Canadian border

Manitoba-Saskatchewan Government Visitor Reception Center
on Highway 1 at Manitoba-Saskatchewan border

Other Manitoba Information Centers

Churchill, Flin Flon, The Pas, Brandon, Dauphin, Grandview, Killarney,
Minnedosa, Neepawa, Roblin, Souris, Swan River, Virden, Carmen, Morris,
Morden, Portage la Prairie, St. Boniface, St. Pierre, Winnipeg, and Beau-
sejour

Other Agencies Providing Travel Literature and Aids

Development and Extension Service
Box 9, 989 Century St.
Winnipeg, Manitoba R3H OW4

Surveys Branch Department of Mines and Natural Resources Room 816, Norquay Bldg. 401 York Ave. Winnipeg, Manitoba R3C OP8	Provincial and county maps, legal survey plans

New Brunswick

New Brunswick Department of Tourism
P.O. Box 1030
Fredericton, New Brunswick E3B 5C3

Information Bureau
Admiral Beatty Hotel
King Square
St. John

Jaycee Tourist Information Bureau
Wilmot Park, Woodstock Rd.
P.O. Box 514
Fredericton

Fredericton Chamber of Commerce
364 York St.
Fredericton

Topographic Reference Maps (50¢ each)

Department of Natural Resources
Room 575, Centennial Bldg.
Fredericton, New Brunswick

Newfoundland and Labrador

Tourist Services Division
Newfoundland Department of Tourism
Confederation Bldg.
St. John's, Newfoundland A1C 5R8

Parks Division
Pleasantville
St. John's

Passenger Sales Department
Canadian National Railways
St. John's

Director of Crown Lands & Administration Department of Mines, Agriculture, and Resources Confederation Bldg. St. John's	Provincial and county maps, surveys

Northwest Territories

Division of Tourism, Travel Arctic
Department of Economic Development
Yellowknife, Northwest Territories XOE 1HO

Secretary
Northwest Territories, Historical Advisory Board
Government of the Northwest Territories
Yellowknife

Supervisor of Arts and Crafts
Department of Economic Development
Government of the Northwest Territories
Yellowknlfe

Yellowknife Public Library
Box 694
Yellowknife

Superintendent
Baffin Island National Park
Pangnirtung, Northwest Territories XOA ORO

Nova Scotia

Nova Scotia Department of Tourism
P.O. Box 130
Halifax, Nova Scotia B3J 2M7

Handcraft Centre
P.O. Box 2147
Halifax

Nova Scotia Communications Information Centre
Box 2206
Halifax

Department of Lands and Forests   Hunting & fishing information
Halifax

Ontario

Ontario Ministry of Industry Tourism
Government of Ontario
Parliament Bldgs.
Toronto, Ontario M7A 1T3

Ministry of Industry and Tourism
Travel Services Branch
Queen's Park
Toronto

CANADIAN CAMPING AND CARAVANING** 163

Other Ontario Travel Information Centers

Open all year: Barrie, Cornwall, Hill Island, Niagara Falls, Sarnia, Sault Ste. Marie, Toronto, and Windsor

Open mid-May-mid-September: Fort Erie, Fort Frances, Hawkesbury, Homer-St. Catharines, Kenora, Lancaster, Pigeon River, Point Fortune, Prescott, Rainy River, and Windsor

Ontario Ministry of Agriculture and Food
Parliament Bldgs.
Toronto, Ontario M7A 1A5

Fall fairs information

Ontario Ministry of Transportation & Communications
Highway 401 and Keele
Downsview, Ontario M7A 1Z8

Road conditions; county maps

Ontario Ministry of Natural Resources
Parliament Bldgs.
Toronto, Ontario M7A 1X5

Provincial parks, canoeing, fishing, hunting, topographical maps

Canadian Hydrographic Service
Marine Sciences Branch
Department of the Environment
615 Booth St.
Ottawa, Ontario K1A OE6

Marine-navigation charts, sailing directions

Canadian Department of National Revenue
Customs & Excise Branch
Connaught Bldg.
Mackenzie Ave.
Ottawa, Ontario

Border crossing and general customs regulations

Canada Immigration
Ontario Region
P.O. Box 23
Toronto-Dominion Bank Building
55 King St. W.
Toronto, Ontario M5G 1V2

Temporary employment information

Ontario Human Rights Commission
400 University Ave.
Toronto, Ontario M7A 1Vi

Prince Edward Island

Tourist Information Centre
Department of the Environment and Tourism
P.O. Box 940
Charlottetown, Prince Edward Island C1A 7M5

Fish and Wildlife Division
Environmental Control Commission
Charlottetown

Department of the Environment and Tourism   Provincial and county maps
Map Library
P.O. Box 2000
Charlottetown

Quebec

Quebec Department of Tourism, Fish, and Game
Place de la Capitale
150 E. Blvd. St.-Cyrille
Quebec, Quebec G1R 2B4

Tourist Branch
Department of Tourism, Fish, and Game
Parliament Bldgs., Complex "G"
Quebec, Quebec G1A 1R4

Other Reception Centers for the Department of Tourism Within Province

12, rue Ste.-Anne
Quebec, Quebec G1A 1R4

2, Place Ville-Marie
Montreal, Quebec 113

Notre-Dame-du-Portage, r. 20
Highway 132

Riviere-Beaudette, r. 20
Highway 20

St.-Bernard-de-Lacolle, r. 15
Highway 15

Information booths open June to September in:
   Côteau-du-Lac, Hull, Rigaud, Armstrong, Black Lake, Huntingdon, Pike River, Rock Island, Sabrevois, Montmorency, Ste.-Foy, St.-Nicholas, Riviere-du-Loup, Ste.-Flavie, Ste.-Luce, Trois-Pistoles

Representatives for Quebec Department of Tourism Outside of Canada

12 Upper Grosvenor St.
London, England

66, rue Pergolèse
Paris, France

30 Konigsallee
Dusseldorf, West Germany

72 West Adams St.
Chicago, Ill. 60664

31 St. James Ave.
Boston, Mass. 02116

17 W. 50th St.
New York, N.Y. 10020

710 W. 6th St.
Los Angeles, Cal. 70014

Other Provincial Agencies Providing Tourist Aids
Photogrammetry and Cartography Division
Department of Lands and Forests
200 Chemin Ste.-Foy, 7th Fl.
Quebec City, Quebec

Saskatchewan
Saskatchewan Tourist Branch   Tel. 306-527-8611
Department of Tourism and Renewable Resources
7th Floor, SPC Bldg.
Regina, Saskatchewan S4P 2Y9

Highway Visitor Information Centers (open May 15-Sept. 2)
Trans-Canada Highway 1
  East: Manitoba-Saskatchewan Border
  Moosomin
  Campgrounds: McLean, Besant, Maple Creek
Yellowhead Routes 14 and 15
  East: Langenburg
  West: Lloydminster
Highway 7
  West: Alsask
Highway 39
  South: North Portal, adjacent to Canadian customs office

Other Unofficial Representatives (often Chamber of Commerce offices)
Battlefords Provincial Park, Blaine Lake, Canora, Eastend, Estevan, Fort Qu'Appelle, Gardiner Dam, Gravelbourg, Indian Head, La Ronge, Lloydminster, Melfort, Melville, Moose Jaw, Moosomin, Muenster, Naicam, North Battleford, Prince Albert, Prince Albert National Park, Regina, St. Walburg, Saskatoon, Strasbourg, Swift Current, Weyburn, Wynyard, Yorkton

Topographical and Forestry Maps
Lands and Surveys Branch
Department of Natural Resources
2340 Albert St.
Regina, Saskatchewan S4P 2V7

Outfitters Association
Secretary-Treasurer
316 10th St. E.
Prince Albert, Saskatchewan

Provincial Park Accommodations

Conservation Information Services
Department of Natural Resources
Administration Bldg.
Regina, Saskatchewan

Fishing and Hunting Information

Tourist Development Branch
Department of Industry and Commerce
7th Fl, Power Bldg.
Regina, Saskatchewan S4P 2Y9

Yukon Territory

Tourism and Information Branch
P.O. Box 2703
Whitehorse, Yukon Territory

Director of Game
Box 2703
Whitehorse

Department of Fiseries
Box 2410
Whitehorse

Superintendent of Forestry
Box 1168
Whitehorse

Mining Recorders   Mining and prospecting
at Whitehorse, Dawson, Mayo, and Watson Lake

Department of Mines and Technical Surveys   Topographical maps, 50¢ each
Box 969
Whitehorse

Department of Education
Box 2703
Whitehorse

Whitehorse Chamber of Commerce   Commercial enterprises
Box 167
Whitehorse
Canada Manpower Centre   Employment
Box 1798
Whitehorse

Supervisor of Lands
Whitehorse or
Land Agents at Dawson, Mayo, and Watson Lake

Department of National Revenue   Border crossing information
Customs and Excise Division, Box 997
Whitehorse

Department of Manpower and Immigration   Immigration
Box 399, 300 Quebec St.
Prince George, British Columbia

HOLIDAYS IN CANADA

All Canada
New Year's Day   January 1
Good Friday   Friday preceding Easter
Easter Monday   Monday following Easter
Victoria Day   Monday preceding May 25
Dominion Day   July 1
Labour Day   First Monday in September
Thanksgiving Day   Second Monday in October
Remembrance Day   November 11
Christmas Day   December 25

Quebec
Ascension Day   40 days after Easter
Newfoundland
Commonwealth Day   May 24
Discovery Day   Second to last Monday in June
Quebec
St. Jean Baptiste Day   June 24
Newfoundland
Orangemen's Day   July 12
Manitoba, Northwest Territories, Ontario
Civic Holiday   First Monday in August
Yukon
Discovery Day   Friday nearest August 17
Quebec
All Saints' Day   November 1
Immaculate Conception   December 8
Alberta, British Columbia, Manitoba, New Brunswick, Newfoundland, Ontario, Prince Edward Island
Boxing Day   December 26

ART GALLERIES, ART MUSEUMS, AND CULTURAL CENTERS

Alberta
Alberta College of Art   Calgary
Calgary Allied Arts Centre   Calgary
Edmonton Art Gallery   Edmonton
Genevieve Yates Memorial Centre   Lethbridge
Glenbow-Alberta Institute   Calgary
Medicine Hat Art Club   Medicine Hat
University of Alberta   Edmonton
University of Calgary   Calgary
Provincial Museum and
   Archives of Alberta   Edmonton

British Columbia

Art Gallery of Greater Victoria	Victoria
British Columbia Provincial Museum	Victoria
Burnaby Art Gallery	Burnaby
Dawson Creek Museum and Art Gallery	Dawson Creek
Kootenay School of Art	Nelson
Lipsett Collection	Vancouver
Maltwood House, University of Victoria	Victoria
Richmond Arts Centre	Richmond
University of British Columbia	Vancouver
University of Victoria	Victoria
Vancouver Art Gallery	Vancouver
Vernon Museum Art Gallery and Archives	Vernon

Manitoba

Brandon Allied Arts Council	Brandon
Gallery 111, University of Manitoba	Winnipeg
Winnipeg Art Gallery	Winnipeg
The Manitoba Museum of Man and Nature	Winnipeg

New Brunswick

Beaverbrook Art Gallery	Fredericton
New Brunswick Museum	St. John's
Owens Gallery-Mount Allison University	Sackville
Provincial Portrait Gallery	Fredericton
Sunbury Shores Art & Nature Centre, Inc.	St. Andrew's
University of New Brunswick	Fredericton
University of Moncton	Moncton

Newfoundland and Labrador

Arts and Culture Centre	St. John's
Gander Airport Exhibition Area	Gander
Memorial University Art Gallery	St. John's
The Newfoundland Museum	St. John's

Northwest Territories

Museum of the North	Yellowknife

Nova Scotia

Acadia University Gallery	Wolfville
Centennial Art Gallery of Nova Scotia	Halifax
Centennial Centre	Amherst
Dalhousie Art Gallery	Halifax
Dartmouth Heritage Museum	Dartmouth
Nova Scotia Provincial Museums	Halifax

* *For complete list, check "Canadian Museums and Related Institutions"*

Ontario

Agnes Etherington Art Centre, Queens University	Kingston
Art Gallery of Hamilton	Hamilton
Art Gallery of Ontario	Toronto
Bobcaygeon Museum-Library	Bobcaygeon
Cobourg Public Library Art Gallery	Cobourg
Eva Brook Donly Museum	Simcoe
Glenhyrst Arts Council	Brantford
Homer Watson Gallery	Doon
Kitchener-Waterloo Art Gallery	Kitchener
London Public Library and Art Museum	London
McIntosh Memorial Art Gallery, University of Western Ontario	London
McMichael Conservation Art Gallery	Kleinburg
National Gallery of Canada	Ottawa
National Museum of Canada	Ottawa
Oshawa Art Gallery	Oshawa
Peterborough Centennial Museum	Peterborough
Rodman Hall Arts Centre	St. Catharine's
Rothmans Art Gallery of Stratford	Stratford
Sarnia Public Library and Art Gallery	Sarnia
Sigmund Samuel Canadiana Museum	Toronto
Sudbury Centennial Museum & Art Gallery	Sudbury
Tom Thompson Memorial Gallery and Museum of Fine Art	Owen Sound
Gallery of the Theatre of the Arts, University of Waterloo	Waterloo
Willistead Art Gallery of Windsor	Windsor
The Royal Ontario Museum Complex	Toronto

Prince Edward Island

Confederation Art Gallery and Museum	Charlottetown

Quebec

Atelier d'Art de l'Academie de Quebec	Quebec
Caisse Populaire St.-Frédéric	Drummondville
Centre d'Art d'Argenteuil	Lachute
Centre d'Art de Boucherville	Boucherville
Centre d'Art du Mont-Royal	Montreal
Centre d'Art de Pérce	Pérce
Centre d'Art de Sorel	Sorel
Centre d'Art de Trois-Riviére	Trois-Riviére
Centre d'Art	Victoriaville
Centre Civique	Rimouski
Centre Culturel d'Amos	Amos
Centre Culturel	Amqui
Centre Culturel de Baie Comeau	Baie Comeau
Centre Culturel de Baie St.-Paul	Baie St.-Paul

Centre Culturel Beauceville	Beauceville
Centre Culturel de la Cote de Beaupre	Beaupré
Centre Culturel de Beloeil	Beloeil
Centre Culturel	Cap-Chat
Centre Culturel Confédératif	Mistassini
Centre Culturel de Dorval	Dorval
Centre Culturel de Farnham	Farnham
Centre Culturel G. P. Vanier	Chateauguay Centre
Centre Culturel (et Récréatif) Régional des Iles, Inc.	Havre;Aubert
Centre Culturel de Jonquiére	Jonquiére
Centre Culturel de La Sarre	La Sarre
Centre Culturel de Longueil	Longueil
Centre Culturel du Nord de l'Outaouais	Hull
Centre Culturel de Pierreville	Pierreville
Centre Culturel de Riviére du Loup	Riviére du Loup
Centre Culturel	Rouyn
Centre Culturel (et Sportif) de St.-Hyacinthe	St.-Hyacinthe
Centre Culturel	St.-Jacques-de-Montcalm
Centre Culturel de la Cité de St.-Michel	St.-Michel
Centre Culturel (et Sportif)	St.-Prosper
Centre Culturel (et Sportif)	Schefferville
Centre Culturel de Shawinigan	Shawinigan
Centre Culturel	Trois-Riviére
Cité des Jeunes	Vaudreuil
Conseil des Arts	Plessisville
Cowansville Art Centre	Cowansville
Cultural Centre of Coaticook	Coaticook
Ecole des Beaux-Arts de Québec	Quebec
Galerie d'Art d'Arvida	Arvida
Galerie d'Art de Chicoutimi	Chicoutimi
Galerie d'Art de l'Université de Sherbrooke	Sherbrooke
Galerie Nova et Vetera	St.-Laurent
Lachine Cultural Centre	Lachine
Maison des Arts La Sauvegarde	Montreal
Maniwaki Cultural Centre	Maniwaki
McCord Museum	Montreal
Montreal Museum of Fine Arts	Montreal
Musée d'Art Contemporain	Montreal
Musée d'Art de Joliette	Joliette
Musée d'Art Primitif de Montréal	Montreal
Musée de L'Artiste	Chicoutimi
Musée du College Bourget	Rigaud
Musée du College Loyola	Sherbrooke
Musée de Québec	Quebec
Saidye Bronfman Centre of Y.M. and Y.W.H.A. and H.H.S. of Montreal	Montreal
Sir George Williams University Art Gallery	Montreal
Stewart Hall Cultural Centre	Pointe Claire

Saskatchewan

Imhoff Art Gallery	Lloydminster
Marquis Hall Art Gallery, University of Saskatchewan	Saskatoon
Mendel Art Gallery and Conservatory	Saskatoon
Moose Jaw Art Museum	Moose Jaw
Norman MacKenzie Art Gallery	Regina
Nutana Collegiate Library and Art Gallery	Saskatoon
Regina Public Library Art Gallery	Regina

NATURAL HISTORY AND HISTORICAL MUSEUMS
Alberta

Banff National Park Natural
   History Museum
Banff Ave.
P.O. Box 900
Banff
Tel. 403-762-2040

Barrhead & District Centennial
   Museum
P.O. Box 910
Barrhead
Tel. 403-674-2160

Glenbow Foundation-Alberta
   Government Museum
7th Ave. and 5th St. S.W.
Calgary
Tel. 403-245-4741

Glenbow Foundation Historical
   Library and Archives
Memorial Park
12th Ave. and 2nd St. S.W.
Calgary
Tel. 403-245-4741

Provincial Museum and Archives
   of Alberta
12845 120th Ave.
Edmonton
Tel. 403-482-5451

British Columbia

Oscar's Wildlife Museum
P.O. Box 211
McBride
Tel. 604-569-2474

City of Vancouver Museums Department

Centennial Museum
1100 Chestnut St. (3)
Vancouver
Tel. 604-736-4431

British Columbia Forest Service Department
Department of Lands, Forests, and Water Resources
Parliament Bldgs.
Victoria
Tel. 604-382-2611

British Columbia Museums Complex
Provincial Museum
Belleville St.
Victoria
Tel. 604-382-6111, ext. 2512

Manitoba

B. J. Hales Museum of Natural History
Brandon University
270   18th St.
Brandon
Tel. 204-727-5401

The Manitoba Museum of Man and Nature
Rupert and Main
Winnipeg
Tel. 204-942-1445   (Human History or
Natural History Division)

Natural History Museum
Department of Zoology
Winnipeg
Tel. 204-474-9245

New Brunswick

Miramichi Natural History
    Museum
149 Wellington St.
Chatham
Tel. 506-773-4213

Grand Manan Museum
Grand Harbour
Grand Manan Island

Sunbury Shores Arts and Nature
    Centre, Inc.
129 Water St.
P.O. Box 100
St. Andrew's
Tel. 506-529-3386

The New Brunswick Museum
Natural Science Department
Human (Canadian) History Department
277 Douglas Ave.
St. John
Tel. 506-693-1196

Newfoundland

Newfoundland Museum
Duckworth St.
St. John's
Tel. 709-726-9733

Northwest and Yukon Territories

McBride (Centennial) Museum
P.O. Box 73
Whitehorse, Northwest Territories

Museum of the North
P.O. Box 335
Yellowknife, Northwest Territories

Nova Scotia

Centennial Centre
City Hall
Amherst
Tel. 902-667-3352

Nova Scotia Provincial Museums
Historical Museum
The Citadel
Halifax
Tel. 902-423-7564

The Ovens Natural Park and Museums
Rose Bay

Ontario

United Empire Loyalist Museum
Adolphustown Park
R.R. 1 Belleville
Adolphustown
Tel. 613-962-4393

Algonquin Provincial Park Museum
Mail Address: Department of Lands and
    Forests Whitney
Tel. 705-633-5613

Quetico Park Museum
French Lake
Mail Address: Department of Lands
    and Forests Atikokan

Black Creek Pioneer Village
Jane St. and Steeles Ave.
Black Creek Village
Tel. 416-633-9901

Presqu'ile Provincial Park Museum
Mail Address: R.R. 5, Brighton
Tel. 613-475-2204

Bancroft Historical Museum
Station St., P.O. Box 163
Bancroft

Bowmanville Museum
37 Silver St.
Bowmanville
Tel. 416-623-3427

Brant Historical Museum
57 Charlotte St.
Brantford
Tel. 519-759-2483

Chatham-Kent Museum
59 William St. N.
Chatham
Tel. 519-352-8540

Gananoque Historical Society Museum
King St., P.O. Box 1390
Gananoque
Tel. 613-382-4663

Muskoka (Huntsville) Museum
Brunel Rd., P.O. Box 936
Huntsville
Tel. 705-789-2788

Kapuskasing and District Memorial
    Museum
11 Mundy St.
Kapuskasing

Museum of Northern History
24 Duncan Ave. N., P.O. Box 966
Kirkland Lake

London Public Library Board Museums Complex
Historical Museum
325 Queen's Ave.
London
Tel. 519-432-7166

Western Manitoulin Historical Museum
Old Gaol
Dawson St.
Gore Bay

Huronia Museum
Little Lake Park
Midland

Rondeau Provincial Park Museum
Mail Address: R.R. 1, Morpeth
Tel. 519-674-5788

The Lundy's Lane Historical
    Museum
1902 Drummond Rd.
Niagara Falls
Mail Address: 1146 Willmott St.
Tel. 416-358-5082

Niagara Historical Society
    Museum
43 Castlereagh St., P.O. Box 208
Niagara-on-the-Lake
Tel. 416-468-3912

Bytown Museum
Canal Locks Rideau Canal
Ottawa
Mail Address: 27 Java St. (3)
Tel. 613-234-4570

National Museum of Man
Victoria Memorial Bldg.
McLeod and Metcalfe Sts.
Ottawa
Tel. 613-992-0483

National Museum of Natural Sciences
Victoria Memorial Bldg.
McLeod and Metcalfe Sts.
Ottawa
Tel. 613-992-0483

County of Grey, Owen Sound Museum
975   6th St. E.
Owen Sound

Champlain Trail Museum
Highway 17, P.O. Box 355
Pembroke
Tel. 613-732-8417

St. Catharine's Historical Museum
343 Merrit St.
St. Catharine's
Tel. 416-227-2962

Bruce County Museum
Southampton
Tel. 519-797-3644

Thunder Bay Historical Society Museum
216 S. Brodie St.
Thunder Bay
Tel. 807-622-6446

Wellington Community Historical Museum
411 Main St., P.O. Box 555
Wellington

Oxford Museum
City Hall Square
Woodstock
Tel. 519-537-8411

Toronto Historical Board
Stanley Barracks, Exhibition Park (2B)
Toronto
Tel. 416-531-4628

Upper Canada Village
Crysler Farm Battlefield Park
P.O. Box 550
Morrisburg
Tel. 613-543-2911

Prince Edward Island

Public Archives of Prince Edward Island
Confederation Centre Library
P.O. Box 1000
Charlottetown

Quebec

Museé Laurier Laurier Museum
16, Ave. Laurier
Arthabaska

Museé Historique   Historical Museum
Case Postale 118
Bonaventure
Tel. 418-534-2930

Carillon Historical Museum
   Musee Historique de Carillon
Carillon
Tel. 514-537-3861

Compton County Historical Museum
   Museé Historique du Comte de Compton
Mail Address: P.O. Box 235,
Sawyerville

Musee Historique de l'Outaouois
Hull

Brome County Historical Society Museum
Museé de la Societe Historique du Comte   de Brome
Knowlton

Museé de la Societe Historique
   Abitibienne Abitlbi Historical
   Society Museum
Fort Iberville
Chalet du Lac

Museé Historique Charles LeMoyne
   Charles LeMoyne Historical Museum
4 est, rue St. Charles
Longueuil
Tel. 514-674-6226

Chateau de Ramezay
290 Notre Dame St. E.
Montreal
Tel. 514-861-3708

Museé Louis Hemon-Maria Chapdelaine
   Louis Hemon-Maria Chapdelaine Museum
Peribonka, Cte. Lac St. Jean
Tel. 418-374-2181

Maison Maillou Maillou House
17, rue St. Louis
Case Postale 128
Quebec 4
Tel. 418-522-7078

Museé du Seminaire de Quebec Quebec Seminary Museum
6, rue de l'Université
Case Postale 460
Quebec 4
Tel. 418-529-9931, poste 40

La Vieille Maison des Jesuites
    Jesuits Old House
2320, Chemin des Foulons
Sillery (6)
Quebec
Tel. 418-683-4640

Museé du College Bourget
    Bourget College Museum
College Bourget
Rigaud
Tel. 514-238-5311

Société D'Histoire et de Genealogie de
    Riviére-du-Loup Historical and
    Genealogical Society of Riviére-du-Loup
Hotel-de-Ville, Case postale 313
Riviére-du-Loup
    Tel. 418-862-2691 or 862-4727

Museé Historique et Galereé D'Art
    Historical Museum and Art Gallery
10,018 Ave. Royale
Basilique Ste.-Anne
Ste.-Anne-de-Beaupré
Tel. 418-263-3781

Maison Laurier Laurier House
Avenue Laurier
St.-Lin

Cornell Mill Museum
    Museé Cornell Mill
Stanbridge East

Maison Chauvin Chauvin House
Postal Address: Canada Steamship
    Lines, Case Postale 100
Montreal 3
Tel. 418-235-4401

Museé D'Archeologie Prehistorique
    Museum of Prehistorical Archeology
1260, rue Royale
Case Postale 500
Trois-Riviéres
Tel. 819-378-2701

Museé Historique de Vaudreuil
    Vaudreuil Historical Museum
31, rue Du Bois Vert
Caste Postale 121
Dorion-Vaudreuil
Tel. 514-234-2092

Saskatchewan

Barr Colony Museum
5011 49th Ave.
Lloydminster
Tel. 306-875-2241

Lund Wildlife Exhibit
River Park
Mail Address: 839 4th St. E.
Prince Albert

Royal Canadian Mounted Police
  Museum
Depot Division
Regina
Tel. 306-569-5481

Saskatchewan Museum of Natural History
Wascana Park
Regina
Tel. 306-527-6608

Western Development Museum
1839 11th St. W.
Saskatoon
Tel. 306-382-0755

Swift Current Museum (Thoreson Memorial)
2nd Ave. N.E.
Swift Current
Tel. 306-773-4301

Historical Chronology of Canada

ca. 1000 A.D.   Leif Ericson believed to have discovered Newfoundland, Lab-
                rador, and Nova Scotia.

1497   John Cabot reached Canada; Britain claimed Newfoundland
                and Nova Scotia.

1534-41   Jacques Cartier explored the Gulf of St. Lawrence; his French
                colony failed.

1576-78   Martin Frobisher sought the Northwest Passage.

1583   Humphrey Gilbert claimed Newfoundland for Britain.

1587   John Davis sought the Northwest Passage.

1605   Samuel de Champlain founded Port-Royal, Nova Scotia—the
                first permanent white settlement in Canada.

1608   City of Quebec founded by Champlain; several Indian tribes
                aided in fur trade.

1610-11	Henry Hudson discovered and explored Hudson Bay while commissioned by Britain to find the Northwest Passage.
1610	First English settlement on Newfoundland.
1633	Champlain appointed first French governor of New France (Canada).
1634-35	Nicolet explored the Great Lakes.
1642	Montreal founded by Sieur de Maisonneuve.
1648-60	Iroquois frequently harrassed the French and their Indian allies; massacred Huron Indians and Jesuit missionaries; threatened New France with extinction.
1666	First census in New France (3,215 population).
1670	Hudson's Bay Company headed by Prince Rupert of England was established.
1673-80	Joliet, Marquette, and LaSalle explored the Great Lakes.
1689-1763	French and Indian Wars—direct armed conflict between French and British colonists for control of the continent.
1713	Treaty of Utrecht—France ceded Nova Scotia to Britain and gave up claim to Newfoundland and the Hudson Bay Territory.
1731-44	La Verendrye explored west to Saskatchewan River; discovered Lake Winnipeg in 1733.
1734	First road opened from Quebec to Montreal.
1743	Son of La Verendrye discovered the Rocky Mountains.
1749-55	Nova Scotia colonized by British; Acadian French expelled; Halifax founded in 1749.
1752-55	First newspaper in Canada (*Halifax Gazette*, 1752); first public gardens in Canada (Halifax, 1753); first post office in Canada (Halifax, 1755).
1759	British took Quebec; Wolfe (Br.) and Montcalm (Fr.) died in battle.
1760	British took Montreal.
1763	Treaty of Paris—France ceded its land east of Mississippi River to Britain.
1765	First book printed in Canada (published in French); first agricultural fair (Windsor, Nova Scotia).
1770-72	Samuel Hearne explored the Northwest Territories.
1774	Britain passed Quebec Act, expanding Quebec boundaries, confirming freedom of religion for Catholics, establishing a combined French-British rule.

1775-83	The American Revolution caused the United Empire Loyalists to flee to Canadian soil; foundation of Ontario and New Brunswick; American attacks on Quebec failed.
1776-93	James Cook and George Vancouver explored the Pacific Northwest coast and opened it to trade; Alexander Mackenzie completed his cross-country expedition.
1783-87	North West Company is formed by Montreal merchants, competing with the Hudson's Bay Company.
1789	First English University in Canada (King's, Windsor, Nova Scotia).
1791	Canada divided into upper and lower provinces, each with elected assemblies.
1792	First legislative assemblies: Upper Canada at Niagara-on-the-Lake; Lower Canada at Quebec City.
1793	Toronto (York) was founded; Alexander Mackenzie reached the Pacific Ocean.
1800	New Brunswick College founded.
1809	First Canadian-built steamer ran from Montreal to Quebec City.
1812	Scottish settlers arrived on the Red River; first circulating library in Canada (Truro, Nova Scotia).
1812-14	War of 1812-between United States and Britain; treaty established boundary settlements; 49th parallel fixed as boundary between United States and Canada from Lake-of-the-Woods to the Rockies (1817).
1821	Hudson Bay Company and North West Company merged.
1825-32	Opening of canals: Lachine Canal (1825); Welland Canal (1829); Rideau Canal (1832).
1827-40	First stationary steam engine in Canada (Albion Mines, Nova Scotia, 1827); first railway in Canada opened from Laprairie to St. John's, Quebec (1836); first paper produced from wood in Canada (Upper Sackville, Nova Scotia, 1839); first mail steamer crossed Atlantic (Liverpool to Halifax, 1840).
1837-38	Political rebellions in Upper and Lower Canada.
1840	Upper and Lower Canada united; capital at Kingston for four years, then moved to Montreal.
1842-46	Treaties established 49th parallel as boundary from Rockies to Pacific Ocean and clarified New Brunswick-Maine boundary.
1847	Lord Elgin became governor of Canada.
1857	Ottawa selected as capital of Canada.

1858	Gold rush in British Columbia (Fraser River).
1864	Agreement for Confederation of British North America reached at conferences at Charlottetown and Quebec.
1867	British North America Act-Dominion of Canada confederated with Ontario, Quebec, Nova Scotia, and New Brunswick as provinces.
1869	Hudson's Bay Company territories in the northwest transferred to Canadian confederation.
1869-85	Louis Riel led two uprisings of Red River settlers and Indians against inclusion in the Dominion; Riel captured and executed for treason.
1870-71	Manitoba became a province of the Dominion in 1870; British Columbia became a province in 1871; Winnipege and Victoria became the capitals.
1871	First census of the Dominion of Canada (3,689,257) population).
1873	North West Mounted Police established; Prince Edward Island became a province.
1881-85	Canadian Pacific Railway built from coast to coast.
1896	Gold rush in the Yukon district (Klondike).
1898	Yukon established as a separate territory.
1901	First trans-Atlantic wireless message received at St. John's, Newfoundland, from England (by Marconi).
1903	Canadian-Alaskan boundary established.
1905	Alberta and Saskatchewan became provinces.
1907	First recorded airplane flight in Canada.
1914-18	Canadian participation in World War I; Conscription Bill developed further antagonism between English and French Canadians.
1916	Fire destroyed Parliament Buildings in Ottawa.
1919-20	Treaty of Versailles signed by Canada; joined League of Nations.
1931	Statute of Westminster—established legal independence and sovereignty of Canadian parliament within Canada.
1934	Newfoundland because of economic depression ceased its self-governing status and reverted to colonial status.
1939-45	Canadian participation in World War II.
1947	Joined the security council of the United Nations.
1949	Joined the North Atlantic Treaty Organization; Newfoundland became the 10th province.

1950	Entered the Korean War.
1952	Queen Elizabeth II first sovereign proclaimed Queen of Canada.
1953-59	Began construction of St. Lawrence Seaway; United States joined in 1954; opened in 1959.
1965	Adopted new flag.
1967	Celebrated Centennial Year; exposition held in Montreal, "Man and His World."
1973	Census: 22,095,000.

CAMPING ASSOCIATIONS

National Office

Canadian Camping Assn.
Suite 203, 102 Eglinton Ave. E.
Toronto 315, Ontario

Alberta Camping Assn.
2402 27th St. S.W.
Calgary 4, Alberta

British Columbia Camping Assn.
1309 McLean Dr.
Vancouver 6, British Columbia

Manitoba Camping Ass'n.
672 Niagara St.
Winnipeg, Manitoba

New Brunswick Camping Ass'n.
Moncton Y.M.C.A.
Moncton, New Brunswick

Newfoundland & Labrador Camping Ass'n.
P.O. Box 248
St. John's, Newfoundland

Nova Scotia Camping Ass'n.
P.O. Box 1622
Halifax, Nova Scotia

Ontario Camping Ass'n.
Suite 203, 102 Eglinton Ave. E.
Toronto 315, Ontario

Quebec Camping Ass'n.
2233 Belgrave Ave.
Montreal 261, Quebec

Saskatchewan Camping Ass'n.
P.O. Box 823
Regina, Saskatchewan

SELECTED SPORTING ORGANIZATIONS

The Alpine Club of Canada
2974 W. 28th Ave.
Vancouver 8, British Columbia

British Columbia Kayak and Canoe Club
Eric Kozak, Representative
P.O. Box 2237
Vancouver 3, British Columbia

British Columbia Mountaineering Club
P.O. Box 2674
Vancouver, British Columbia

Bruce Trail Ass'n.
Ray Lowes, Representative
33 Hardale Crescent
Hamilton, Ontario

Canadian Wheelmen's Ass'n.
Paul Suave Center
4000 Beaubien St. F.
Montreal, Quebec

Canadian Youth Hostels Ass'ns.
455 12th St., N.W.
Calgary, Alberta

1407 W. Broadway
Vancouver 9, British Columbia

6405 Quinpool Rd.
Halifax, Nova Scotia

86 Scollard St.
Toronto 185, Ontario

1324 Sherbrook St.
Montreal 109, Quebec

Island Mountain Ramblers
Ron Facer, Representative
440 Chestnut St.
Nanaimo, British Columbia

Montreal Voyageurs
Rene Bureaud, Representative
360 Barberry Pl.
Dollard des Ormeaux
Montreal 960, Quebec

National Campers and Hikers Ass'n.
Bill Robb, Representative
8 Thorpe Rd.
Weston, Ontario

Niagara Escarpment Trail Council
P.O. Box 1
St. Catharine's, Ontario

Skyline Trail Hikers of the Canadian Rockies
622 Madison Ave. S.W.
Calgary, Alberta

Toronto Hiking and Conservation Club
Box 121, Station F
Toronto 5, Ontario

Trail Hikers of the Canadian Rockies
622 Madison Ave. S.W.
Calgary, Alberta

Trail Riders of the Canadian Rockies
P.O. Box 6742, Station D
Calgary 2, Alberta

Walker Mineralogy Club of Toronto
Bill Ince, Representative
12 Redwing Pl.
Don Mills, Ontario

CANADIAN NATURE FEDERATION AFFILIATES

**Canadian Nature Federation
46 Elgin St.
Ottawa, Ontario K1P 5K6
Tel. 613-233-3486**

British Columbia

Central Okanagan Naturalists Club
Mrs. E.M. Palmer, Secy.
925 Bernard Ave.
Kelowna

North Okanagan Naturalists Club
Miss K. Bartholomew, Sec.-Treas.
Box 473
Vernon

Okanagan Similkameen Parks Society
Miss Catherine R. Madsen, Secy.
Box 787
Summerland

Pinegrove Garden Club
Miss L. Owen, Secy.
Mt. Lehman Rd., R.R. 1
Mt. Lehman

Vancouver Natural History Society
Mrs. H. Pinder-Moss, Corr. Secy.
P.O. Box 3021
Vancouver

Victoria Natural History Society
Mrs. Katherine Sherman, Pres.
2168 Guernsey St.
Victoria

Alberta

Calgary Field Naturalists Society
Secretary, P.O. Box 981
Calgary

Edmonton Bird Club
Miss M. J. Wade, Secy.
6519 94th St.
Edmonton

Lethbridge Natural History Society
Mrs. Frances Schultz, Pres.
1054 Henderson Lake Bldg.
Lethbridge

Saskatchewan

Saskatchewan Natural History Society
Miss Margaret Belcher, Secy.
2601 Winnipeg St.
Regina

Ontario

Barrie Horticultural Society
Mrs. J. H. Gable, Secy.
23 Wellington St.
W. Barrie

Canadian Beekeepers' Council
Mr. R. H. Taylor, Exec. Secy.
1568 Carling Ave.
Ottawa 3

Federation of Ontario Naturalists
Mr. Gerald McKeating, Exec. Dir.
1262 Don Mills Rd.
Don Mills

Hamilton Naturalists Club
Mr. W. A. T. Gilmour, Secy.-Treas.
Main Post Office, Box 384
Hamilton

Huntsville Nature Club
Mrs. Phil Bailey, Secy.-Treas.
Box 103
Huntsville

Kingston Field Naturalists
The Secretary
Box 831
Kingston

North Grey Region Conservation Authority
Mr. M. D. Kirk, Field Officer
715 3rd Ave. E.
Owen Sound

Sauble Valley Conservation Authority
Mr. M. D. Kirk, Field Officer
715 3rd Ave. E.
Owen Sound

Rideau Kiwanis Club of Ottawa
Conservation Committee, Mr. F. S. Gray
671 Pleasant Park Rd.
Ottawa 8

South Peel Naturalists' Club
The Secretary, P.O. Box 91
Port Credit

Women's Division, Toronto Humane Society
The Secretary
11 Wollesley St. W.
Toronto 5

Willow Beach Field Naturalists Club
Mrs. Henry Marsh, Pres.
R.R. 3
Cobourg

Quebec

Barbara Richardson Wildlife Foundation
Mrs. Therese D'Amour
18 Hillside Ave.
Ste. Agathe des Monts

Canadian Society for the Prevention of Cruelty to Animals
Mr. L. P. Poirier, Exec. Dir. Administration
5215 Jean Talon West
Montreal 308

Provancher Society of Natural History of Canada
Mr. V. E. Lyon, Exec. Dir.
1160 Bourlamaque Ave.
Quebec 6

Province of Quebec Society for the Protection of Birds
Mrs. E. Brosseau, Secy.
Apt. 208, 500 Francois Park
Montreal 201

Manitoba

Natural History Society of Manitoba
c/o Manitoba Museum of Man and Nature
147 James St.
Winnipeg

New Brunswick

Gerrish House Society
Mr. Elmer Wilcox, Secy.
Seal Cove Grand Manan

Prince Edward Island

Prince Edward Island Natural History Society
Miss Margaret Mallett, Secy.
53 Fitzroy St.
Charlottetown·

Nova Scotia

Nova Scotia Bird Society
Secretary, c/o Nova Scotia Museum of Science
Summer St.
Halifax

Newfoundland

The Newfoundland Natural History Society
The Secretary
P.O. Box 1013
St. John's

ETHNIC GROUPS

Selected Ethnic Organizations

Austrian

Austrian Club, Edelweiss Inc.
207 Beverley St.
Toronto, Ontario

Australian

International Australia-New Zealand Ass'n.
3 W. 5th Ave.
Vancouver 1,
British Columbia

Byelorussian
Byelorussian Alliance in Canada
524 St. Clarens Ave.
Toronto 4, Ontario

Byelorussian National Ass'n. in Canada
c/o Joe Babrowski
55 Ellington Dr.
Scarborough, Ontario

"Pahonia" Byelorussian Organization
Publishers' and Arts Club
524 St. Clarens Ave.
Toronto 4, Ontario

Chinese *
Chinese Benevolent Ass'n.
108 Pender St. E.
Vancouver, British Columbia

Chinese National League
10 Hagerman St.
Toronto 2, Ontario

Chinese Nationalist Party
1816 Osler St.
Regina, Saskatchewan

Croatian
Croatian Peasant Society
c/o Mr. Steve Bradica
16 Martimus St.
Hamilton, Ontario

Czechoslovakian
Czechoslovak National Ass'n. of Canada
740 Spadina Ave.
Toronto, Ontario

Estonian
Estonian Federation in Canada
958 Broadview Ave.
Toronto 6, Ontario

French
Ass'n. France-Canada
3425 St. Denis
Montreal 18, Quebec
    and
P.O. Box 195, Terminal "A"
Toronto, Ontario

* Key national organizations

Alliance Francaise de Toronto (L'Alliance Francaise)
6 St. Thomas
Toronto, Ontario
Tel. 922-1389

Finnish

Central Organization of Loyal Finns in Canada, Inc.
c/o Aulis Kangas
468 Antwerp St:, P.O. Box 171
Sudbury, Ontario

Finnish Society of Toronto
957 Broadview Ave.
Toronto, Ontario

German *

Trans-Canada Alliance of German Canadians
Henry Weiseach, Pres.
8 Bobolink Rd.
Hamilton 51, Ontario
Tel. 388-3523

Alliance of Danube-Swabians in Canada
214 Main St.
Toronto, Ontario

Central Organization of Sudeten-German Clubs
     in North America
179 Durant Ave.
Toronto 6, Ontario

German Benevolent Society (1835) Montreal
3579 Hutchison
Montreal, Quebec

Greek

Greek American Progressive Ass'n. (GAPA)
Officer i/c Group A
Hellenic Community
8 Sherbrooke St. W.
Montreal, Quebec

Officer i/c Group B
Hellenic Community
115 Bond St.
Toronto, Ontario

Canadian Hungarian Federation
519 Dundas St. W.
Toronto 2B, Ontario

Hungarian Helicon Society
Adelaide, P.O. Box 96
Toronto, Ontario

Icelandic
Icelandic National League
Winnipeg, Manitoba

Irish
Irish-Canadian Social and Athletic Club
665 St. Clair Ave. W.
Toronto, Ontario

Italian *
Order Sons of Italy in Canada
505 Jean Talon St.
Montreal, Quebec

Order Sons of Italy
Petrona Lodge
150 Culford St., Apt. 217
Toronto, Ontario

Japanese *
National Japanese Canadian Citizens' Ass'n.
415 Spadina Ave.
Toronto 2B, Ontario

Jewish *
Canadian Jewish Congress
493 Sherbrooke St. W.
Montreal, Quebec

Canadian Young Judaea, National Office
188 Marlee Ave.
Toronto 19, Ontario

Jewish Ass'n. of Hungarian Descent
12 Hollaman Rd.
Toronto 19, Ontario

Latvian
Latvian National Federation in Canada
491 College St.
Toronto, Ontario

Lebanese
Canadian Lebanon Ass'n.
Westmorland Rd. E.
St. John, New Brunswick

Lithuanian
Lithuanian Canadian Community
1129 Dundas St. W.
Toronto, Ontario

New Zealand
International Australia-New Zealand Ass'n.
3 W. 5th Ave.
Vancouver 1, British Columbia

North American Indian *
National Indian Council of Canada
Calgary, Alberta

Department of Indian and Northern Affairs
Ottawa, Ontario

Norwegian
Sons of Norway
Lodge North Star
Nahaimo, British Columbia

Polish *
Canadian Polish Congress
783 College St.
Toronto, Ontario

Polish National Union of Canada
1087 Queen St. W.
Toronto 3, Ontario

Polish Combatants Ass'n. in Canada, Inc.
206 Beverley St.
Toronto 2B, Ontario

Portuguese
Portuguese Ass'n. of Canada
3609 St. Lawrence Blvd.
Montreal 18, Quebec

Roumanian
Union & League of Roumanian Societies of America
2585 Seminole St.
Windsor, Ontario

Russian
Russian Cultural Educational Society
72 Ossington Ave.
Toronto 3, Ontario

Canada U.S.S.R. Ass'n.
84 Avenue Rd.
Toronto 5, Ontario

Serbian
Serbian League of Canada
175 Barons Ave. N.
Hamilton, Ontario

Serbian National Shield
1297 Drouillard Rd.
Windsor, Ontario

Slovak
Canadian Slovak League Bldg. Ltd.
P.O. Box 53, Station "N"
7220 Hutchison St.
Montreal, Quebec

Slovene
Slovenian National Federation in Canada
646 Euclid Ave.
Toronto, Ontario

Spanish
Ass'n. Espagnole, Inc.
485 Sherbrooke St. W.
Montreal 2, Quebec

Swedish
The Executive of the Vasa Order of America
c/o Lodge Strindberg No. 259
Scandinavian Centre
360 Young St.
Winnipeg, Manitoba

Syrian
Canadian Syrian Ass'n.
834 St. Matthews
Winnipeg 10, Manitoba

Ukrainian *
Ukrainian Canadian Committee
456 Main St.
Winnipeg, Manitoba

Ass'n. of United Ukrainian Canadians, National Office
42 Roncesvalles Ave.
Toronto 3, Ontario

Ukrainian National Ass'n.
297 College St.
Toronto 2B, Ontario

REGIONAL FOODS

Throughout the world, to know a country is to know its foods. This is no less true in Canada, where nationalities the world over are represented. Climate, soil, geography, as well as cultures, speak out in the foods of the region. Make a study of regional and provincial food specialties and all it your—food for thought!

Festivals, fairs, and farm vacations offer tourists opportunities for tasting home-prepared provincial specialties. See the Farm Vacations section in this appendix for some addresses of farm families equipped to house and feed tourists. Many have special facilities and rates for camping tourists, and offer child-care service as well. Similar accommodations may be obtained at many guest ranches throughout Canada, but especially in Alberta, where it is possible to include horseback riding among the advantages of experiencing farm vacations and guest ranches.

ALBERTA: Beef, above all else, is the province's specialty: Most notable are the rare steak, the standing rib roast, the ranch stew (vegetables and beef stewed in a broth). Lesser known but worth experiencing if the opportunity arises are buffalo, venison, and Arctic char. Perhaps, if you are lucky, you will even find their favored honey rhubarb pie on the menu, their wild rose-hip catsup, and watermelon pickles in the store.

BRITISH COLUMBIA: The geography has made seafood, particularly salmon, fruits, and wines the provincial specialties. Although the Okanagan Valley, in the southeast corner of the province, is the primary fruit source, you will find fruit pies and dumplings are popular everywhere. Along the coast, accompanying salmon on the menu, are King and Dungeness crab, prawns, oysters, black cod, sole, and halibut. Crab Louie salad is a favorite, although seafood casseroles and fish and chips are equally popular—and less expensive. Victoria is British: Tea and scones and delectable candies will delight your sweet tooth.

Aside from sampling ethnic foods at the many ethnic restaurants, primarily in Vancouver, a unique eating experience might be had at the Portuguese Festival in New Westminster, late in June. Two salmon barbecues and derbies might also win your favor; one is on Saturna Island in early July and the other is held at Parksville in mid-August.

MANITOBA: With Manitoba's high percentage of recent, and not so recent, immigrants, the province has become best known for its ethnic foods. Festivals offer tourists a fine opportunity for sampling home-prepared foods. Check the festival list for Manitoba in the appendix. A partial listing of festivals held during July and August includes: Sunflower Festival in Altona; Indian Pow-Wow in Griswold; National Ukrainian Festival in Dauphin; National Icelandic Festival in Gimli; Mennonite Pioneer Days in Steinback; and Corn and Apple Festival in Morden. The most concentrated selection of ethnic foods, however, is found in mid-August at Winnipeg's Folkorama, where over 50 ethnic groups participate.

Wild rice of the region has a long history of use by the Indians (particularly the Ojibways of eastern Manitoba) and the explorers, for whom it served not only as a mainstay in the diet but also as a trading commodity. Although the rice harvesting season lasts only two or three weeks from late August to early September, because of its durability the rice is seen on menus throughout the year. If interested in preparing it in the campground, a wild rice recipe is included for your convenience in the chapter, Coping with Camp Cooking.

You may also wish to sample other locally harvested or produced foods: honey, blueberries (often found in muffins), game, caviar (from lake sturgeon), sunflower seeds, and the now rather famous Winnipeg goldeye (half-cooked, half-smoked fish).

NEW BRUNSWICK: The sea is responsible for most of this province's specialties: lobster, salmon, cod, clams, oysters, mackerel, haddock, herring. Try them all! Whatever you do, don't miss an opportunity to boil your own freshly caught lobster (directions are found in the chapter on cooking), and to dig your own clams, then steam or chowder them. It is these indigenous activities that linger long, that color your memories of the trip.

Dried Seaweed, called *dulse*, is worth at least one nutritious but nippy nibble. And while gorging on greens, gather a few fiddlehead ferns of the ostrich variety for your next salad or for combining with your cooked vegetable of the day, seasoned with butter or cream sauce. Perhaps you will grow so fond of fiddleheads that you will purchase the canned variety for the days when spring has gone, when the fern is no longer tender. Blueberries and cranberries, too, crop up occasionally.

NEWFOUNDLAND AND LABRADOR: Although salmon, tuna, halibut, flounder, crab, and shrimp are popular catches from the sea, it is cod that is the basic food in the diet—fried cod, dried cod, baked cod, boiled cod. Fish and chips, codfish chowder, and cod au gratin may not offer the tourist a new eating experience but perhaps cod roe or cod tongue will. Sliced, buttered, and fried, cod tongue is said to have a taste resembling scallops. Flipper pie, too, sounds intriguing made from salt pork, vegetables, and—flippers of young seals. Moose soup, salmon smoked over blackberry twigs, and cod with brewis are other dishes native to the province. Brewis, we are told, is a hardtack that has been softened in water and brought to the boiling point, then seasoned with salt pork drippings. Salt beef, fish, bannock, and canned vegetables dominate the winter diet, while summer berries—squash berries, partridge berries, cloudberries, blueberries—appear in desserts, jellies, and jams.

The Folkfestival held in St. John's in late August is the only festival we can recommend that may provide the tourist with homecooking.

NORTHWEST TERRITORIES: Indian and Eskimo foods predominate with game (buffalo, caribou, bear, moose, seal, duck, grouse, Arctic ptarmigan) and fish (Arctic char, lake trout, Arctic grayling) providing the basis of the diet. It is possible to buy seal meatballs and char canned in the Northwest Territories.

NOVA SCOTIA: When we think of Nova Scotia, we think of lobster and learning to eat *everything*, except the shell, as the Acadians do. You will not find lobster cheaper or tastier anywhere. Other seafoods to enjoy after your fill of lobster are scallops, salmon, shrimp, halibut, haddock, and cod—sauteed, fried, baked, or in chowder. Salted herring and onion (soaked in a vinegar and spice brine for a week) is a zesty appetizer called *Solomon Grundy*—a must for anyone with Scandinavian ancestry. Cranberries and apples, too, are harvested in quantity and frequently find their way into the same stewing pot.

Most festivals—and there are many throughout the summer—include barbecues or home-cooked suppers; Friday night church dinners may still provide summer tourists a sampling of local foods. Pleasant eating experiences can be had at some of the July festivals (see the appendix for a more complete list): Gathering of the Clan in Pugwash; Chowder Carnival in Milford; Feast of SolomonGrundyat Blue Rocks; and Strawberry Festivals at Concession, Maplewood, Masstown, and Dominion. Antigonish is the site of a seafood supper as part of the Highland Activities, and Parrsboro has home-cooking for the public during most of Old Home Week, both in July.

ONTARIO: Owing to the climate, southern Ontario has a variety of vegetables and fruits: apples, peaches, pears, cherries, to name just four. Cheeses (particularly cheddar), honey, and maple syrup—all provincial specialties—frequently flavor fruit and vegetables dishes resulting in countless culinary combinations. Since much of Canada's wine originates from Ontario's Niagara peninsula, you may wish to sample a liter—just to taste.

If sampling ethnic foods, too, is your pleasure, then read carefully the festival list for Ontario in the appendix. You will note the Kitchener-Waterloo region is particularly interesting, for the Mennonites and Amish offer their kitchen and garden products at the Farmer's Market every Wednesday and Saturday, June through November. Although the market is becoming quite commercial, it is worth experiencing anyway. Throughout the year patrons of the German restaurants in Kitchener and Waterloo stuff themselves on *sauerbraten* and *schweineschnitzel*, "maintaining" fitness for the annual *Oktoberfest*. Elmira has a maple syrup festival in early April where not only maple syrup specialties are available, but German ones as well.

Twice a year St. Catharine's highlights its ethnic heritage: late in May, gourmet foods are part of the Folk Arts Festival and late in September, featured in the Niagara Festival are wine and cheese parties. The Mennonites of New Hamburg, in late May, have an auction relief sale where a pancake-sausage breakfast and a smorgasbord dinner are prepared along with other food and craft items. And about the same time of year, but in Cornwall, French-Canadian food is featured at the Festival de la Semaine Francaise. Toronto (also in late May) sponsors the Metro Toronto Caravan, where the city's many cultural groups—and their foods—may be discovered. Come August, September, and October there are countless festivals for ol' time fun and eatin', featuring corn and apples and beans in Bancroft, Zurich, Meaford, Kleinburg, Ingersoll, London, Jordon.

North of Lake Erie are a concentration of Scots (described in John Kenneth Galbraith's *The Scotch*, where barley broth, shortcake, bannock, and haggis are still enjoyed.

Trout, perch, smelt, and other fresh water fish from Ontario's many lake round out the provincial specialties.

PRINCE EDWARD ISLAND: If you enjoy seafood, you'll enjoy Prince Edward Island. Lobster, oyster, clam, crab are harvested from the surrounding waters, prepared in every manner imaginable and served hot and cold. Tuna—800, 1,000 lb. and over—are caught along with cod, halibut, hake, mackerel, and herring. Trout, salmon, and perch are fished from inland streams. Locally grown fruits and vegetables round out the diet, with potato pancakes (pork, bacon, onion, potato, and egg—mixed and fried) remaining a favorite.

Tourists to "Spud Island"—a name fondly given the province by fellow Canadians—may find home-cooking at the Acadian Festival in Egmont Bay, late in August.

QUEBEC: Fresh produce from local farms, combined with the French flair in food preparation, and the tourist is destined to delight while eating in Quebec. Soups—particularly the favored cabbage, pea monjettes, onion, or fish varieties—remain an integral part of each main meal. Although the cuisine is directly inspired by dishes from the old provinces of western France, it is considered a less refined, a more hearty fare—because of the climate—than food traditionally associated with France. Meats and flour combinations dominate, with the French-Canadians doing wonders with game, eel, and pork—particularly pork pie (tourtiere), pork roast, pig's feet stew, and pork meatballs.

Quebec is second only to France in its cheese production, with its cheddar, ermite, oka, and raffine most widely appreciated. A delightful delicacy without doubt is a cheddar-caribou combination. (That's even fun to say!) Fun, too, no doubt will occur if you linger long with caribou (a mixture of sweet red wine and whiskey), for even the Quebecois declare it liquid dynamite. Locally produced rice beer, champagne, and cider are also favorite liquid refreshments. Some of the favored desserts include a dried raisin and maple syrup combination (tarte a la ferlouche), sugar pie, eggs cooked in boiling maple syrup, and the springtime delicacy of fresh snow with a hot maple sap topping (torquettes).

While traveling through the province—in fact, throughout Canada—you find maple syrup and wines bottled in Quebec. While sampling the variety of wines, sample too the famous maple syrup pie; your sampling could begin in any one of Montreal's 4,000 restaurants.

SASKATCHEWAN: The province, sometimes called the "breadbasket of the world," is best known for its wheat (bread, biscuits, pancakes) and occasionally its berries (pinchberry, boysenberry, Saskatoon), its fish (lake trout, pike, and whitefish) and its small game (geese, duck). Bannock, a quickbread of Scottish origin, is served in the homes of the province and for this reason is included in the In-Camp Cooking section. Although a number of agricultural fairs are held annually, where a few home-prepared foods such as Saskatoon-berry pie are offered for sale, there are few ethnic festivals where one might sample provincial specialties. One ethnic festival worth investigating is held in Yorkton in early June: write the Yorkton Chamber of Commerce for specific information.

YUKON: Eskimos and Indians, fish and game prevail. As you would expect, prices of fresh and canned produce reflect the distance it was transported. King crab from the Gulf of Alaska, boiled and served with melted lemon butter and bannock, is bound to please any cavorting camper.

MANUFACTURERS OF FREEZE-DRIED FOODS

Alpine Recreation
455 Central Park Ave.
Scarsdale, N.Y. 10583

Bernard Food Industries
Box 487, St. James Station
222 S. 24th St.
San Jose, Cal. 95103

Chuck Wagon Foods
Micro Drive
Woburn, Mass. 01801

Dri-Lite Foods
11333 Atlantic Ave.
Lynwood, Cal. 90262

E-Z Food Products
1420 S. Western Ave.
Gardena, Cal. 90247

Freeze-Dri & Dehydrated Foods
Cohasset, Mass. 02025

National Packaged Trail Foods
632 E. 185th St.
Cleveland, Ohio 44119

Oregon Freeze Dry Foods, Inc.
P.O. Box 666
Albany, Ore. 97321

Rich Moor Corp.
Box 2728
Van Nuys, Cal. 91404

Seidel Trail Packets
1245 W. Dickens Ave.
Chicago, Ill. 60014

Stow-A-Way Products
103 Ripley Rd.
Cohasset, Mass. 02025

Trail Chief Foods
Box 60041, Terminal Annex
Los Angeles, Cal. 90060

Trail Meals, J. B. Kisky
1829 N.E. Alberta St.
Portland, Ore. 97211

Trailwise Products,
c/o Ski Hut   1615 University Ave.
Berkeley, Cal. 94703

Catalogs from some sporting equipment dealers—such as Recreational Equipment, Inc., 1525 11th Ave., Seattle, Wash. 98122—list freeze-dried foods from various companies including kind of food, quantity, and price, enabling the consumer to order by mail with ease.

Canadian Events

Traveling, for some, is being led from place to place as a herd, remaining an island unto itself. If you like traveling when it brings you into individual and direct contact with local peoples, in their natural settings, in their natural activities, then you will wish to include folksy gatherings (fairs, flea markets, festivals) in your travels. Conversation develops easily in such informal settings. Provincial and ethnic foods, handicrafts, music are studied with equal ease. Antique shows, sporting events (curling, cricket, golf, regattas, and rodeos are especially popular), Indian Pow-Wows—all reveal a different aspect of life in Canada.

Each provincial tourist bureau offers the most complete listing of events available for each province (see appendix for addresses); the CGTB in Ottawa will send on request a more abbreviated but all-Canada events brochure for the current spring and summer, fall and winter.

Since specific dates of events change from year to year, we have chosen to indicate time of month in this way:

Early	ca.	1-9
Mid	ca.	10-20
Late	ca.	21-31

ALBERTA

January/February

	Edmonton and Calgary	Chinese New Year Celebrations (date varies)

February
Early	Calgary	Ethnic Arts and Handicrafts Exhibition
Early	Vermilion	Winter Carnival
Early	Red Deer	Snow Festival
Mid	Wetaskiwin	North American International Snowmobile Races and Carnival
Mid	Lethbridge	Ethnic Festival and Exhibit during Winter Games
Late	Whitecourt	Winter Carnival
Late	Peace River	Peace Winter Carnival

March
Unknown	Calgary	Music Festival of Ethnic Groups
Mid	Calgary	Rodeo Royal
Mid	Drayton Valley	Winter Ice Carnival
Late	Fort Macleod	Ice Carnival

April
Mid	Calgary	International Food Fair
Mid	Red Deer	Silver Buckle Rodeo
Mid	Lloydminster	Indoor Professional Rodeo
Late	Jasper	Kobasa Kapers

May

Early	Berwyn	Arts and Crafts Display
Mid	*Calgary	International Horse Show
Mid	Stavely	Indoor Rodeo
Mid	Sundre	Annual Downriver Race
Mid	Medicine Hat	Victoria Day Golf Tournament
Mid	Jasper	Jasper Aquathon
Mid	*Taber	Rodeo
Mid	Caroline	Rodeo
Mid	*Hanna	Pioneer Days
Mid	Rycroft	Golf Tournament
Mid	Sundre	Canoe Races (A.M.)
Late	Cardston	Rodeo
Late	Grand Centre	Rodeo
Late	Youngstown (20 miles south of)	Big Stone Rodeo
Late	Sundre	Provincial Downriver Championships
Late	Stony Plain	Giant Steak BBQ
Late	Wainwright	Open Golf Tournament
Late	Rimbey	Rodeo
Late	St. Paul	Silver Dollar Jamboree
Late	*Red Deer	"Arts and You"
Unknown	Ukrainian Heritage Village (35 miles from Edmonton, Highway 16)	Ukrainian Heritage Day
Unknown	Lac Ste. Anne	Indian Days
Early	Vauxhall	Rodeo
Early	Lloydminster	Rock and Gem Club Show
Early	Writing-On-Stone Provincial Park	Rodeo
Early	Calgary	Strathcona Tweedsmuir Downriver Race
Early	Edmonton	Thoroughbred Racing
Early	*Big Valley	River Regatta and Raft Races
Early	Nanton	Annual Open Golf Tournament
Early	Irma	Open Golf Tournament
Early	*Hinton	Big Horn Rodeo
Early	Buck Lake	Buck Mt. Fish Derby
Early	Coronation	Rodeo
Early	*Rocky Mt. House	Agricultural Fair and Stampede
Early	Waterton Park	Early Bird Golf Tournament
Early	Drayton Valley	Evergreen Rodeo
Early	Hardisty	Men's Golf Tournament
Early	Wetaskiwin	Gold Cup House Show
Early	Edson	Gymkhana
Mid	*St. Albert	Rodeo Week
Mid	Slendon	Agricultural Fair
Mid	Stony Plain	Annual Handcraft Show
Mid	Brooks	Farmers' Day Rodeo

* *Indicates special events.*

Mid	Hardisty	
	aBattle River Light Horse	
		Rodeo and Show
Mid	Spruce Grove	Hootenany Days
Mid	Olds	Rodeo
Mid	High Level	Rodeo and Agricultural
		Exhibition
Mid	Calgary	Provincial Slalom Championships
Mid	Ponoka	Rock and Gem Show
Mid	High River	Old Time Ranch Day
Mid	Trochu	Golf Tournament
Mid	Consort	Gooseberry Lake Rodeo
Mid	Lloydminster	Men's Open Golf Tournament
Late	High Level	Midnight Golf Tournament
Late	*Wainwright	Stampede
Late	*Didsbury	Little Britches Rodeo
Late	Marwayne	Lea Park Rodeo
Late	Castor	Open Golf Tournament
Late	Fort Macleod	Golf Tournament
Late	Torrington	Frontier Day
Late	Red Deer	Highland Games
Late	Hanna	Amateur Rodeo
Late	Bonnyville	Fish Derby
Late	*Ponoka	Stampede
Late	Redcliff	Annual Golf Tournament
Late	Drumheller	Stampede and Exhibition
Late	Red Deer	International Folk Festival
Late	High Level	Rodeo and Sports Day
Late	Whitecourt	Rodeo
Late	Lloydminster	Ladies' Open Golf Tournament

July

Early	Edmonton	Highland Games
Early	*Blairmore	River Race
Early	Boyle	Golf Tournament
Early	Fort Macleod	Canada Day Celebrations
Early	Raymond	Stampede
Early	Bassano	Stampede
Early	*Peace River	12 Ft. Davis Open Golf Tournament
Early	Fort McMurray	Canada Day Celebrations
	Jasper	
Early	*Drumheller	Exhibition and Stampede
Early	Thorhild	Stampede
Early	Benalto	Rodeo
Early	*Banff	Summer Showcase-Banff Centre
Early (1st Thurs.		
to next week Sat.)	*Calgary	Calgary Stampede and Exhibition
Early	*Fort Macleod	Midnight Days
Early	Calgary	Highland Games
Early	Red Deer	Oilmen's Golf Tournament

Early	Goodfish Lake	Goodfish Lake Rodeo
Early	Irma	Golf Tournament, Sports Day, BBQ
Mid	Saddle Lake	Saddle Lake Rodeo
Mid	Boyle	Fiesta Days
Mid	Entrance	Indian Days
Mid	*Red Deer	Exhibition
Mid	*Lethbridge	Whoop Up Days
Mid	Trochu	Golf Tournament
Mid	*Edmonton	Klondike Days and Exhibition
Mid	Edmonton	Thoroughbred Racing
Mid	Lethbridge	Rodeo
Mid	Edmonton	Beerfest
Late	Fairview	Waterhole Rodeo
Late	Pembina Provincial Park	Arts and Crafts Family Camp
Late	High Prairie	Stampede
Late	Medicine Hat	Exhibition and Stampede
Late	Lloydminster	Exhibition
Late	Fairview	Frontier Days
Late	Black Diamond	Old Timers' Golf Tournament
Late	Legal	Fete Au Village
Late	Fort Saskatchewan	Klondike Days Square Dance and Camp-Out
Late	Bruce	Rodeo
Late	Fairview	Frontier Days
Late	Bragg Creek	Indian Days; Sarcre Indians
Late	Grande Prairie	Teepee Creek Stampede
Late	Grande Prairie	Rio Grande Stampede
Late	Mayerthorpe	Agricultural Day and Mardi Gras
Late	Vegreville	Exhibition
Late	Cremona	Rodeo

August

Early	Edmonton and Calgary	Heritage Day
Early	Vermilion	Agricultural Fair
Early	Edmonton	Canadian Nature Art. (PMA)
Early	Edmonton	Summer Craft Activities (PMA)
Early	*Grimshaw	Lac Cardinal Stampede
Early	Berwyn	Stampede Fiesta
Early	Grande Prairie	International Days
Early	*Lac La Biche	Pow Wow and Blue Feather Fish Derby
Early	*Rocky Mt. House	D. Thompson Highway Cavalcade
Early	Rycroft	Agricultural Fair
Early	Bonnyville	Stampede
Early	Slave Lake	Riverboat Daze
Early	Irma	Agricultural Show and Sports Day
Early	*Banff	Banff Festival of the Arts
Early	Bashaw	Elks' Annual BBQ

Early	Grande Prairie	Muskoseepi Sunday
Early	Edson	Rodeo
Early	Blackfalds	Blackfalds Day Rodeo
Early	Wetaskiwin	Men's Open Golf Tournament
Early	Oyen	Agricultural Fair
Early	Grande Prairie	County Fair
Early	Camrose	Agricultural Fair
Early	Donnelly	Smoky River Agricultural Fair
Early	Bentley	Amateur Rodeo/Town and Country Fair
Mid	*Banff	Banff Indian Days
Mid	Lougheed	Agricultural Fair
Mid	Fairview	Agricultural Society Flower Show
Mid	Wainwright	Flower Show
Mid	Peace River	Peace River and District Agricultural Fair
Mid	Wasdatenau	Agricultural Fair
Mid	Stony Plain	Flower and Garden Show
Mid	Wildwood	Fair
Mid	Leduc	Black Gold Rodeo
Mid	Redwater	Discovery Days
Mid	Edmonton	Thoroughbred Racing
Mid	Berwyn	Flower Show
Mid	Three Hills	Horticultural Show
Mid	Eckville	Annual Indoor Rodeo
Mid	Edson	Gymkhana
Mid	Bonnyville	Agricultural Fair
Mid	Vilna	Annual Open Golf Tournament
Mid	Skaro	Polish Annual Pilgrimage to Marian Shrine
Late	Acme	Flower Show
Late	Ponoka	Agricultural Fair
Late	Cardston	Fair and Rodeo
Late	Hanna	Agricultural Fall Fair
Late	Vilna	Agricultural Fair Days
Late	Grande Cache	Coal Dust Daze
Late	Three Hills	Provincial Horticulture Show
Late	Two Hills	Annual Rodeo
Late	Fox Creek	Kinsmen Beer Fest
Late	High River	Summer Festival
Late	Lloydminster	Horticultural Flower and Vegetable Show
Late	Onoway	BBQ and Car Raffle
Late	Rycroft	Agricultural Fair
Late	Manning	Agricultural Fair and Rodeo
Late	Spirit River	Fun Fair Days
Late	Hobbema	Hobbema Indian Days
Late	Dogpound	Dogpound Rodeo
Late	Pincher Creek	Agricultural Fair
Late	Westlock	Agricultural Fair
Late	Carmangay	Agricultural Fair

September

Early	*Ponoka	Rifleman's Rodeo
Early	Camrose	Men's Open Golf Tournament
Early	Edmonton	Thoroughbred Racing
Early	Cochrane	Rodeo and BBQ
Early	Medicine Hat	Golf Tournament
Early	Peace River	Club Championship Golf Tournament
Early	*Fort McMurray	Blueberry Festival
Early	*Jasper	Totem Golf Tournament
Mid	Calgary	Strathcona Tweedsmuir Slalom
Late	Edmonton	Oktoberfest
Late	Forestburg	Annual Indoor Rodeo
Late	Wainwright	Fall Fair
Late	Edmonton	Oktoberfest
Late	Edson	Fall Festival
Late	*Calgary	101-Mile Antique Car Rally

October

Early	Lacombe	Indoor Rodeo
Early	*Edmonton	Oktoberfest
Early	*Calgary	Oktoberfest
Early	Bon Accord	Annual Turkey Supper
Mid	Edmonton	Gem and Mineral Show
Mid	Vermilion	Kinsmen Indoor Rodeo
Mid	High River	Fall Fair
Late	Caroline	Stampede
Late	Edmonton	Cultural Heritage Performances
Late	Manning	Klondike Days
Late	Red Deer	Oktoberfest

November

Early	Lethbridge	Lethbridge Multicultural Festival (art, folk dances, song, historical lectures)
Late	Edmonton	Csardas Ball (Hungarian Cultural Society)

BRITISH COLUMBIA

April

Early	Victoria	Annual Spring Show, Vancouver Island Rock & Alpine Garden Show
Early	Surrey	Arts & Crafts Spring Show
Early	Burnaby	Burnaby Arts Council's Craft Market
Mid	Kamloops	Hockey: International Bantam Tournament
Mid	Keremeos	Annual Easter Barbeque and Rodeo, Chap-aka Indian Reserve
Mid	Duncan	Easter Arts Fair
Mid	Trail	Caledonian Society Annual Scottish Tattoo and Highland Games

Mid	Chilliwack	Spring Flower Show
Late	Surrey	Rhododendron Society Show
Late	Nelson	Rock and Gem Show
Late	Kamloops	Annual Indoor Rodeo
Late	Ladysmith	Easter Arts Fair
Late	Revelstoke	Art Display
Late	Richmond	Annual Gem and Mineral Club Exhibit
Late	Quesnel	Annual Quesnel Amateur Rodeo

May

May thru Sept.	Bella Coola	Indian Arts and Crafts Exhibition
Early	Campbell River	Arts and Crafts Show
Early	Vancouver	Open International Fencing Tournament
Mid	Burnaby	Burnaby Arts Council Craft Market
Mid	Whitelake	Outdoor Fun Carnival Canoe Races
Mid	Creston	Creston Valley Blossom Festival
Mid	New Westminster	Hyack Canoe Marathon
Mid	Golden	Loggers' Sports Day
Mid	Denman Island	Annual Oyster Festival
Mid	North Vancouver	Capilano International White-Water Races (Kayak)
Mid	Kelowna	Blossom Time Sailing Regatta
Mid	Port Coquitlam	Invitational Lacrosse Tournament
Mid	Cloverdale	Rodeo
Mid	Parksville	Annual Victoria Day Golf Tournament
Mid	*Victoria	Victorian Days
Mid	Maple Ridge (Fraser River)	Raft and Kayak Races
Mid	Keremeos	Annual International Rodeo
Late	Campbell River	Salmon Derby
Late	Chetwynd	Loggers' Sports Day
Late	Kitamaat Village	Kitamaat Indian Village Sports Day
Late	Victoria	Highland Games
Late	New Westminster	Hyack Festival (Pancake Breakfast, Bavarian Night)
Late	Nanaimo	Bottle Show
Late	Port Moody	Invitational Canoe Championship

June

Early	West Vancouver	North Shore Artists and Craftsman Show
Early	Merritt	Merritt Annual Spring Rodeo
Early	Castlegar	Arts and Crafts
Early	Chilliwack	Indian Festival, Cultus Lake
all June	Victoria	Vancouver Island Crafts
June-Aug.	Bella Coola	Historical Indian Dances
June-Oct.	Burnaby	Lawn Bowling (visiting bowlers welcome), South Burnaby Lawn Bowling Club

Early	Burnaby	Western Pacific International Kayak Championship
Early	Vancouver	Display of Pottery, House of Ceramics
Early	New Westminster	Highland Games
Early	Duncan	Cowichan Indian Celebrations
Mid	Victoria	Esquimalt Buccaneer Days
Mid	Vancouver	Craft Market
Mid	Victoria	Annual Curling Esquimalt
Mid	Prince Rupert	Indian Salmon Days
Mid	Nelson	Sea Food Smorgasbord
Mid	Penticton	Flower Show
Mid	Revelstoke	Loggers Sports
Mid	Nanaimo	Lawn Bowling
Mid	Port Alberni	Ladies' West Coast Open Golf Tourney
Mid	Victoria	Lawn Bowling Tournament
Late	North Vancouver	"Longhouse Fair" Capilano Indian Reserve
Late	Victoria	Victoria Horticultural Society
Late	Port Alberni	Men's West Coast Open Golf Tourney
Late	Campbell River	World's Oyster Eating Contest, Foreshore
Late	Campbell River	Campbell River Salmon Festival
Late	*Williams Lake	Stampede
Late	New Westminster	Portuguese Festival
Late	Revelstoke	Kinsmen Alpine Days
Late	White Rock	White Rock Sea Festival
Late	Campbell River	Salmon Festival of Arts and Crafts

July

Early	Bridge Lake	Annual Stampede
Early	Qualicum Beach Saturna Island	Salmon Derby and Barbecue
Sundays (July-Aug.)	Burnaby	Craft Market
Mid	*Nelson	Nelson's Annual World Midsummer Championship Curling Bonspiel
Mid	Nanaimo	Highland Games, Caledonia Park
Mid	Revelstoke	Ethnic Group Craft Showing
Mid	Penticton	Canadian Flying Dutchman Championship
Mid	Quesnel	Billy Barker Days and Rodeo
Mid	Kimberley	Bavarian July Fest
Mid	Quesnel	Rodeo
Mid	*Sooke	Loggers' Sports, Cookouts
Mid	Bella Coola	MacKenzie Day
Mid	Nanaimo	Kinsmen's "Bavarian Gardens"
Late	*Vancouver	Sea Festival
Late	Mission	Nationality Festival
Late	Victoria	Flower Show
Late	West Vancouver	Western Canadian Daysailor Championship

August

Early	*Penticton	Peach Festival
Early	Galiano Island	Arts and Crafts Show
Thursdays all Aug.	Victoria, Butchart Gardens	Pipes and Drums of the Canadian Scottish Regiment, Dancers, Singers
Mid	*Kelowna	Kelowna International Regatta
Mid	Howe Sound	Annual Fishing Derby
Mid	Parksville	Salmon Derby and Barbeque
Mid	Nanaimo	Dancers and Indian Crafts Display
Mid	Victoria	Gladiola and Dahlia Society Flower Show
Mid	Prince George	Simon Fraser Open Golf
Mid	Keremeos	All Indian Rodeo and Indian Days
Mid	*Vancouver	Salmon Derby
Mid	*Vancouver	Pacific National Exhibition
Mid	Vernon	Annual Kayak and Canoe Races
Late	Victoria	North American Single-Handed Sailboat Championship
Late	Prince George	Flower Show
Late	Clinton	Annual T.R. Bar Ranch Roping Event Barrel Racing, Roping, Barbeque, Barn Dance
Late	Coombs	Fall Fair
Late	Bella Coola	Fall Fair
Late	Denman Island	"Farmers' Market" (Handicrafts and Sports Program)
Late	Trail	Annual International Horse Show
Late	Williams Lake	Annual Kinsmen Loggers' Sports Days
Late	Vernon	Annual Indian Days, Six Mile Creek

September

Early	*Nelson	Annual Highland Scottish Games, (Kiltie Bands, Piping, Dancing, "Highland Tattoo")
Early	Qualicum	Salmon Derby and Barbeque
Early	*Hudson's Hope	Big Dam Canoe Race, 50 miles
Early	*Trail	Horse Show
Early	*Taylor	Taylor Day Festivities (Gold Panning)
Early	Port Alberni	Alberni Valley Fall Fair
Early	Oliver	"Vinyard Pow-Wow," Indameep Vinyard, Northeast of Oliver, Osoyoos Indian Band
Early	Summerland	Annual Fall Fair
Early	Duncan	Annual Agricultural Fair
Early	Rossland	"Golden City Days"
Early	Lillooet	Fall Fair
Early	Sooke	Fall Fair
Mid	*Creston	Fall Fair
Mid	Victoria	Fall Horticultural Show
Mid	Princeton	Annual Fall Fair

Mid	*Lillooet	Lillooet Rodeo
Late Sept.- early Oct.	*Vancouver	Oktoberfest

October

Mid	*Vancouver	Annual British Columbia Gem Craft Show
Late	Richmond	Arts and Crafts Seminar and Display

MANITOBA

February

	St. Boniface	Festival du Voyageur
	The Pas	Trappers' Festival
	Beausejour	Winter Farewell

March

Late	Churchill	Aurora Show Festival

April

Early	Brandon	Royal Manitoba Winter Fair

May

Mid	Morden	Apple Blossom Festival
Mid	Winnipeg	Ukrainian Festival

June

Early	Winnipeg	Annual Canoe Race
Early	Winnipeg	Highland Dancing Championships
Early	Beausejour	Horseshoe Tournament
Mid	Dauphin	Flower Show
Mid	St. Claude	French Celebration
Mid	Winnipeg	Manitoba Highland Dancing Championships
Late	Winnipeg	Red River Exhibition
Late	La Broquerie	Fete Franco Manitobaine
Late	*Flin Flon	Trout Festival
Late	Winnipeg	Cricket
Late	Landmark	Landmark (Mennonite Centennial Day)
Late	Winnipeg	Lithuanian Week
Late	Dauphin	Dauphin Fair
Late	Neepawa	Neepawa Fair
Late	Killarney	Killarney Fair

July

Early	Winnipeg	Canada Day
Early	Winnipeg	Scottish Sports and Highland Dancing
Early	Neepawa	Holiday Festival of the Arts
Early	Miami	Miami Fair

Early	Minnedosa	Peony Fair
Early	Manitou	Fair
Early	Carberry	Agricultural Fair
Early	Selkirk	Fair
Early	Selkirk	Red River Days
Early	Hartney	Fair
Early	Winnipeg	Scottish Games
Early	Morden Winkler	Pembina Threshermen's Reunion
Mid	*Selkirk	Highland Gathering
Mid	*Thompson	Nickel Days
Mid	Winnipeg	Mid-Canada Highland Dancing Championships
Mid	Winnipeg	Highland Games
Mid	Winnipeg	Highland Dancing Championships
Mid	Oak River	Fair
Mid	Strathclair	Fair
Mid	Russell	Fair
Mid	Minnedosa	Fun Festival
Mid	Gilbert Plains	Fair
Mid	Winnipeg	Annual International Gem and Mineral Exhibition
Late	*Morris	Manitoba Stampede (2nd largest in Canada)
Late	*Austin	Threshermens' Reunion
Late	*Swan River	Northwest Roundup and Agricultural Fair
Late	Altona	Sunflower Festival (Mennonite)
Late	Langruth	Rodeo
Late	Roblin	Fair
Late	Minnedosa	Fair
Late	Reston	Fair
Late	Dugald	Fair
Late	Virden	Fair
Late	Steinbach	Fair
Late	Griswold	Indian Pow-Wow
Late	Winnipeg	Canadian National Tennis Championships

August

Early	*Steinbach	Pioneer Days
Early	*Dauphin	Canada's National Ukrainian Festival
Early	St. Pierre	Frog Follies
Early	Boissevain	Turtle Derby (curling and farmer's market)
Early	*Gimli	Icelandic Festival
Early	Brandon	Provincial Exhibition and Agricultural Fair
Early	Winkler	Fair
Early	St. Pierre	Horticultural Show
Early	Birtle	Horticultural Show
Early	Portage la Prairie	Antique Car Rally
Early	The Pas	The Pas Rodeo and Exhibition

Early	McCreary	Rodeo
Early	Bowsman	Horticultural Show
Early	Boissevain	Horticultural Show
Early	Hartney	Horticultural Show
Early	Winnipeg	Horticultural Show
Early	Arborg	Agricultural Fair
Mid	Rossburn	Harvest Festival
Mid	Reston	Horticultural Show
Mid	Souris	Horticultural Show
Mid	Niverville	Community Fair
Mid	Notre Dame de Lourdes	Agricultural Fair
Mid	*Winnipeg	Folklorama
Mid	*The Pas	Opasquia Indian Days
Mid	Gimli	Creative Arts Week
Mid	Winnipeg	Horticultural Show
Mid	Winnipeg	Horticultural Show
Mid	Pilot Mound	Horticultural Show
Mid	Winnipeg	Golf-Manitoba Senior Championships
Mid	Winnipeg	Hi Neighbour Festival
Mid	Deloraine	Horticultural Show
Mid	Dominion City	Horticultural Show
Mid	Winnipeg	Canadian Canoe Championships
Mid	Toulon	Agricultural Fair
Late	Winnipeg	Canadian Amateur Golf Championships
Late	Flin Flon	Horticultural Show
Late	Poplar Point	Horticultural Show
Late	Dauphin	Garden Show
Late	Winnipeg	Winnipeg International Flower Show
Late	Winkler	Oldtime Days
Late	Fisher Branch	Rodeo
Late	Morden	Horticultural Show
Late	*Morden	Corn and Apple Festival

September

Early	Gimli	Community Fair
Mid	Virden	Western Days Rodeo
Mid	Winnipeg	Horse Show
Mid	Winnipeg	Fall Shoot
Late	Kelwood	Fair
Late	Minnedosa	Nature Trek

October

Early	Mayville	Fair
Early	*Winnipeg	Oktoberfest
Mid	Russell	Beef and Barley Festival
Mid	St. Claude	Horseshoe Tournament
Mid	Winnipeg	Turkey Shoot
Mid	Waskada	Fair

NEW BRUNSWICK

January

Mid	Millville	Winter Carnival
Late	New Maryland	Winter Carnival
Late	St. John	New Brunswick Ladies' Lassie Curling Championship
Late	Fredericton	St. Thomas University Winter Carnival
Late	Sackville	Mt. Allison University Winter Carnival

February

Early	Beresford	Carnaval du Siffleux (Ground Hog Carnival)
Early	Fredericton	University of New Brunswick Winter Carnival
Mid	Woodstock	Winter Carnival
Mid	Sussex	Winter Carnival
Mid	Richibucto	Winter Carnival
Late	Moncton	MacDonald Canadian Lassie Curling Bonspiel

March

Early	Mactaquac	Maple Candy Parties and Sugar Bush Tours

April

Early	Moncton	Craft and Hobby Fair
Mid	Houlton	Arts and Crafts Festival
Mid	Port Elgin	Craft Center Show

May

Early	Loch Lomond (St. John)	Flower Festival
Early	Moncton	Flea Market
Early	St. John	"Loyalist Day" Celebrations

June

June-Aug.	Prince William	Kings Landing Historical Settlement Season
June-Aug. (every Sunday)	Berwick	Flea Market
June-Aug. (every Wed.)	St. John	The Flea Market Ltd.
Early	McNamee	Fair Days
Early	Kingston	Loyalist Days Celebration
Early	New Denmark	New Denmark Day
Early	Dalhousie	Bon Ami Festival
Mid	Oromocto	Pioneer Days
Late	Grand Falls	Potato Festival
Late	Campbellton	Salmon Festival

Late	Newcastle	Canada Days
Late	Petit Rocher	Festival de la Traverseé de la Baie des Chaleurs (The Crossing of the Bay of Chaleur Festival)
Late	Val Comeau	Festival des Pecheurs (Fishermen's Festival)
Late	Fredericton	Art and Crafts Show and Sale, Good Neighbor Days
Late	Sussex and area	Canada Days Festivities
Late	Savage Island (Island View)	Fiddlehead Festival
Late	Canterbury	Canterbury Community Fair Days
Late	Fredericton-Oromocto	Confederation Canoe Race
Late	Newcastle	Miramichi Folk Song Festival
Late	Fairvale	Fair Week

July

Early	Hartland	Potato Festival
Early	Richibucto and area (Tri-Community)	Scallop Festival
Early	St. Andrews	Antique Fair and Sale
Early	(Bas) Lower Carquet	Festival Marina (Marine Festival)
Early	*St. John	"The Alexander Memorial" Harness Race
Early	Shediac	Laser Class Regatta
Early	Shediac	Lobster Festival and Regatta
Mid	Val Comeau	Festival Val Comeau
Mid	St. Martin's	Old Home Week
Mid	Grand Lake	"BASH"—New Brunswick Annual Sailing Holiday
Mid	Shippagan	Festival des Pecheries (Fisheries Festival)
Mid	Shediac-Charlottetown	Crusing Classes Yacht Race
Mid	Robinsonville	Strawberry Festival
Mid	Prince William	Annual Auction
Mid	Moncton	Frolic Acadien
Late	Woodstock	Old Home Week
Late	*St. John	Loyalist Days
Late	Loch Lomond (St. John)	Craft Exhibition
Late	Boiestown	Fair
Late	Lameque	Peat Moss Festival
Late	St. John	New Brunswick Antique Show and Flea Market
Late	Fundy National	Fundy Craft Festival D'Artisanat
Late	Renforth	New Brunswick Highland Gathering
Late	Riverview	Causa Games
Late	Mactaquac	Commodore's Regatta
Late	Grand Lake	Village Festival
Late	Doaktown	Fair

August
Early	Pointe Verde	Villagers' Festival
Early	*Renforth	Renforth Regatta (international sculling)
Early	Cape Pele	Blessing of the Fleet
Early	Moncton	Brouhaha "Codiac Hubbub"
Early	Moncton	Canadian National Annual Atlantic Regional Golf Tournament
Early	Deer Island (Fairhaven)	Sea Festival
Early	St. Stephen-Milltown-Calaquet	International Festival
Early	Nauwigewauk	Fair
Early	Moncton	Flea Market
Mid	Caraquet	Acadian Festival
Mid	Cocagne	Bazaar Acadien
Mid	Chatham	Old Home Week and Pioneer Days
Mid	Chatham	Miramichi Agricultural Exhibition
Mid	Harvey	Fair
Mid	Stanley	Fair
Late	St. Basile	Madawaska Fair
Late	*St. John	Atlantic National Exhibition (largest agricultural fair in New Brunswick)
Late	Petitcodiac	Westmorland County Fair
Late	Fredericton	Flower Show
Late	Moncton	Horticultural Show
Late	Maisonnette	Oyster Festival
Late	Mactaquac Provincial Park	New Brunswick Craftsmen Festival
Late	Fredericton	Canadian Film Festival
Late	Bathurst	Agricultural Show
Late	Moncton	Horse Show
Late	Nashwaaksis	Carnival Day
Late	Perth-Andover	Fair
Late	Oromocto	Summer Fair
Late	Lincoln	Fair
Late	Milltown	Fair
Late	(Grand Lake) Young's Cove	Fair

September
Early	Shediac	Sailing Races
Early	Fredericton	Exhibition and Livestock Show
Early	Plaster Rock	Fall Fair
Early	Albert	Fair
Early	Sussex	Fair
Early	Gagetown	Fair
Early	Nackawic	Community Days
Early	Charlo	Fair
Early	*Campbellton Edmundston	New Brunswick Multicultural Festival

Early	Chipman	Fair
Early	Loch Lomond	Fair
Mid	Albert	Fair

October

Early	Fredericton	Annual International Intercollegiate Wood-smen Competition
Early	Woodstock	Kinsmen Annual Walking Marathon

November

Early	Moncton	Monctonion Curling Bonspiel and Donkey Bar-B-Q

NEWFOUNDLAND AND LABRADOR

May-October	Conception Bay	Sailing Races
June	Grand Falls	Invitational Golf Tournament
June	Clarenville	Trade Fair

July

Early	St. John	Summer Festival of the Arts
Early	St. John	Canada Day Pageant
July & Aug.	St. John	Signal Hill Military Tattoo
Early	Killigrew	Soiree
Late	Placentia	Intertown Regatta
Late	Harbour Grace	Regatta
(often runs into early Aug.)		

August

Early	Port-aux-Basques	Bruce Arena Fair
Early	St. John	Annual Regatta (old-time country fair)
Mid	St. John	Folkloric Arts Festival
Late	St. John	Folkfest
September	Various courses	Golf Championship
September	Harbour Grace	Trinity-Conception Trade Fair
September	Grand Bank	Annual Fall Fair
September	Various cities	Regional agriculture exhibitions and fairs

NORTHWEST TERRITORIES

March

Mid	Inuvik	International Curling Bonspiel
Mid	Fort Smith	Southern Mixed Open Curling Bonspiel

Mid	Fort Smith	Wood Buffalo Frolics (celebrating the coming of spring: snowmobile racing, muskrat skinning, log chopping, hockey, cross-country skiing)
Late	Pine Point	Bradford Snowmobile Race (50 miles; $5,000 prize)
Late	Yellowknife	Caribou Carnival (ice skulptures, dog derby)

April

Early	Inuvik	Top of the World Ski Meet (cross-country)
Early	Yellowknife	Open Snowmobile Race ($5,000 prize)
Mid (Easter weekend)	Yellowknife	Annual 'Spiel ($12,000 prize)
Mid	Sachs Harbour	White Fox Jamboree
Late	Tuktoyaktuk	Beluga Jamboree
Late	Frobisher Bay	Toonik Tyme (celebrating spring's arrival: seal skinning, igloo building, ice sculpture, tobaggan race)

May

End	Yellowknife	Square Dance Jamboree

June

Mid	Holman	Sports Day
Mid	Fort Smith	$2,000 Fast Ball Tournament (barbecue)
Late	Pine Point	Pine Days
Late	Yellowknife	Midnight Golf Tournament
Late	Fort Smith	Square Dance Camporee (in the midnight sun)

July

Early (3 days)	Inuvik	Arctic Fly-in (for private aircraft)

September

Early	Inuvik	Delta Daze

NOVA SCOTIA

June

Early	*Wolfville	Annapolis Valley Apple Blossom Festival
Early	Forties Settlement	Spring Flower Show
Early	Sydney Mines	Spring Flower Show
Early	Windsor	Maritime Quarter-Horse Show
Early	*Meteghan	Blessing of the Fleet (colorful ceremony with decorated boats on parade)
Mid	Bridgewater	Horse Show

Mid	Broad Cove	Corpus Christi (spring flowers church procession)
Late	*Dartmouth	Maritime Old-Time Fiddling Contest
Late	Truro	Chicken Barbecue
Late	Lawrencetown	Lawrencetown Country Fair
Late	Maplewood	Hobby Show and Sale (antiques, handicrafts; home-cooking, smorgasbord)
Late	Elmsdale	Goat Field Day (goat products; goat meat meal)
Late	Canso	Fair
Late	Halifax	Atlantic Regatta Canada (smaller classes)
Late	Westville	Westville Dominion Day Festival
Late	*Lockeport	Seaside Festival (dory and canoe racing, handicraft market)

July

Early	*Westville	Dominion Day Festival
Early	Middleton	Dominion Day Celebrations
Early	Parrsboro	St. Brigid's Picnic and Ham Supper
Early	Clark's Harbour	Dominion Day Celebrations
Early	Pugwash	Gatherine of the Clans (highland piping and dancing, boat races, ox pulls, lobster dinners)
Early	Hantsport	Community Fair (horse shoe tournament, chicken barbecue)
Early	Lackeport	Dominion Day Celebrations (handicraft market, dory races)
Early	Windsor	Eastern Stock Horse Association Riding School and Show
Early	Bear River	Western Nova Scotia Rose Show
Early	Sydney	Provincial Golf Tournament
Early	*Port Hawkesbury	Festival of the Strait
Early	Milford, Hants County	ChowderCarnival
Early	*Pictou	Lobster Fisheries Carnival
Early	Blue Rocks	Solomon Grundy supper (sale of handicrafts, country picnic)
Early	Sydney	Highland Games
Early	New Glasgow	Provincial Golf Tournament
Early	Concession, Digby County	Strawberry Festival
Early	Mabou	Scottish Concert (fiddling, Gaelic singing, dancing)
Early	Antigonish	Highland Activities (pipe band, kilted golf tournament, seafood supper)
Mid	Parrsboro	Old Home Week
Mid	North Sydney	Cape Breton Rose Show
Mid	Maplewood	Strawberry Festival
Mid	Canning	Handicraft Demonstration and Sale

Mid	*Canning	Glooscap Festival (arts and crafts shows, market, country and western show)
Mid	Halifax	Provincial Rose Show
Mid	*Meteghan River	Acadian Festival (artcrafts, canoeing and boat races, barbecue, folk singing)
Mid	Antigonish	Highland Games
Mid	Kingston	Kingston Steer Barbecue
Mid	Glendale	Scottish Concert
Mid	New Glasgow	Junior Golf Championships
Mid	Springhill	Old Home Week (garden parties, carnival atmosphere)
Mid	Masstown	Strawberry Festivals
Mid	*Wolfville	Theatre Arts Festival International (multicultural folk arts program; arts and crafts displays)
Mid	Annapolis Royal	Western Nova Scotia Handicraft Demonstrations and Sale
Mid	Musquodoboit	Musquodoboit Harbour Fair and Exhibition
Mid	Milton	Milton Days (water sports, garden party, suppers, pony pulling)
Mid	Thorburn	East Pictou Annual Fair (handicrafts, steak barbecue)
Late	Dartmouth	Dartmouth Festival of Piping
Late	Englishtown	St. Anthony Daniel Day (pageant, outdoor concert)
Late	Guysborough	Guysborough Come Home Week
Late	Margaree	Margaree Summer Festival (fishing derby, bicycle marathon, handicraft displays, suppers, woodmen's contests)
Late	Windsor	Sam Slick Days (contests, concerts, auction, sports events, re-enactment of historical events)
Late	*Stillwater	Sportmen's Meet (log-rolling, wood-chopping and power-saw competitions, canoe races, flycasting)
Late	Chapel Island Cape Breton	Indian Mission (colorful religious ceremony, canoe races, ball game, horseshoe competitions)
Late	Bear River	Bear River Cherry Carnival (home-cooking, auction)
Late	Truro	Pork Barbecue and Open House, Nova Scotia Agricultural College
Late	Middle Musquodoboit	Summer Flower Show
Late	Broad Cove, Inverness County	Scottish Concert Under the Stars
Late	Parrsboro	Chicken barbecue, Glooscap Park
Late	Digby	Natal Day (parade, barbecue, canoe races)

Late	Halifax	Halifax Natal Day (6-mile road race, concerts, barbecue, sports events)

August

Early	Bridgewater	South Shore Exhibition (international horse and ox pulls, parades)
Early	Lunenburg	Swiss Carnival
Early	New Glasgow	Antique Car Show
Early	Iona	Highland Village Day (Highland dancing and piping competitions, concert, dance)
Early	Port Greville	Firemen's Field Day
Early	French Vale	Scottish Concert
Early	Parrsboro	St. Brigid's Lobster Supper
Early	Annapolis Royal	Annapolis Royal Natal Day (children's parade, grand parade)
Early	Yarmouth	Western Nova Scotia Exhibition
Early	St. Ann's	Nova Scotia Gaelic Mod
Early	Dartmouth	Dartmouth Natal Day
Early	Weymouth	Flower Show
Early	Parrsboro	Rockhound Round-Up (displays of rocks, demonstrations, lectures, home crafts, home-cooked meals)
Early	New Glasgow	Festival of the Tartans
Mid	Goffs, Halifax County	Goffs Country Fair
Mid	Stewlacke	Stewlacke Town Day
Mid	Upper Selma	Old Home Weekend
Mid	Big Pond	Scottish Concerts
Mid	Concession, Digby County	Parish Picnic
Mid	Blue Rocks	Garden Party (seafood feast, home-crafted goods for sale, games)
Mid	Lawrencetown, Anna County	Annapolis County Exhibition
Mid	Digby, Great Village	Flower Shows
Mid	Middle Musquodoboit	Halifax County Exhibition
Mid	Hubbards	Annual Scuba Diving Meet
Mid	New Ross	Farmer's Exhibition (ox pull, agricultural exhibits)
Mid	Canso	Canso Regatta
Mid	Waterville	Field Day
Mid	Advocate Harbour	Hospital Bazaar (parade, church supper, auction)
Mid	Dartmouth	Nova Scotia Sprints Rowing Championships
Late	*Halifax	Nova Scotia Festival of the Arts
Late	Truro	Nova Scotia Provincial Exhibition
Late	Bear River	Flower Show
Late	Shelburne	Shelburne County Exhibition
Late	Shelburne	Loyalist Days

Late	Bear River	Digby County Exhibition
Late	Riverport	Flower Show
Late	Walton	Firefighters' Field Days
Late	New Glasgow	Flower Show
Late	Halifax	Flower Shows
Late	Halifax	Bluenose Class Sailing Championships
Late	Maplewood	Field Day and Bazaar
Late	Parrsboro	St. Brigid's Lobster Supper
Late	Wedgeport, Cape St. Mary	International University Sports Fish Seminar
Late	North Sydney	Cape Breton County Exhibition
Late	Oxford	Cumberland County Exhibition
Late	Dominion, Westmount, Forties Settlement	Flower Shows
Late	Antigonish	Eastern Nova Scotia Exhibition
Late	Truro	Nova Scotia Sheep Fair (sheep dog trials, shearing demonstrations, weaving, spinning and knitting, tanning, soap and candlemaking workshops)
Late	Tremont	Western Kings Community Club Fair (light horse show, horse and ox pulls, exhibits of fruit, vegetables, and crafts, home-cooked meals)
Late	Shelburne	Nova Scotia Marathon (26-mile road)
Late	Greenwood	Horse Show
Late	Beaver Dam, Shelburne County	Beaver Dam Sports Meet (water sports, woodsmen's events)

September

Early	Amherst and area	Blueberry Harvest Festival
Early	Berwick	Gala Day
Early	Hantsport	Horseshoe Tournament
Early	Pictou	Pictou-North Colchester Exhibition (woodsmen's competitions, exhibits, handicraft)
Early	*Wedgeport, Cape St. Mary	International Tuna Cup Match
Early	Sheffield Mills	Sheffield Mills Harvest Festival (horse, ox and tractor rides, barbecue, games of skill)
Early	Truro	Powder Puff Derby (free-for-all harness races with female drivers)
Mid	Windsor	Hants County Exhibition (Canada's oldest agricultural fair)
Mid	*Lunenburg	Nova Scotia Fisheries Exhibition

| Late | Lockeport | Handicraft Bazaar (handicraft display and sale, art show, sale of homebaked goods) |
| Late | Caledonia | Queens County Exhibition |

October
Early	Halifax	Joseph Howe Festival
Mid	Halifax	Atlantic Winter Fair (horse show, home-crafts, floriculture)
Mid	Auburn	Fall Auction (new and used items, antiques, fruit and vegetables)

ONTARIO

All Year	**Antique Shows**	
	Aylmer	Antique Fun Fair (2nd and 4th Sun. each month)
	Cambridge	Flea Market (4th Sun. each month) in Galt
	Clappison Corners	Circle 'M' Ranch Flea Market (Sundays)
	Comber	Antique Market and Show (1st and 3rd Sun. ach month)
	Dundas	Flea Market (Sat. and Sun.)
	Hamilton	Flea Market (Sun.)
	Oakville	Granary Antique Market (1st and 3rd Sun. each month)
	Richmond Hill	Antique Show and Sale (1st Sun. each month)
	Scarborough	Collectors' Corner Historical Society Antique Market (Sun.)
	Thornhill	Portabello Market (4th Sun. each month)
	Woodbridge	Antique Market and Show (3rd Sun. each month)
	Art	
	Kleinburg (north of Toronto)	McMichael Canadian Collection of Art (900 paintings by the Group of Seven and their contemporaries, Tom Thomson, Emily Carr, David Milne, Clarence Gagnon, Indian and Eskimo works of art; pioneer furniture and artifacts, all in a 300-acre wooded park)
	Market	
	Kitchener	Kitchener Market (Amish and Mennonite farmers sell produce, home crafts; in summer, Wed. and Sat. until noon; in winter, only Sat.)

March
| Early | North Bay | Winter Fur Carnival (sled dog derby, snowmobile races) |

Mid	Toronto	Canadian National Sportsmen's Show (displays of camping gear, sporting goods, travel products, recreational activities)

April

Early	Elmira	Maple Syrup Festival (craft exhibits, German food, pancakes and maple syrup, tours)
Mid-April-Dec.	Toronto	Black Creek Pioneer Village (rural village life 100 years ago; 20 buildings restored and furnished)

May

Mid	Niagara Falls	Blossom Festival (parades, ethnic dances, sporting events, blossoms)
Late	Ottawa	Canadian Tulip Festival
Late	*St. Catharine's	Folk Arts Festival (ethnic concerts, gourmet food, art and crafts displays, parade)
Late	New Hamburg	Mennonite Auction Relief Sale (handicrafts, paintings, quilts, smorgasbord)
Late	Cornwall	Festival de la Semaine Francaise (French-Canadian food, entertainment, and events)

June

Early	Welland	Rose Festival
Early	Beeton	Antique Show
Early	Norwich	Annual Historical Show
Early	Orangeville	Arts and Crafts Show
Early	Thornhill	The Willowdale Artisans Show
Early	Scarborough	Annual Artscraftsantiquickity (auction, flea market, country kitchen, craft sale)
Early	Unionville	Village Festival (crafts, antique cars, old-fashioned cooking)
Early	Streetsville	Bread and Honey Festival (arts/crafts, antique show, fishing derby, bread baking contest)
Early	Cornwall	Annual Festival de la semaine Francaise (French-Canadian food, events)
Early	Stoney Creek	Canada Flag Week (strawberry social, bar-b-q)
Early	Durham	Huskyfest (German food, events)
Early	Ottawa	Annual Rose Show
Early	Wilfred	June Flower Show
Early	Hamilton	Iris Society Show
Mid	Beeton	Antique Steam Show
Mid	Toronto	Annual Outdoor Art Exhibition

Mid	Niagara-on-the-Lake	Sidewalk Art Show
Mid	Windsor and Essex County	Folkloric Arts Festival
Mid	Keene	Kawartha Folk Arts Festival
Mid	Richmond Hill	Iris and Peony Show
Mid	Ottawa	Annual Flower Show
Mid	Etobicoke	Festival Weekend and Flower Show
Mid	Brampton	Annual Flower Festival and Highland Games
Mid	Oshawa	Irish Show
Mid	Hamilton	International Peony Exhibition
Mid	Milton	Annual Flower Show
Mid	Kitchener	Scottish Weekend (food, dancing)
Mid	Walkerton	Family Fair and Wild West Show
Mid	Toronto	Eastern Canadian Championships (horse)
Mid	Welland	Horse Show
Late	Hamilton	Annual Open Sailing Regatta
Late	Welland	Art Festival
Late	*Toronto	Mariposa Folk Festival
Late	Hamilton	Irish Festival
Late	Morrisburg	Annual Old Home Week
Late	Meaford	Old Home Week
Late	Orillia	Bavarian Festival
Late	Gravenhurst	Canada Day Celebrations
Late	*Toronto	Metro Caravan (international foods, handicrafts, souvenirs, entertainment)
Late	*Toronto	Queen's Plate (running of top Canadian thoroughbred horses)
Late	Toronto	Flower Show
Late	Clinton	Rose Show
Late	Gore's Landing	Rose Show
Late	Oshawa	Rose Show and Tea
Late	Toronto	National Rose Show (over 1,000 exhibits)
Late	Cobourg	Rose Show and Strawberry Social
Late	Ottawa	Highland Games
Late	Orangeville	Lord Dufferin Horse Show
Late	Leamington	Rodeo
Late	Elliot Lake	Annual Uranium Festival

July

Early	*Fort Frances	Fun in the Sun (canoe race, fish fry)
Early	*Cobourg	Highland Games
Early	Gravenhurst	Arts and Crafts Show
Early	Brockville	Arts and Crafts
Early	Leamington	Annual Arts and Crafts Show and Bazaar (ethnic displays, wine and cheese party, fish fry)
Early	Wawa	Summerfest
Early	Sudbury	Festival Canada Weekend (arts and crafts, food)

Early	Toronto	Annual International Picnic
Early	Sudbury	Rose Show
Early	Embro	Annual Zorra Caledonian Society Highland Games
Early	*Brantford	Highland Games
Early	Sarnia	Chippewa Pow Wow
Early	St. Catharine's	International Regatta
Mid	Ridgetown	Annual Antique Sale and Show
Mid	Stratford	Annual Festival of Arts and Crafts (juried)
Mid	Ottawa	Annual Artarama Contest
Mid	Bracebridge	Annual Muskoka Arts and Crafts
Mid	Goderich	Summer Festival and Art Mart
Mid	Tweed	Annual International Peace Festival and Crafts Show
Mid	Richmond Hill	Delphinium, Rose and Lilly Show
Mid	Kettle Point	Pow-Wow
Mid	Sarnia	Sarnia-Mackinac Sailboat Race
Late	*St. Catharine's	Royal Canadian Henley Regatta
Late	*St. Catharine's	Horse Show (Canada's largest outdoor horse show)
Late	Walkerton	Annual Chickenfest (rodeo, chicken-eating contest)
Late	Hamilton	Annual Lilly Show
Late	Lion's Head	Flower Fantasy (plants, arrangements, crafts)
Late	Teeswater	Ontario Championships in Pipes; Highland Games
Late	Walpole Island	Pow-Wow

August

Early	Caledonia	Display of Antique Cars, Arts and Crafts
Early	Peterborough	Historical Autos of Canada
Early	Lucknow	Craft Festival and Show of Canadian Crafts and Antiques
Early-end	Willowdale	Display and Demonstration of 19th-Century Handcrafts at Three Historic Houses
Early	Harrow and Colchester S.	Corn Festival
Early	Orillia	Leacock Festival of Humour
Early	Middleville	Pioneer Days
Early	Toronto	Simcoe Day (Fort York)
Early	Port Perry	Summer Festival (Western days, regatta, parade)
Early	Spring Bay	Flower Show and Tea
Early	*Maxville	Glengarry Highland Games (largest Highland gathering in North America)
Early	Brockville	International Highland Games
Early	Timmins	Annual Horse Show (Western and English)

Early	Little Current	Annual Lions Haweater Weekend (Pow-wow, beerfest, fish fry, horse show, horseshoe tournament)
Early	*Brantford	Six Nations Indian Pageant (displays, dances)
Early	*Manitoulin Island	Wikwemikong Indian Pow-Wow (dances, ceremonies)
Early	Curve Lake	Indian Pow-Wow Regatta
Early	Rankin	Pow-Wow
Early	*Bancroft	Gemboree (rock swapping, gemstone jewelery, demonstrations, corn roasts, square dancing)
Early	*Cobalt	Miners' Festival (ethnic days, canoe race)
Early	*Lake of the Woods	International Sailing Regatta (Kenora)
Early	Shelburne	Canadian Old Time Fiddlers Contest
Mid	*Fergus	Highland Games
Mid	*Toronto	Canadian National Exhibition (oldest and largest annual exhibition in the world plus Scottish World Festival)
Mid	Brigden	Annual Western Ontario Steam Threshers and Antique Association Show
Mid	Petawawa	Annual Steam Show
Mid	Port Dover	Summer Festival (fish fry, arts and crafts, antiques)
Mid	Orillia	Summer Festival
Mid	Richmond Hill	Summer Flower Show and Social
Mid	Creemore	Flower Show and Tea
Mid	Watford	Annual Flower and Vegetable Show
Mid	Lindway	Stampede
Mid	Kingston	Annual International Mineral and Gem Show
Mid	Thunder Bay	Mid-Canada Tennis Championships
Mid	Toronto	Canadian Canoe Championships
Mid	Madawaska	Annual Madawaska and Downriver Races
Late	*Zurich	Bean Festival (farm produce sold, outdoor bean meal)
Late	Etobicoke	Annual World of Antiques
Late	Bowmanville	Annual Flower Show
Late	Lion's Head	Annual Flower Show
Late	Clinton	Annual Flower Show
Late	Niagara Falls	Annual Flower and Vegetable Show
Late	Oshawa	Annual Flower and Vegetable Show
Late	Toronto	Annual Flower Show and Auction
Late	Willowdale	Annual Flower Show
Late	Brooklin	Annual Summer Flower Show
Late	London	Canadian Junior Golf Championships
Late	Sarnia and Mooretown	Ontario Senior's Gold Championship Rodeo
Late	Exeter	
Late	Meaford	HorseshoeTournament

Late	Burleigh Falls	Slalom Race (annual)

September
Early-late

(every Sunday)	Aberfoyle	Flea Market and Artisans' Market
Early	Milton	Ontario Steam and Antique Preservers
Early	Markham	Annual Antique Exhibition and Sale
Early	Barrie	Annual Canadian National Auto Flea Market
Early	Toronto	Annual Arts, Crafts and Hobbies Show
Early	Cornwall	Handicraft Exhibition and Bazaar
Early	Beamsville	Lincoln County Fair
Early	*London	Western Fair
Early	Meaford	Corn Roast
Early	Kleinburg	Binder Twine Festival (arts and crafts, flea markets, home-cooking)
Early	Sudbury	Mum Show
Early	Oshawa	Dahlia Show
Early	Cobourg	Flower Show
Early	Grimsby	Flower Show
Early	Brighton	Annual Flower Show and Tea
Early	Stouffville	Annual Flower Show
Early	Don Mills	Flower Show
Early	Toronto	Canadian National Equestrian Horse Show
Early	Thamesville	Moravian Indian Celebrations
Early	Ohsweken	Six Nations Indian Fair
Early	Sarnia	North American Wayfarer Championships
Early	Toronto	North American Laser Championships
Early	Owen Sound	Fall Fair
Mid	Belleville	Annual Antique Show and Sale
Mid	Fonthill	Annual Antique Mart
Mid	Willowdale	Craft Festival (tole painting, chair caning)
Mid	Welland	Niagara Regional Exhibition (agricultural fair) and Rodeo
Mid	Minesing	Pioneer Day
Mid	Toronto	Autumn Flower Show
Mid	Richmond Hill	Fall Flower Show and Corn Roast
Mid	Toronto	Horticultural Society Flower Show and Bazaar
Mid	Scarborough	Annual Flower Show
Mid	Hamilton	Fall Flower Show
Mid	Agincourt	Chrysanthemum and Dahlia Show
Mid	Stouffville	Autumn Show (flowers)
Mid	Newmarket	Autumn Show (flowers)
Mid	Deseronto	Annual Mohawk Indian Fair
Mid	Toronto	Canadian Sailing Championships
Mid	Toronto	Ukrainian Festival on Ice
Late	*Toronto	Pioneer Festival at Black Creek Pioneer Village

Late	Belle River	Flea Market
Late	Barrie	Annual Antique Show and Sale; Horticultural Fair
Late	Rolphton	Arts and Crafts Annual Exhibit
Late	Sarnia	German-Canadian Oktoberfest
Late	Ingersoll	Annual Cheese andWine Festival
Late	Point Edward	Bluewater Oktoberfest
Late	Flesherton	Split-Rail Festival
Late	Oshawa	Oktoberfest
Late	Ottawa	Garden Chrysanthemum Show
Late	Brooklin	Mum Show
Late	Newcastle	Fall Show
Late	Colborne	Trade Fair and Flower Show
Late	Hamilton	Chrysanthemum Show
Late	Georgetown	International Plowing Match and Machinery Show (Canada's largest)

October

Early	Point Edward	AntiqueShow
Early	St. Catharine's	Annual Antique Show and Sale
Early	Toronto	Pioneer Crafts
Early	Gore's Landing	Golden Harvest Fall Flower Show
Early	Oshawa	Mum Show
Early	Richmond Hill	Chrysanthemum Show
Early	Simcoe	Fair and Horse Show
Early	London	Oktoberfest
Early	Sault Ste. Marie	Algoma Fall Festival
Early	Port Hope	Oktoberfest
Mid	Saltford	Arts and Crafts Sale
Mid	Lang	Thanksgiving Harvest Festival
Mid	Lang	Pioneer Harvest Festival
Mid	Bancroft	Oktoberfest
Mid	Jordan	Annual Pioneer Day Celebration (Mennonite food)
Mid	Ottawa	Winter Fair and Horse Show
Mid	Kitchener-Waterloo	Oktoberfest (10 days in Ontario's oldest German settlement)
Late	Kingsville	Migration Festival
Late	*London	Arts and Crafts Sale
Late	Welland	Silent Auction and Flea Market
Late	Don Mills	Exhibition and Sale of Arts/Crafts
Late	Meaford	Apple Festival
Late	Barrie	International Night
Late	Kitchener	North America International Figure Skating
Late	Brooklin	Mum Show
Late	Orono	Fall Flower Show
Late	Don Mills	Winter Bouquet Sale

November

Early	Toronto	Annual Ceramic Sale
Early-late	Windsor	Annual Sale of Canadian Art, Paintings, Sculpture
Early	Don Mills	Chrysanthemum Show
Mid	Toronto	Annual Antique Show (display of period costumes)
Mid-late	Barrie	Several church bazaars
Mid	Toronto	Royal Winter Fair and Horse Show; Flower Show; Figure Skating Display
Mid	London	Mardi Gras at German-Canadian Club
Late	London	Christmas Flower Show
Late	Orono	Christmas Flower Show
Late	Don Mills	Christmas Flower Show

PRINCE EDWARD ISLAND

June

Late	Charlottetown	Natal Day

July

Mid	Charlottetown	Provincial Rose Show
Late	Summerside	Lobster Carnival and Livestock Exhibition (harness racing, lobster dinners)
Late	Charlottetown	Sailboat Race

August

Early	O'Leary	Prince Edward Island Potato Blossom Festival
Early	Eldon	Highland Games
Early	Charlottetown	Country Days
Mid	Charlottetown	Old Home Week (handicrafts, flower shows, livestock)
Late	Alberton	Prince County Livestock Show and Exhibition
Late	Dundas	Prince Edward Island Plowing Match and Agricultural Fair
Late	*Egmont Bay	Acadian Festival (Midway and Acadian Dinners)
Late	Abrams Village	Acadian Festival of Evangeline

September.

Early	Brudenell	Harvest Moon Open Golf Tournament

QUEBEC

January

Mid	Montreal	Montreal International Auto Salon

Late	Quebec	International Bonspiel
Late	Quebec	Canadian National Skating Championship

February
Mid	Quebec	Quebec Winter Carnival
Mid	Chicoutimi	Carnival-Souvenir of Chicoutimi
Late	Rimouski	Quebec Winter Games

March
Late	Montreal	Camping, Leisure and Travel Show

April
Unknown	Piessisville	Maple Festival (taffy-pulling, French-Canadian suppers, evenings at the sugar shack)
Early	Montreal	Flower, Garden Show

June
Late June-early Sept.	Montreal	Man and His World (permanent cultural exhibition)
Late	Province de Quebec	St.-Jean-Baptiste Day Celebrations

July
Unknown	Quebec	Summer Festival
Unknown	Riviere-du-Loup	Summer Festival
Early	Hull	Raftsman's Festival (lumberjack events)
Mid	Valleyfield	International Regatta
Mid	La Tuque	Les 24 Heures de la Tuque (International Swimming Relay Race)
Late	Chicoutimi	Swimming Marathon
Late	Baie-St.-Paul	Baie-St.-Paul Folklore Festival (paintings, drawings, rugs, pottery, tapestries, handicrafts; concerts, recitals)
Late	Montreal	Golf Championship

August
Early	Péribonka/Roberval	International Lac St.-Jean (swim crossing, between Peribonka and Roberval—25 miles)
Late	Chicoutimi	National Folklore Festival
Late	La Tuque/Trois-Rivières	La Classique Internationale de Canots de la Mauricie (canoe race)
Late	Chicoutimi	Kayak Canoe Race

September
Early	*Quebec	Expo Quebec (provincial agricultural exhibition)

Early- mid	Perce	Handicrafts exhibition
Early	Coteau-du-Lac	Agricultural Fair
Early-mid	*St.-Tite	St.-Tite Western Festival (rodeo, beef-tasting)
Early	Montreal	Cycletouring: regional outing (Tel.: 514-389-9461)
Early	Rigaud	Notre-Dame-de-Lourdes Shrine Centenary Celebrations
Early	Jonquiére	Agricultural Fair
Mid	St.-Georges (Beauce)	Winter Salon
Mid	Shawville	Agricultural Fair
Mid	Havelock	Agricultural Fair
Mid	Montreal	Field Hockey Tournament
Mid	Ste.-Agathe-des-Monts	Fall Festival of the Hautes Laurentides (paintings, handicrafts, photography; wine and cheese parties)
Mid	Caughnawaga	Champion of Champions Golf Tournament
Late	Tadoussac	Sand Skiing
Late	Montreal	Fiesta Folklorico
Late	Sherbrooke	Annual Autumn Antiques Showsale

October

Early	Chicoutimi	Olden Times Soap Sale (carnival)
Early	Tadoussac	Sand Skiing
Early	*Rimouski	Rimouski Fall Festival (open-air activities, recreative and socio-cultural)
Mid	St.-Stanislas	Pheasant Festival
Mid	*St.-Michel-des-Saints	Provincial Hunting Festival (visit to Nonourville Village: log cabins, wild animals, moose-calling contest, portages)
Mid	*Montreal	Salon du Sport-Winter and Indoor Sports
Late	*Montmagny	Snow Goose Festival
Late	Chicoutimi	Motocross Race
Late	Montreal	International Salon of Food and Agriculture

November

Mid-Nov-mid-Dec.	Montreal	Chrysanthemum Fall Exhibition
Late Nov.-mid-Jan.	Quebec	Sun and Snow Culture
Late	Quebec	Antiques of Old Quebec
Late	Kenogami	Curling Bonspiel

December

Early	Chicoutimi	Art Crafts Festival
Early	Granby	Gala of Granby Song Festival
Mid	Quebec	National Curling Week
Mid	*Montreal	Salon des Metiers d'Art du Quebec
Mid	*Quebec	Salon des Artisans de Quebec
Mid-Dec.-		
mid-Jan.	Montreal	Christmas Plants Exhibition
Mid	Hull	Hockey Tournament

SASKATCHEWAN

March

Mid	Lloydminster	Farmers' Interprovincial Bonspiel
Mid	Carrot River	Mixed Curling Bonspiel
Mid	Saskatoon	Alpine Fest
Mid	Alameda	Auction Mart Annual Bull Show and Sale
Mid	Cupar	St. Patrick's Bazaar
Mid	Fort Qu'Appelle	Ice Carnival
Mid	Wilkie	Farmer's Day
Mid	*Meadow Lake	Winter Festival
Mid	Moose Jaw	Provincial Curling Bonspiel
Mid	Yorkton	Figure Skating Competitions
Mid	Moose Jaw	Saskatchewan Open Fencing Championships
Mid	Saskatoon	Saskatchewan Indoor Speed Skating
Mid	Regina	Rothmans Archery Tournament
Mid	Weyburn	Spring Bonspiel
Mid	Carrot River	Mens' Curling Bonspiel
Late	Moose Jaw	Annual Adult Education Art Exhibition
Late	Regina	Winter Fair
Late	Moose Jaw	Regional Curling Bonspiel
Late Mar.-		
early Apr.	Regina	Horse Show and Bull Sale

April

Early	Yorkton	Yorkton Purebred Cattle Show and Sale
Early	Yorkton	Bantam Hackey Tournament
Early	Maymont	Memorial Hall Smorgasbord
Early	Swift Current	The Family Sportsman's Show
Early	Ituna	Ham Shoot
Mid	Yorkton	Yorkton Purebred Swine Show and Sale
Mid	Lloydminster	Bull Sale
Late	*Saskatoon	Sportsman Show
Late	Moose Jaw	Kinsmen Sport and Home Show
Late	Indian Head	Them Good Ole Days Tea
Late	Balcarres	Art Show
Late	North Battleford	Annual Bull Show and Sale

Late	North Battleford	Kinsmen Indoor Rodeo
Late	Lumsden	Tea-Bake Sale and Bazaar
Late	Lloydminster	Registered Trapshooting Tournament
Late	Humboldt	St. Dominic and St. Augustine Art Show

May

Early	Lumsden	Lumsden Canoe Races
Early	Saskatoon	Ukrainian Dance Recital
Early	Saskatoon	Ukrainian Folk Heritage in Canada
Early	Estevan	Tattoo
Mid	Elbow	Norway Day
Mid	Regina	Provincial Open Regatta
Late	Glen Ewen	Annual Sports Day
Late	Moose Jaw	Golf Tournament
Late	Spalding	Annual Museum Opening and Outdoor Tea and Bake Sale
Late	*Bengough	Big Muddy Rodeo
Late	Saskatoon	Registered Trapshooting Tournament
Late	Maple Creek	Rodeo
Late	Swift Current	Victoria Day Golf Tournament
Late	Unity	Annual Open Golf Tournament
Late	*Swift Current	Frontier Days Bull Show and Sale

June

Early	Lloydminster	Rock and Gem Show
Early	Lloydminster	Art Show and Sale
Early	Porcupine Plain	Open Fastball Tournament
Early	Nipawin	Men's Open Golf Tournament
Early	Briercrest	Sports Day and Arts and Crafts Show
Early	*Weyburn	Antique Car and Gun Club Show
Early	*Yorkton	Ethnic Festival
Early	Rosetown	Saskatchewan Provincial Shoot and Rosetown Annual Registered Trapshooting Tournament
Early	Goodsoil	Annual Sports Day and Softball Tournament
Early	Churchbridge	Fish Derby
Mid	North Battleford	Territorial Days
Mid	Alameda	Alameda Agricultural Society Summer Fair
Mid	Lashburn	Bavarian Beer Gardens
Mid	Kamsack	Rodeo and Sports Day
Mid	Moose Jaw	Saskatchewan Sailing Club Open Regatta
Mid	Regina	Registered Trapshooting Tournament
Mid	Lloydminster	Men's Open Golf Tournament
Mid	Moose Jaw	Antique Automobile Club Spring Rally and Black Powder Shoot
Mid	Lampman	Annual Golf Tournament
Late	Assiniboia	Rodeo
Late	Bruno	Annual Community Day

Late	Meadow Lake	Stampede
Late	Veregin	Veregin's Peter's Day at Russian Prayer Home
Late	Moose Jaw	"Crabgrass" Rugby Tournament
Late	*	Saskatchewan Sailing Club Open Regatta
Late	Wadena	Wild West Days
Late	Watrous	Art Salon
Late	*Nipawin	Pike Festival
Late	Hanley	Pioneer Days

July

Early	Weyburn	Exhibition
Early	*Swift Current	Frontier Days Rodeo and Fair (largest rodeo in Saskatchewan)
Early	Estevan	Fair
Early	*Indian Head	Them Good Ole Days—"Reunion Days"
Early	Saskatoon	"Louis Riel" Rugby Tournament
Early	Foam Lake	Open Golf Tournament
Early	Moose Jaw	Traveller's Day Parade
Early	Moose Jaw	Exhibition
Early	Saskatoon	Pioneer Days
Early	Wynyard	Perennial Flower Show
Mid	Indian Head	Them Good Ole Days-"Participation Days"
Mid	*Wood Mountain	Rodeo
Mid	Weyburn	Antique Car Show
Mid	Maple Creek	Stampede
Mid	*Yorkton	Saskatchewan Stampede and Yorkton Exhibition
Mid	Norquay	Key Indian Sports Day and Rodeo
Mid	Arcola	Annual Agricultural Fair and Sports Day
Mid	Dundurn Ranges	Saskatchewan Provincial Rifle Association Shoot
Mid	Kindersley	All Breed Horse Show
Late	Ogema	Annual Fair and Sports Day
Late	Greig Lake	Saskatchewan Provincial Water-ski Championship Competition
Late	*Indian Head	Them Good Ole Days-Open Golf Tournament
Late	Watson	Open Golf Tournament
Late	Prince Albert	Canadian Archery Championships
Late	Creelman	Fair
Late	Kennedy	Annual Rodeo
Late	Creelman	Summer Fair
Late	Kindersley	Quarter Horse Show and Cutting Horse Competition
Late	*North Battleford	Exhibition
Late	Saskatoon	Rothman's Open Tennis Tournament
Late	*Lloydminster	Three-Day Exhibition

Late	Abernethy	Agricultural Society Fair
Late	*Regina	Buffalo Days
Late	Central Butte	Agricultural Fair
Late	North Portal	Golf Tournament
Late	Madge Lake	amsack Fish and Game League Fish Derby
Late	Perdue	Agricultural Fair
Late	Regina	Pile-O-Bones Day
Late	Nipawin	Agricultural Fair and Rodeo
Late	*Regina	Exhibition and Fair
Late	Saskatoon	Saskatchewan Sailing Club National Enterprise Championship
Late	*Prince Albert	Exhibition

August

Early	Invermay	Agricultural Society Annual Fair
Early	Leader	Bavarian Festival
Early	Nokomis	Annual Fair and Exhibition
Early	Radisson	Annual Agricultural Fair
Early	Kelvington	Annual Fair and Race Meet
Early	North Battleford	Saskatchewan Sailing Club Open Regatta
Early	Kerrobert	Jamboree Days
Early	Goodsoil	Fish Derby
Early	Edam	Annual Mixed Open Golf Tournament
Early	Porcupine Plain	Shand Agricultural Exhibition
Early	Somme	Summer Fair
Early	Turtleford	Agricultural Fair
Early	Kennedy	Annual Fair
Early	Saskatoon	Saskatchewan Open Pro-Am Golf
Early	Saltcoats	Agricultural Fair
Early	Unity	Canadian National Senior Baseball Championship Playoff
Early	Churchbridge	Flower Show
Early	Churchbridge	Cattle and Horse Show
Early	Churchbridge	Summer Fair
Early	*Saskatoon	Peter Jackson Saskatchewan Open Golf Championship
Early	Lloydminster	Interprovincial Registered Trapshooting Tournament
Mid	Senlac	Fish Derby
Mid	Fort Qu'Appelle	Highland Dancing, Piping and Drumming
Mid	Wadena	Kinsmen Saskin Sunfest
Late	*Lloydminster	Silver Spur Galaxy Horse Show
Late	Wagrous	Provincial Horticultural Show
Late	Saskatoon	Labour Day Tennis Tournament
Late	*Regina	"Prairie Cities" Rugby Tournament
Late	*Prince Albert	Saskatchewan Sailing Club Open Regatta
Late	*Swift Current	Labour Day Golf Tournament
Late	*Maple Creek	Threshing Bee and Hobby Show

September

Early	*Swift Current	International Golf Tournament
Early	Dundurn Ranges	Saskatchewan Province Rifle Association Prairie Provincial Shoot
Early	*Moose Jaw	Antique Automobile Club of Saskatchewan Fall Threshing Bee
Early	Carrot River	Pasquia Club Golf Tournament
Late	Canora	Bonus Days
Late	*Frobisher	Threshermen's Reunion, Parade and Threshing Demonstration
Late	Lumsden	Anglican Church Fowl Supper

October

Early	*Swift Current	Western Canadian Amateur Championship Fiddling Contest
Early	*Goodsoil	Homecoming
Mid	*Kindersley	Annual Goose Festival
Mid	Radisson	Farm-Urban Day
Mid	Lancer	Chokecherry Festival
Mid	McLean	Fowl Supper
Mid	Rabbit Lake	Annual Thanksgiving Fowl Supper
Mid	Maymont	United Church Annual Turkey Supper
Mid	Lumsden	United Church Fowl Supper
Mid	Unity	Annual Turkey Shoot
Mid	*Cutknife	Rodeo, Tomahawk Days
Mid	Saskatoon	Welsh Guards and Argyll and Southern Highlanders
Mid	Alameda	Agricultural Society Fall Fair
Mid	Grenfell	Agricultural Fall Fair
Late	Hodgeville	Turkey Shoot
Late	Unity	Agricultural Fair
Late	Rama	Fall Festival

November

Early	*Climax	Annual Carnival
Mid	Edam	Annual Turkey Shoot
Mid	*Frontier	Fall Carnival
Mid	*Kindersley	Kinsmen Annual Turkey Shoot and Carnival
Mid	St. Victor	Annual Masquerade
Mid	*Saskatoon	Exhibition and Fall Fair
Late	*Regina	Western Canadian Agribition
Late	*Spalding	Annual Winter Festival
Late	Kendal	Parish Bazaar

December

Early	Maymont	United Church Annual Bean and Casserole Supper
Early	Kinistino	Kinette Novelty Bazaar
Mid	*Swift Current	Annual Carol Festival

Mid	Ituna	Turkey Shoot
Late	Spalding	Annual Men's Open Curling Bonspiel
Late	Saskatoon	Indoor Games

YUKON

February
Late Feb.-
early Mar.   Whitehorse   Sourdough Rendezvous

March
Early   Mayo   Winter Carnival (dog racing, tug-o-war)

June

June-Sept.	Dawson City	Gaslight Follies (Gay 90's vaudeville, melo-drama, gold-panning)
June-Sept.	Dawson City	Klondike Nights
June-Sept.	Dawson City	Robert Service's Cabin (the ghost of Robert Service returns to recite the ballads of the Yukon poet)
June-Sept.	Whitehorse	Frantic Follies (turn-of-the-century vaudeville stage show of fun and nostalgia for the entire family)
June-Sept.	Whitehorse	Tours of Historic Sternwheeler S.S. *Klindike*
Mid	Tagish	Fishing Derby
Late	Dawson City	Midnight Picnic (picnic under the midnight sun)

July
Early   Simpson Lake   Community Picnic

August

Mid	Dawson City	Discovery Day (commemorating the discovery of gold in the Klondike on Aug. 17, 1896; horticulture, handicrafts display, raft races)
Late	Whitehorse	Kiwanis Club Horticultural and Hobby Show
Late	Faro	Pelly River Revelry; Faro 400 Tricycle Race, Ball Tournament

FARM VACATIONS/GUEST RANCHES

Have you considered camping on a Canadian farm or ranch where it is possible to join the host's family for home-cooked meals, for riding instructions, or for just observing farm life? Some farm families will arrange for hay rides, hikes, cookouts for guests—and even provide child-care service by the day or week. Rates vary: $12-$15 per week per family is frequently charged for camping; $50-$80 per adult is commonly charged for room and board in the farmhouse. Camping families making arrangements to eat one or more meals a day in the farmhouse must write directly to the farm family to obtain prices.

Several provinces (notably Alberta, Saskatchewan, Manitoba, and Ontario) have begun publicizing "back-on-the-farm" opportunities for travelers. Quoting a farm vacation leaflet from Saskatchewan: "Commodious and lovely farm houses have taken the place of the log shacks of the pioneers, and the land is vocal with the sound of husbandry. This transformation has been accomplished by the steady labour and indomitable courage of the first settlers through many seasons. Most of those who laid the first foundation have gone down the last trail and those who are left to carry on as farmers have a Farm Vacation to offer for all seasons and people of all ages. It can be busy or relaxed as you want it to be. We offer a holiday with a difference: hospitality, wholesome food, fresh air and much more."

Since accommodations differ considerably from farm to farm, it is recommended you write requesting information from several listed here or from the provincial office's more current list. Then, when you have narrowed the field, a phone call may provide added insight before a reservation and deposit (often a 10% minimum) are made. When requesting information from specific farm owners, tell about your family, ages of the children, your special interests, and so on. The quality of information received will likely represent the quality of care the farm and its facilities receive.

Do's and Don't's Suggested for Farm Vacations

Do take along some old clothing and lots of extra shoes—you'll need shoes that thrive on mud. (Not a sidewalk in sight, thank goodness!)

Do instruct your children to wipe feet before entering the farmhouse.

Do pack a supply of books and games—as well as clothes—for rainy weather.

Do remember your hosts are busy people. Help them keep the property free of litter.

Do plan some sightseeing in the countryside, even if you can't pry the children off the farm.

Do be willing to belong to another way of life. Part of the fun is adapting to a routine completely different from the one at home. Be prepared to fit into the farm routine, meet the house rules.

Do be friendly, give a little, take a little, behave as you'd like guests to behave in your home.